SUBVERTING GLOBAL MYTHS

Theology and the Public
Issues Shaping Our World

Vinoth Ramachandra

IVP Academic

An imprint of InterVarsity Press
Downers Grove, Illinois

InterVarsity Press
P.O. Box 1400, Downers Grove, IL 60515-1426
World Wide Web: www.ivpress.com
E-mail: email@ivpress.com

InterVarsity Press® is the book-publishing division of InterVarsity Christian Fellowship/USA®, a student movement active on campus at hundreds of universities, colleges and schools of nursing in the United States of America, and a member movement of the International Fellowship of Evangelical Students. For information about local and regional activities, write Public Relations Dept., InterVarsity Christian Fellowship/USA, 6400 Schroeder Rd., P.O. Box 7895, Madison, WI 53707-7895, or visit the IVCF website at <www.intervarsity.org>.

Scripture quotations, unless otherwise noted, are from the New Revised Standard Version of the Bible, *copyright 1989 by the Division of Christian Education of the National Council of Churches of Christ in the USA. Used by permission. All rights reserved.*

Design: Cindy Kiple
Images: Louie Psihoyos/Getty Images

ISBN 978-0-8308-2885-2

Printed in the United States of America ∞

 InterVarsity Press is committed to protecting the environment and to the responsible use of natural resources. As a member of Green Press Initiative we use recycled paper whenever possible. To learn more about the Green Press Initiative, visit http://www.greenpressinitiative.org

Library of Congress Cataloging-in-Publication Data

Ramachandra, Vinoth
Subverting global myths: theology and the public issues shaping our
world / Vinoth Ramachandra.
    p. cm.
Includes bibliographical references and index.
ISBN 978-0-8308-2885-2 (cloth: alk. paper)
1. Religion and social problems. 2. Social problems—Moral and
ethical aspects. I. Title.
HN31.R36 2008
261.8—dc22

2008008911

P	21	20	19	18	17	16	15	14	13	12	11	10	9	8	7	6	5	4	3	2	1
Y	26	25	24	23	22	21	20	19	18	17	16	15	14	13	12	11	10	09	08		

CONTENTS

Prologue 9

1 MYTHS OF TERRORISM 17

Reaping the Whirlwind 17

The Globalization of Islamist Militancy 24

Deconstructing the "War on Terror" 33

Applying Just-War Reasoning 42

Needed: Humility and Courageous Imagination 50

2 MYTHS OF RELIGIOUS VIOLENCE 57

Escaping Parochialism 58

The Complexities of "Religious Violence" 62

Two Asian Case Studies 69

Atheist Polemics and Collective Deception 74

Recovering Christian Integrity 81

Mutual Criticism 85

3 MYTHS OF HUMAN RIGHTS 91

The Language of Rights 91

Questioning the Standard Liberal Story 93

Toward an Alternative Story 99

Individual Rights 105

Relationality and Rights 115

Legislating for Rights 119

Recovering a Tradition 123

4 MYTHS OF MULTICULTURALISM 127

Understanding Cultures 130

Multicultural Nationhood 138

A Defense of Multicultural Society 143

Reconfiguring the Multicultural State 147

Secularist Fundamentalism 154

Rights of Refugees and Asylees 156

Ethics of Freedom 161

5 MYTHS OF SCIENCE 169

Science as Ideology 171

Two Widespread Myths 181

Scientific Research and Moral Responsibility 192

Genetic Engineering 197

The Return of Eugenics 204

Post/Transhumanism 209

Gods or Nothings: The False Choice 213

6 MYTHS OF POSTCOLONIALISM 217

Decentering World History 217

The Colonial Legacy 224

Postcolonialism 228

Toward a More Nuanced Understanding 233

Postcolonialism and Resistance from the Margins 242

Some Theological Reflections 245

Notes 263

Name Index 289

Subject Index 293

The rainbow shines, but only in the thought

Of him who looks. Yet in not that alone,

For who makes rainbows by invention?

And many standing round a waterfall

See one bow each, yet not the same for all,

But each a handsbreadth further than the next.

The sun on falling waters writes the text

Which yet is in the eye or in the thought.

It was a hard thing to undo this knot

GERARD MANLEY HOPKINS,
"IT WAS A HARD THING TO UNDO THIS KNOT"

In Thornton Wilder's novel *The Bridge of San Luis Rey,* the collapse of "the finest bridge in all Peru" on July 20, 1714, sent shockwaves among all those who had previously crossed it with misplaced confidence:

> The bridge seemed to be among the things that would last forever; it was unthinkable that it should break. The moment a Peruvian heard of the accident he signed himself [with the cross] and made a mental calculation as to how recently he had crossed by it and how soon he had intended crossing by it again. People wandered about in a trance-like state, muttering: they had the hallucination of seeing themselves falling into a gulf.[1]

Some years ago I wrote a book called *Gods That Fail.*[2] It was an attempt to show how every society turns around some deity or deities that claim the total allegiance of its citizens. Even the most "secular" of states worships such surrogate gods as "national security," "market forces," "technological imperatives," "economic growth" and "patriotism." The biblical term for such prostration before human creations is *idolatry*, and the propensity to idolatry is endemic in all human individuals and societies. Idols not only blind us to ultimate realities, but they exact a heavy price. They demand human sacrifices and, as we have learned painfully in recent years, wreak havoc on the nonhuman world.

All who experience the world as a safe and secure place tend to assume

that has been so always and is so for everybody. When familiar sources of
security fail us, we are left adrift in a meaningless void until we can latch
onto other idols. And then the never-ending cycle of optimism and despair
is reenergized once more. In the absence of biblical hope, which is grounded
neither in futurology nor in romantic utopias but in the promises of God,
entire societies are held captive to the merchants of fear and death.

Why is it so often said that September 11, 2001, was a benchmark in
the history of our era, a turning point for the world? For the vast majority
of the world's peoples, especially the poor of all nations, life went on as before. Nothing had changed. Moreover, this was not the first time that many
lives were lost in terrorist attacks and war in the United States. The violence and terrorism of the Civil War and the 1960s social protest movements
also brought destruction and death. The bombing of the Murrah building in
Oklahoma City claimed more than two hundred lives. Lynchings of men,
women and children of African descent by terror groups such as the Ku Klux
Klan, and the continued fire bombings of black churches in the American
deep South, have taken the lives of thousands.

In an essay written soon after 9/11, the theologian John Milbank stated:
"The question that one should ask in response to the immediate aftermath of
the events of September 11th 2001 is this: why was there outrage on such a
gigantic scale?"[3] Milbank's own answer—that it posed a threat to sovereign
power (the power of the state being the highest authority in secular modernity) and that it gave an opportunity to strengthen the policing of the market
system in whose service the state stands—is not very convincing, but the
question is significant, nevertheless.

On February 13, 2001, an earthquake, the second within a month, hit the
tiny Central American country of El Salvador. Two-thirds of the country
was affected by the earthquake. The El Salvadorean theologian Jon Sobrino,
in a lengthy reflection on the earthquake, has observed that such tragedies
serve as an x-ray of a country: "The earthquake has pointed out where sin,
poverty, and injustice are most cruelly focused: on women and children, on
peasant men and women, on those who have lost jobs and those who cannot
get credit, on those who have practically no decision-making power over their
own lives and future."[4] He points out that

an earthquake, like a cemetery, reveals the iniquitous inequality of a society, and thus also its deepest truth. Some tombs are huge, sumptuous pantheons of luxurious marble, in prestigious locations. Others, almost without names and without crosses, are piled up in hidden places and consigned to anonymity. They are the majority.[5]

The role of the global media is crucial. Despite all the liberal rhetoric about "equality," who in the world of the media or the academy really believes that the life of a Nepali peasant, say, is as valuable as that of a Hollywood actress or a football star? Hurricane Katrina, which struck the Gulf Coast in August 2005, killing about 1,300 people, generated forty times more Western print coverage than Hurricane Stan that killed more than 1,600 people in Guatemala a month later. On the same day that the second earthquake struck El Salvador, a soccer game was played between Real Madrid and Lazio. The combined market value of the players on the field was $650 million, slightly less than half of what it took to rebuild the entire physical infrastructure of El Salvador after the earthquake. The press reported the value of the soccer players with enthusiasm bordering on veneration.[6]

The October 20, 2005, issue of the *New York Review of Books* carried a full-page advertisement for a book by one Sam Harris called *The End of Faith*. It was hailed as a "New York Times Bestseller" and had won the 2005 PEN Award for Nonfiction.[7] The advertisement carried a string of rave reviews from Richard Dawkins to Natalie Angier. The latter praised the book for articulating "the dangers and absurdities of organized religion so fiercely and so fearlessly," and said that she "felt relieved" as she read it, "vindicated, personally understood." The review from British newspaper *The Independent* saluted Harris's "brave, pugilistic attempt to demolish the walls that currently insulate religious people from criticism."

The same issue of the *New York Review* also carried an essay by Richard Lewontin, an eminent biologist and one of the sanest critics of evolutionary psychology, on the topic "The Wars Over Evolution." Unfortunately, the only reference in the entire essay to any Christian (or other religious) argument was a lengthy quotation contrasting evolution unfavorably with "special creation" by a Reverend Ron Carlson, described by Lewontin, as a "popular preacher, lecturer, and author." If Harris's pugilism has inspired Lewontin, then this is like Muhammad Ali in his prime knocking out a lightweight reporter. There was no engagement with the best of Christian philosophers or theologians on what the biblical doctrine of creation means. And since then we have been treated to many such one-sided offensives against orthodox Christianity and Islam in the scholarly as well as popular Western media.

For a non-Western observer like myself, there is something interesting afoot here. Is the benign disregard for religion in the West giving way to a strident assault on religion, with the comforting stereotyping of the "other" that we have come to associate with racism and colonialism? Once liberals have tasted on their own soil the violence that their societies have inflicted on others, does fear expose the Achilles' heel in their rhetoric of human dignity and human rights? American, British and Australian governments, which have patronizingly lectured their Third World counterparts about civil liberties and respect for the rule of law, have, since September 11, 2001, and their own "war on terrorism," taken more than a leaf out of the book of the worst Third World regimes.

The near adulation with which prominent liberal journals responded to Harris's book is far more intriguing, indeed fascinating, than the book itself. Ironies abound. The weapons of mass destruction, under whose cloud Harris writes, were created and developed by men (perhaps a few women, too) of scientific, enlightened reason, under the aegis of secularized liberal government. Now that such horrific weapons lie within reach of Islamist movements and states, we are told that the West can no longer afford the luxury of tolerance. The battle lines are drawn. And they are once more drawn between "us rational, civilized, progressive types" and "them out there—religious, ignorant and backward." Will men and women of faith be the last defenders of liberal values in the West?

What frightens a people serves as a reliable guide to their idolatries. Idols are sustained by myths—public, large-scale narratives that engage our imaginations and shape the way we experience the world. Myths are an intrinsic part of human existence. They give meaning to our lives, sometimes at the expense of truth. The eminent literary critic Northrop Frye points out that "Certain stories seem to have a particular significance: they are the stories that tell a society what is important for it to know, whether about its gods, its history, its laws, or its class structure."[8] Global capitalism, Marxism, behaviorism, evolutionism, social contract theories, all represent particular ways of seeing that employ metaphors and symbols embedded within an overarching story of the human condition. They all contain a central truth which is then inflated and used to exclude other, perhaps more important, ways of seeing. The modern market system, for instance, places an artificial scarcity at the heart of human existence. It envisages human beings as creatures with insatiable desires. It leads to a conception of human life centered on competition, acquisitiveness and unqualified consumption. As such it militates against other myths, often present in the same society, that speak of "the sacredness of nature" or the "inherent dignity of human beings."

The British philosopher Mary Midgley has argued that not only are myths central to worldviews but they are strongly influenced by the dominant technology of the day. Mechanistic views of the natural world, and of human beings' relationship with nature, flourished in a world of clocks and steam engines. In an age of computers, everything (including human intelligence) becomes information and information-processing. The rise of genetic engineering diverts attention to the search for biochemical solutions to complex social, political, psychological and moral problems. "For instance," she writes, "much of the demand for liver transplants is due to alcohol. But it is a lot harder to think what to do about alcohol than it is to call for research on transplants. Similarly, infertility is largely caused by late marriage and sexually transmitted diseases. But changing the customs that surround these changes calls for quite different and much less straightforward kinds of thinking."[9]

The "quite different and much less straightforward kind of thinking" is characteristic of the theological approach that undergirds the present book. Christian theology is more than a set of doctrinal beliefs or systematic arguments. It is a way of seeing, of so dwelling in a particular language and doing new things with that language so that its revelatory and transformative power is manifest in the world. That language arose out of specific historical events that both constitute us as the *ekklesia* of Christ and call forth characteristic social practices such as thanksgiving, forgiving, exposing evil, truth-telling, welcoming the broken and the hopeless, and bearing testimony to grace.

Such a theology seeks comprehensiveness, because it seeks to bear prophetic witness to One whose speech-acts heal, renew and transform the world in its entirety, but its own speech is always broken, sharing in the not-yet-redeemed character of the world.

This book brings together essays that have grown out of talks given in various parts of the world. The essays take up six areas of contemporary, global discourse where powerful myths energize and mobilize a great deal of public funding as well as academic production. They are addressed not primarily to theological specialists but to all thoughtful men and women who are concerned about the public issues that shape our increasingly interconnected and interdependent world.

Chapters one and two explore the ways politics and international relations have come to be dominated in recent years by public narratives in which slogans such as "the war on terror," "combating religious violence" and "secular reason versus fundamentalist faith" play a central role. If they are not thought through carefully and critically they only obscure the truth of what is actually happening around the world. These chapters draw on my own experience working as a pastor-theologian among university students and professors against a backdrop of militant religious and secular ideologies in a country (Sri Lanka) which has suffered from "terrorism" and a "war on terror" that has claimed over sixty thousand lives since the late 1970s and shows no signs of abating. They also reflect the experience of living and traveling extensively not only in the West but in several of the "trouble spots" in Asia today.

The language of human rights is fast becoming a universal discourse and is promoted with a missionary zeal that often disguises its hypocritical practice. In chapter three I present a biblical, Christian approach to human rights and argue that if we are to promote that in a way that is both intellectually coherent and morally consistent, we need to move beyond a secularist paradigm of humanness. Can we practice respect for human dignity without taking seriously the role of cultural communities in human formation? What rights attach to cultures and when do these become problematic? What are the benefits of a multicultural society and how do we reconfigure a multicultural state? These issues have been the stuff of incendiary political debates from Canada to Fiji in recent years. In chapter four I try to bring a Christian mind to bear on some of these complex but pressing questions. Early versions of chapters three and four were first given as part of the Josiah Mann Lectures in Pastoral Theology at the China Graduate School of Theology, Hong Kong, in 2003.

Chapter five addresses the way that science and technology have become the site of powerful global myths from sociobiology to transhumanism. Scientific research has come to be dominated by political, military and huge corporate interests in India and South Korea no less than the United States, and this has important implications for what is presented to the public as science. No one who cares deeply about science (as I do) can be indifferent to such developments. This essay critiques the popular antireligious myths that lie behind the hegemonic role that science has assumed in the media and much of the academy. The identification of evolution with atheism is promoted both by scientific fundamentalists and their religious counterparts. I seek to clarify the real issues behind contemporary debates over evolution, biotechnology, stem-cell research and a posthuman future. Early versions of this chapter have been delivered as public lectures in places as far afield as Delhi, Uppsala and New Jersey.

Chapter six is an extensive revision of an essay that was delivered and later published in the proceedings of the British and Irish Association of Mission Studies annual conference in Belfast in June 2005.[10] It brings a historical and theological challenge to both Eurocentric readings of globalization and postcolonial theorizing about the Third World today. It begins by sketching the decentering of histories of modernity that have been undertaken in recent years by a new breed of historians; and proceeds to describe the abiding colonial legacy and how that has provoked the fruitful and important academic discourse known as "postcolonial theory." I dialogue critically with the latter, questioning some of its assumptions but also welcoming its relevance for doing theology today.

Obviously, these essays do not aim at exhaustive coverage of any given topic; but nor, on the other hand, do they provide the sound bytes that some readers prefer. "My novels are not fast food," Salman Rushdie recently told an audience of journalists in India, with understandable impatience. It is a line every serious writer today must be tempted to use. To find a humanities student, let alone a scientist or engineer, who has actually read a whole book from cover to cover during his or her university career, is a rare pleasure. Baroness Susan Greenfield, the eminent British neuroscientist, has warned her government that a new generation is growing up, immersed in cyber worlds and mobile communication technology, but lacking what we have long identified as the hallmarks of critical intelligence: curiosity, attentive listening, the ability to place information in context, the weighing of evidence, retentive memory, independent judgment and articulate expression. She has set up an all-parliament group comprising former education secretaries and brain scientists to investigate the way that the changing cultural environment is affecting the brain circuitry of children and the implications of this for parenting and educational practice.[11]

In fairness it must be said that the myths that hold us captive were not generated by the present teenage generation but by their very literate and articulate forebears. Also, enveloped as we are in a global media that is obsessed with mindless celebrities and owned by a few powerful tycoons, we all struggle to sort out the significant from the trivial. Slow, thoughtful and critical readers who care to explore reality rather than flip from one reality show to another do actually exist. To them this book is offered as an invitation to journey with the author in heretical subversion of the present reality in order to make way for another.

1

MYTHS OF TERRORISM

"Alas the Afghanistan of our youth is long dead.
Kindness is gone from the land and you cannot escape the killings.
Always the killings. In Kabul, fear is everywhere, in the streets,
in the stadium, in the markets, it is a part of our lives here."

A CHARACTER IN KHALED HOSSEINI'S *THE KITE RUNNER*

REAPING THE WHIRLWIND

The U.S. Central Intelligence Agency coined a term for it: *Blowback.* The
explosive boomerang that governments throw when, either by propaganda or
through covert military operations, they deliberately stoke up the flames of
ethnic, religious or nationalist rivalries for political gain. Faustian monsters
are created who then threaten to overwhelm the very governments that gave
them birth. Blowback was first used by the CIA to describe the unintended
consequences of their covert activities in Iran in 1954. The agency warned of
the possible repercussions of the coup d'etat it had engineered to overthrow
the elected government of Mohammed Mossadeq a year earlier. The joint
operation with Britain's MI6 was undertaken in order to prevent the nation-
alization of Iran's oil reserves. For the next twenty-five years a despotic Shah
was armed and protected by the United States and Britain so that their oil
companies could have a free hand. The blowback was a long time in coming,
but when it did the results were catastrophic: the creation of a Shia Islamic

Republic that became an implacable enemy of the United States and inspired Muslims all over the world to confront the West.

The Soviet Union made its fatal move into Afghanistan on Christmas Eve 1979, not long after the Shah had fled Iran, two events that redefined geopolitics for generations to come. The Afghan communist party (the Peoples' Democratic Party of Afghanistan) had participated, along with the Afghan army, in a bloodless revolution in 1973 against feudal rule. It took power directly in April 1978 and pushed through progressive reforms. It introduced free medical care in the poorest areas, educated women, recognized the rights of ethnic minorities and freedom of religion. (By the late 1980s half the university students in the country were women, and women made up 40 percent of Afghanistan's doctors and 30 percent of its civil servants.) The reforms were opposed by Islamic parties and tribal warlords collectively known as the mujahedin. The Soviet Union sent its army to help the PDP government fight off the warlords, but before they did so the CIA had already begun a covert action program in support of the mujahedin.[1] Ironically, the Soviets justified their incursion into Afghanistan in the same terms that the American government used to justify their invasion in November 2001: they were combating "religious fundamentalism" and "terrorism."

Afghanistan has been a battleground for rival global powers for many centuries. While it boasts of having never been colonized, its feuding warlords have sustained their personal fiefdoms by becoming stooges of foreign powers, provided the price was right. The outside world has been willing to pay because of the importance of Afghanistan's location as a strategic gateway between the Middle East, India and Central Asia. When Ronald Reagan was elected President of the United States in 1980, the U.S. intelligence community informed him that the Soviet Union could be seriously weakened by a protracted war in Afghanistan. The president enthusiastically supported a plan to provide more funds and military training to mujahedin fighters and the militant Arabs (later to be known as Afghanis) who were flying in from North Africa and the Middle East to join the mujahedin in the war against the PDP government and the Soviets.

My first of several visits to Pakistan was in 1988, the year that saw the beginning of the death throes of the Soviet empire. The war in Afghanistan had drained its failing economy, and it was in no position to claim military parity with the United States. The dusty, chaotic town of Peshawar in north-west Pakistan had been home not only to hundreds of Christian, Muslim and secular relief agencies that worked among the massive tide of Afghan refugees, but also to hundreds of foreign journalists and spooks from the CIA, MI6 and the Pakistani intelligence services, the ISI. Its narrow lanes and alleys were congested with rickshaws, horse-drawn carts and cyclists. The seven main mujahedin parties had their offices in the city. Mujahedin fighters and Afghanis would drive recklessly through these lanes in their over-crowded Land Cruisers, waving their gleaming automatic rifles and shouting to passersby "Allah-u-akhbar!" (God is great).

I learned from local Pakistanis that the U.S. government's support for the mujahedin and Afghanis went beyond the provision of sophisticated weapons and military training. The American taxpayer was also funding the vigorous program of Islamization by Pakistani Islamists among the millions of refugees in Peshawar and the tribal trust territories.[2] Pamphlets with Qur'anic texts were distributed in the madrasas (religious schools), reviving the inter-pretation of jihad as holy war against the enemies of Islam, an idea that had largely lain dormant for centuries.

The best known among the mujahedin leaders was the brutal Gulbud-din Hekmatyar, the biggest opium trafficker in the region. His fanaticism extended to throwing acid on women who refused to wear the veil. Brit-ish Prime Minister Margaret Thatcher invited him to London in 1986 and hailed him as a freedom fighter. The West's closest ally in South Asia was the Islamist dictator General Zia ul-Haq of Pakistan, who enforced shari'a law in Pakistan and supported the recruitment of jihadi fighters from all over the Arab world. Zia's enthusiasm for Hekmatyar meant that the bulk of armaments and cash flowing into the anti-Soviet cause were diverted to the latter's militant party (Hizb-I-Islami). Such was the overpowering influence of Hizb-I-Islami both in the refugee camps and aid distribution network that incoming refugees soon realized that joining Hekmatyr's party was the fast track to receiving relief.[3]

Little did I understand at the time that what was being forged in Peshawar and beyond the Khyber Pass was a new ideology that would inspire a pan-

Islamic army of "holy warriors" and eventually strike terror in the cities of the United States and Europe. Nor did I realize that one of the most influential people in Peshawar at the time was a lanky, gaunt Saudi billionaire by the name of Osama bin Laden, who had set up an office in the city in 1984. Al-Qa'ida (The Base) began as a private recruitment agency for Arabs wanting to fight in Afghanistan alongside the mujahedin. It was financed by the nephew of King Faisal and head of the Saudi external intelligence service, the Mukhabarat. Bin Laden, the scion of a family construction business close to the Saud dynasty, administered the agency. He brought lavish funds for arms and drilling equipment to the mujahedin, and later joined them as commander of an armed unit. Bin Laden broke irrevocably with the Saudi regime and eventually became their most wanted enemy. When Saudi Arabia suspended its support to the Arab "Afghani" cause after the withdrawal of Soviet forces, bin Laden went rogue, setting up a private base near Jalalabad and activating links with Saudi exiles in Iran and Syria. His lieutenant, Ayman Zahawir, an Egyptian surgeon from an eminent medical family in Cairo, was the mastermind behind the carnage in Manhattan on September 11, 2001.

In 1988 an international agreement was reached in Geneva under which the Soviet Union agreed on a phased withdrawal of its troops from Afghanistan. After the final withdrawal a year later, the Reagan administration continued its support of the mujahedin struggle against the PDP government. The fall of the government, however, in 1992 only led to further savage bloodletting as the tribal warlords fought for control of the country. By the time the Soviets withdrew, Afghanistan was awash with weapons. In addition to MiG jetfighters, helicopter gunships, tanks and rocket launchers supplied to the Afghan army by the Russians, the United States and Saudi Arabia had channeled an estimated $6 billion in weapons and cash to the mujahedin warlords during the war. The U.S. provision of Stinger heat-seeking missiles after 1985 turned the tide of the war by destroying Soviet air superiority. The CIA sought to buy back these missiles after 1989, but much of the weaponry ended up in the arms bazaars in the tribal trust territories along the Pakistani border.[4]

The unremitting internecine violence among the mujahedin reduced Kabul, which had largely been protected during the Soviet occupation, to rubble. The freelance journalist Michael Griffin, who also served briefly with UNICEF in Afghanistan, has written:

> No city since the end of the Second World War—except Sarajevo—had suffered the same ferocity of jugular violence as Kabul from 1992 to 1996. Sarajevo was almost a side-show by comparison and, at least, it wasn't forgotten. An official of the International Committee of the Red Cross, one of only three foreign organizations to remain after the rocketing of January 1994, said: "Afghanistan seems to have disappeared off the face of the earth." This was true both figuratively and literally, as first 50 percent—rising to 80 percent in 1996—of the built up areas of Kabul were turned into a rubble resembling Dresden after the fire-bombing.[5]

The Taliban (the word means "religious students") movement originated among the southern Pashtun clans, the largest tribalized society in the world, and had its initial political base in Kandahar. Pakistan and Saudi Arabia financed the Taliban and supported their drive to power in 1994-1996, an act later condoned by the United States and other Western states. By the middle of 1995 it had taken control of one-third of the country, disarming local populations and imposing on them the harsh Pashtun customary law combined with an idiosyncratic interpretation of what constituted Islamic propriety. Their misogyny made the Iranian Ayatollahs look like feminists. Not only did they demand that women must wear the all-enveloping *burqa*, which covers the body from head to foot and leaves only a narrow lace grill to look through, but their first act in taking power in Kabul (a year later) was to evict tens of thousands of women from their places of work, paralyzing a government administration in which 25 percent of the staff were female. Girls were denied education, and the eight thousand women undergraduates of the recently rebuilt Kabul University were sent home. Those who defied the regime were publicly beaten or escaped abroad. While women bore the brunt of the repression, men were also forced to conform: growing long beards, replacing Western clothing with the *salwar kameez*, and being forced to go to mosques five times a day.

Here, in the particular brand of militarized Islam represented by the Taliban and Osama bin Laden's al-Qa'ida network we see a new fusion of radical movements based in the Arab world and those influenced by South Asian Islamism. Initially, the "religious fundamentalism" of the Arabs and the Afghans were very different: the former were adherents of the austere Islam promoted in the eighteenth-century by the Wahhabi movement, whose political power increased with the creation of Saudi Arabia and the elevation of the House of Saud by British colonialism in 1926. The Afghans were influenced by a conservative strand of Indian Islam, called Deobandi, after the town in which this movement had its training school. The Deobandis were initially weak in Afghanistan, but through a Pakistani group that promoted their ideas, Jamiat-ul-Ulema-I Pakistan, they came to have significant influence over young Afghans, especially those in the refugee camps of Pakistan. A climate of militancy and intellectual obscurantism among these young men, taught only by mullahs from an early age and without contact with family or women, bred the recruits for what was to become the Taliban.

Once the Cold War ended, the West lost interest in the internecine bloodshed in Afghanistan. Public attention focus shifted to Iraq and the eruption of war in Europe as Yugoslavia unraveled. The leaders of the mujahedin were forgotten until September 2001. But ever since the Taliban took power in Kabul, with the support of Pakistan and Saudi Arabia, they were wooed by the American oil lobby. Taliban leaders were flown to Texas, then governed by George W. Bush, and entertained by senior executives of the oil giant Unocal in Houston. The lack of democracy and the persecution of women and minorities mattered as little for most Americans as they did in Saudi Arabia, America's closest ally in the Middle East next to Israel. The *Wall Street Journal* hailed the Taliban as "the players most capable of achieving peace in Afghanistan" and declared that their success was crucial in securing Afghanistan's status as a "prime trans-shipment route for the export of Central Asia's vast oil, gas and other natural resources."[6]

The oil and gas of the Caspian region are worthless without the means to carry them to deep-water ports. In 1998 Dick Cheney, then a consultant on oil pipelines to several Central Asian republics, told a conference of oil industry executives, "I cannot think of a time when we have had a region emerge suddenly to become as strategically significant as the Caspian."[7] President

Clinton's Energy Secretary, Bill Richardson, candidly described the former Soviet Asian republics as "all about America's future energy security," and added, "We would like to see them reliant on Western commercial and political interests rather than going another way. We've made substantial political investment in the Caspian, and it's very important to us that both the pipeline map and the politics comes out right."[8] A trans-Afghanistan route would preserve the boycott of Iran and weaken the Russian oil and gas monopolies. "It was ideal for the United States and Saudi Arabia," comments Michael Griffin, "the two countries with the easiest access to oil industry finance and the greatest interest in the continued isolation of Iran. A trans-Afghanistan route could shift the region's center of gravity well out of the Russian orbit, while remaining far from the attractions of Iran's developed system of pipelines and ports."[9]

When Unocal eventually signed a memorandum of understanding with the Taliban to build the pipeline from Turkmenistan to Pakistan via Afghanistan, it did so on behalf of a consortium of Amoco, British Petroleum, Chevron, Exxon and Mobil. Those who forged the deal were Dick Cheney, James Baker (the former Secretary of State) and Brent Scowcroft (former National Security Advisor). All had served in the cabinet of George H. W. Bush (the "oil man's president"). Another party to the pipeline negotiations was Enron, the notoriously bankrupt energy trader. Enron's disgraced chairman, Ken Lay, a former Pentagon economist, was one of the biggest single investors in George W. Bush's campaign for president. In return, Lay was able to appoint White House regulators, shape energy policies and block the regulation of offshore tax havens. The Unocal deal fell through a few months after the U.S. embassies in Nairobi and Dar es Salaam were bombed in August 1998 and bin Laden (who was a guest of the Taliban) was blamed. But as late as the summer of 2001 representatives of the Taliban were still being invited to Texas.

After the withdrawal of the Soviets from Afghanistan, the demobilized international brigades spread to other countries, eager to find new jihads against repressive, secular rulers of Muslim-majority states. Supporting the secessionist movements in Kashmir and Chechnya were the next moves in the evolution of militant Sunni Islam into a globalized phenomenon.

THE GLOBALIZATION OF ISLAMIST MILITANCY

When, in 1964, the Iranian Parliament granted US citizens extraterrito-
rial rights in Iran, in exchange for a $200m loan, Ayatollah Khomeini's
howl of rage spoke for all Muslims who had felt powerless in the face of
a bullying West, from the bombardment of Alexandria in 1882 to the
brutal treatment of the Palestinians in the present: "they have reduced
the Iranian people to a level lower than that of an American dog."[10]

The resurgence of Islam is a "broad-based, complex, multifaceted phenomenon that has embraced Muslim societies from Sudan to Sumatra," write
John Esposito and John Voll, "Its leaders and organizations are as varied as
its manifestations."[11] In these societies an intellectual and political battle
has raged among Muslim thinkers and activists to rethink the Qur'an and
the prophetic traditions in the light of modern challenges. The longer-term
backdrop is the humiliating experience of Western political and intellectual
domination since the early nineteenth century.[12] In their survey of contemporary Muslim public intellectuals, Esposito and Voll have suggested that
"The failure of the old-style ulama [religious scholars] to provide any real
alternative to the secular intellectuals in the nineteenth and early twentieth
centuries may be the single most important aspect of the rise of the contemporary Muslim activist intellectual."[13] The more recent backdrop is provided
by the despotism and corruption of many allegedly Islamic governments, the
cultural penetration of Western lifestyles, and the failure of secular models of
economic development. Among the modern educated classes, a new style of
Muslim intellectual has emerged, committed to the transformation of society
but within the framework of ideologies and programs that could be identified
as authentically Islamic.

Richard Bulliet, a Middle East historian at New York's Columbia University, has observed that today's Islamic political culture draws its mobilizing
force from the unintended consequences of three developments in the last
century and a half: the marginalization of the ulama [religious scholars] by
"modernizing" states, the nineteenth-century print revolution, and mass education that followed in the wake of nationalist governments after World War
II.[14] Whenever a Muslim community feels threatened it looks to its religious

leaders for guidance. This is why so much of the energies of the modern state was expended in undermining the authority of the ulama who traditionally had been the chief critics of political tyranny. These anticlerical objectives were often mislabeled "secularism" by Western observers.

As for the transition in the nineteenth century from a classroom and pulpit culture to a print culture, this gave birth to new religious authorities who sprang up from outside the traditional seminaries. Just as in Europe centuries before, the widespread dissemination of printed materials destroyed the intellectual monopoly exercised by learned preachers in religiously oriented schools. These new authorities effectively supplanted the old authorities whose power had been based on seminary education, judicial office and income from pious endowments. "The Muslim public at large, both male and female, increasingly learned about their religion from a torrent of books, magazines, newspapers, and pamphlets, written in large part by people who lacked the credentials to be classified as ulama."[15]

Bulliet notes:

> People who followed Hasan al-Banna into the Muslim Brotherhood, or who listened raptly to Ali Shariati denouncing the Iranian monarchy, or who joined Osama bin Laden in al-Qa'ida, would have followed a self-proclaimed Mahdi in previous centuries, or a militant Sufi, or a mufti proclaiming his opposition to an act of imperial tyranny. The manifestos of the nonreligious print ideologues ultimately came to naught for lack of roots in an indigenous political culture. The preachings of the religious print ideologues sank deep because the roots were already in place. What went on, then, was not just a media revolution, but a media revolution that favoured those who could credibly cite Muhammad as their inspiration over those who took their cues from Voltaire, or Thomas Jefferson, or Karl Marx.[16]

When I was a university student in London in the 1970s, some of my Muslim friends from the Middle East were members of the Muslim Brotherhoods in their native countries. They were deeply influenced by an Egyptian writer, Sayyid Qutb (1906-1966), who was a role model for them of a devout Muslim. Qutb had been employed in the Egyptian education department and had sojourned in the United States from 1948 to 1950 to study the schooling system there. Not only was he unimpressed with what he saw, but he returned with feelings of deep repugnance toward what he saw as a soulless, racist and materialist society. His experience of American life convinced him that Islam provided a superior path to progress, not just for Egypt but for the world. Long before Samuel Huntington, Qutb was writing about the "clash of civilizations" and of the irreconcilable differences between "Islam and the West." He became not only the most vocal and literate ideologue of the Muslim Brotherhood but its chief tactician and strategist. He was imprisoned and executed by order of President Nasser in 1966. His writings from the early 1960s were smuggled out of prison by women associated with the Brotherhood and became the basis for a revolutionary Islamic ideology. Qutb himself attained the status of a martyr for Islamists, and his book *Milestones (Ma'alim fi al-tariq)* inspired the development of a militant Islamic ideology by the 1970s in a number of different places in the Sunni Muslim world.

Links were already being established in the mid-twentieth century between Islamist nationalisms in the Middle East and South Asia. Qutb himself had been influenced by the writings of Maulana Mawdudi (1903-1979), founder of the Jamaat-I-Islami party in Lahore in 1941. Critical of Muslim dependence on the West, Mawdudi advocated a gradual Islamization of all aspects of Muslim life. He wrote, "In human affairs the most important thing is, 'who holds the bridle reigns?' If these are in the hands of righteous people, worshippers of God, then it is inevitable that the whole of social life be God-worshipping. . . . None of the purposes of religion can be accomplished so long as control of affairs is in the hands of kafirs."[17] His goal was to train and produce a dynamic nucleus of change agents who would constitute a new elite, creating a true Islamic society in the subcontinent. The Jamaat-I-Islami recruited its members from schools, universities and mosques. Modern learning and religious devotion came together in the creation of a new educated elite that would give leadership in every sector of society.

In many Muslim-majority nations today, it is Islamists who have created much of the organizational and ideological framework for middle- and lower-middle class Muslims to enter the workings of the modern economy and state. They support bureaucratization and promotion by merit, the use of the ballot box, the rule of law, and the codification of that law, shari'a, into forms that may be applied by modern judiciaries. Their schools, clinics, hospitals and neighborhood meeting places have often grown up because the state has failed to provide the infrastructure to support the tens of millions who have moved in recent times from the countryside to the cities.[18] These institutions contribute substantially to the structure of civil society. However, the Western schedule of human rights is vigorously opposed, especially religious liberty and equality for religious minorities and women. (Though in some nations women have made considerable progress in education and employment.)

In rejecting the secularist, individualistic values which have accompanied the modernization process in the West, the new Islamists have provided an important focus for alienated social groups. Students have often been the target of repressive governments, such as in Indonesia under General Suharto. They were critical of the failures of development, corruption, the growing disparity between rich and poor, and conspicuous consumption in a society with limited opportunities for the younger generation. When student organizations were banned in Indonesian universities, mosques became rallying centers for disaffected students. Islamic discourse, often initiated by Muslim intellectuals educated in Europe and the Middle East, now became the chief vehicle to express dissent. With the political door now closed, the stress was placed on the relevance of Islam to social and economic development.

The current struggle in Indonesia, the world's most populous Muslim nation, is instructive for what is happening elsewhere. Indonesia boasts a rich pluralist heritage, especially in Java, where ancient Hindu, Buddhist and animist traditions have coalesced and created a uniquely Javanese worldview and tolerant culture. In large measure the ideological battle now being waged is a clash of two cultures: between this indigenous, pluralist Islam (what some writers call "cosmopolitan Islam") and the legalistic, Arabic Islam propagated by proselytizing movements from Saudi Arabia, Yemen and Egypt.

Cosmopolitan Islam is more concerned with political culture than political institutions. It is expressed in the individual lives and morality of the people, informing the social ethics of the community and its sense of a transnational or universal identity. Many local Muslim intellectuals, as well as broad segments of the public, endorse a pluralist understanding of nationhood. "Civil pluralist Muslims," writes Robert Hefner, "deny the necessity of a formally established Islamic state, emphasize that it is the spirit and not the letter of Islamic law (shari'a) to which Muslims must attend, stress the need for programs to elevate the status of women, and insist that the Muslim world's most urgent task is to develop moral tools to respond to the challenge of modern pluralism."[19]

Just as there have been some strands of Christian thinking that have always been deeply antagonistic toward Islam, so within Islam there have been schools of thought that have always harbored a deep hostility toward Christians, Jews and other non-Islamic religions and civilizations, notably the Wahhabi and Salafi schools dominant in modern Saudi Arabia. Until the twentieth century, however, the Wahhabis were a theological movement of only localized significance. It is the oil wealth of modern Saudi Arabia that has allowed the Wahhabis to spread their intolerant brand of Islam, notably by the funding of extremist Wahhabi and Salafist religious schools across the Islamic world since the mid-1970s.[20] Saudi Arabia has played a central role in the nurturing of a violent form of Islamism. The kingdom took in Salafist leaders expelled by secular regimes such as Syria, Egypt and Iraq. It was among Saudis engaged in the Afghan conflict of the 1980s that the fatal fusion took place between Wahhabi puritanism and the jihadist ideas of the Muslim Brotherhood, leading to the creation of the al-Qa'ida network.

Many Muslim intellectuals in the Middle East had hoped that the ending of the Cold War would usher in an era of peace and democracy. But the 1990s proved to be a decade of further humiliation. When a popular Islamist party was set to win the Algerian elections in 1992, the French-backed military junta annulled the elections. Although the antidemocratic move was initially criticised by the U.S. and British governments, they too eventually acquiesced. In Egypt and Saudi Arabia, authoritarian regimes continued to imprison, torture and kill thousands of Islamists, while Western powers continued to provide them with arms and other forms of "aid." In Palestine the Oslo peace accord collapsed and the intifada against Israeli occupation began. As the Iranian Revolution, which had triggered an Islamic revival worldwide, led to disillusionment in many quarters, so the killing of Muslims in Bosnia;

the crippling economic sanctions against Iraq, which resulted in the deaths of over a million children; Hindu nationalist violence against Muslim communities in north India (often supported by the federal or central governments); and the razing of whole towns and villages by the Russian army in Chechnya only added to the feelings of humiliation and helpless rage on the part of Muslims in many parts of the world.

I was traveling again in Pakistan in February 1991, when an international coalition of armed forces, led by the United States, began its onslaught on Iraq in what was called Operation Desert Storm. I watched with embarrassment, alongside Muslim university students, as the well-known evangelist Billy Graham was shown on CNN praying with the American president, George H. W. Bush, for "victory for the forces of justice and righteousness." My Muslim neighbors and I knew perfectly well that this was not about "justice and righteousness" but about securing the West's oil supplies. The importance of remembering history was brought home to me. After the collapse of the Ottoman empire in the 1920s, British colonial administrators carved out the modern state of Iraq, drawing its boundaries in such a manner that all its huge oil reserves would belong to them and not the Turks, and denying the local puppet regime that they installed in Baghdad access to the sea by creating a buffer state called Kuwait. In the 1980s, when Iraq and Iran were locked in a bloody war that saw over a million casualties on both sides, the Reagan and Thatcher governments illegally engaged in sales of arms and weapons technology to Saddam Hussein, violating the United Nations-imposed trade embargo on both nations. Right up until the invasion of Kuwait in August 1990, Saddam was hailed by senior American and British politicians as their staunchest ally, next to Israel and Saudi Arabia, in the region! So much so that when Saddam used chemical weapons in the mass murder of over five thousand Kurds in 1989, the United States and Britain turned a blind eye. (In 1992 a Congressional inquiry found that George H. W. Bush and his top aides had ordered a cover-up to conceal their secret support for Saddam and the illegal arms shipments sent via third countries.)[21]

The first Gulf War did not end with the "liberation" of Kuwait. In the eighteen-month period from May 31, 1998, to January 14, 2000, the U.S. Air Force and naval aircraft flew 36,000 sorties over Iraq, including 24,000 combat missions. During 1999, American and British aircraft dropped more than 1,800 bombs and hit 450 targets. The Western media routinely ignored such bombings, so the public were left largely in the dark. In a rare acknowledgment the *New York Times* of August 13, 1999, reported, "American warplanes have methodically and with virtually no public discussion been attacking Iraq. . . . [P]ilots have flown about two-thirds as many missions as NATO pilots flew over Yugoslavia in seventy-eight days of around-the-clock war there."[22]

The Clinton administration's response to the East African embassy bombings in August 1998 was another unwarranted propaganda gift to Islamist radicals worldwide. Floundering around to find targets worthy of American vengeance, the U.S. intelligence services chose Osama bin Laden's training camps in the valleys around Khost and the Al-Shifa pharmaceutical plant near Khartoum, a factory allegedly built with bin Laden's money during his Sudanese sojourn in the early 1990s and which the CIA claimed was producing biochemical weapons. On August 20, 1998, as the American nation was bracing itself for Monica Lewinsky's sexual revelations before a grand jury later that day, President Clinton authorized the launching of seventy to one hundred Tomahawk cruise missiles on Khost and al-Shifa. Bin Laden escaped, his resolve to kill Americans strengthened.

The Sudanese government insisted that the Al-Shifa factory only produced medicines for children and vaccines for cattle. They demanded an independent UN inquiry. The U.S. government refused to divulge its intelligence and suppressed the UN inquiry. On the first anniversary of the attack an article in the *Boston Globe* reported that

> without the lifesaving medicine produced, Sudan's death toll from
> the bombing continued. . . . [T]ens of thousands of people—many of
> them children—have suffered and died from malaria, tuberculosis, and
> other treatable diseases. . . . [Al-Shifa] provided affordable medicine
> for humans and all the locally available veterinary medicine in Sudan.
> It produced 90% of Sudan's major pharmaceutical products. . . . Sanc-
> tions against Sudan make it impossible to import adequate amounts of
> medicines required to cover the serious gap. . . . Millions must wonder

how the International Court of Justice in the Hague will celebrate this anniversary.[23]

What would the reaction have been if al-Qa'ida had blown up half the pharmaceutical supplies in the United States and the facilities for replenishing them?

Western powers, and especially the United States, have long been criticized by Islamists for the way they prop up dictatorial, corrupt and self-serving rulers whom they dub "the Eunuchs." The hypocrisies and ostentatious displays of wealth on the part of the royal families of Saudi Arabia, Kuwait and other Gulf states are detested by large numbers of Arabs. The consistent way the United States has used its veto in the United Nations to undermine every UN resolution criticizing atrocities committed by Israeli armed forces in Palestine and the Lebanon, has played into the hands of those Islamists who believe that their local struggles against un-Islamic re gimes cannot succeed without taking on the West itself.

When established religious leaders, such as Sayyid Tantawi, the Grand Sheikh of the Al-Azhar in Cairo, became discredited in the Muslim world as merely mouthpieces for corrupt regimes, a leadership vacuum emerged in the Muslim world. It sucked in men with little or no religious training, such as Osama bin Laden and Ayman Zawahri. It was in 1996 that Osama bin Laden issued his first fatwa, or religio-judicial opinion: "A Declaration of War Against the Americans." He declared that the suffering of Muslims was orchestrated by "Zionist-Crusaders." The ultimate insult to Islam, he announced, was the permanent presence of U.S. troops in Saudi Arabia after Operation Desert Storm: they represented the nadir of Muslim humiliation at the hands of the non-Muslim West. The Saudi king, the protector of the holy shrines of Mecca and Medina, was a mere puppet, being protected himself by the American army. Bin Laden's strategy has been to attack Americans so as to provoke a backlash strong enough to radicalize the Muslim world, topple pro-Western governments and so install a new Islamic caliphate.

British Broadcasting Corporation journalist Phil Rees, who has interviewed the leaders of insurgent groups all over the world, writes of the fascination bin Laden exercised even among moderate Muslims:

Here was a man who was able to give America a bloody nose and many
nonviolent Muslims that I have met, while grieving for the families
of the victims, felt that America had it coming. The 'Eunuch' leaders, endless Arab summits, even the United Nations when it passed
resolutions in favour of Muslim nations, were powerless to challenge
America. . . . Thousands of Islamic radicals who had fought for specific national objectives, from Malaysia to Morocco and Bangladesh to
Indonesia, found al-Qa'ida ideologues joining them at conferences and
they began discussing the idea of a common goal. Many of these groups
spurned al-Qa'ida's global ambitions as irrelevant to their local fight but
they often maintained informal links.[24]

Everything that has happened since 9/11 has reinforced the sense among
Muslims of being under siege. America's overreaction played right into the
hands of al-Qa'ida. Arab men from eighteen to fifty were harassed in public
and questioned by the FBI. Student visas to the United States from Muslim-
majority nations were restricted. The United States and Europe branded as
"terrorists" and confiscated funds from scores of Islamist organizations, including educational organizations and charities. Many Islamist militants had
no quarrel with the United States but found themselves pushed into a corner,
forced to choose between surrendering what they saw as a legitimate struggle
against state repression and joining bin Laden's network of jihadis. Many
have chosen the latter.

Much of the Western media fell silent in September 2004 when the Iraqi
city of Fallujah was almost completely destroyed by U.S. troops. But this
event, as well as the crimes against humanity committed in the mountains
of Afghanistan, Guantánamo and Abu Ghraib, have been broadcast all over
the Arab world. They fuel the helpless rage that many young Muslims feel
in the face of American tactics of so-called shock and awe. This rage is easily exploited by al-Qa'ida and other militant networks. The support of the
United States and Britain for the despotic rulers of countries such as Saudi
Arabia, Uzbekistan, Bahrain, Kuwait and Egypt, not to mention the hypocritical stance toward Iran's nuclear program and the one-sided denunciation
of Palestinian violence, plays right into the hands of Islamist demagogues as

well as those like Osama bin Laden who can translate demagogy into brutality. At a time when the Muslim landscape is so barren of heroes and feelings of humiliation and despair are rampant in many Muslim societies, it is hardly surprising that bin Laden (with his selective manipulation of Qur'anic texts) should present himself as the divinely appointed leader of the Muslim Ummah against the West.

The Muslim Brotherhood, along with the emir of the Jamaat-I-Islami in Pakistan and Sheikh Ahmed Yassin, the founder of Hamas, were deeply critical of al-Qa'ida and signed a joint statement soon after 9/11 expressing their "deepest sympathy and sorrow" with the American people and condemning unequivocally the events that were "against all human and Islamic norms." Two years later, following the Israeli assassination of Sheikh Yassin, Hamas changed its rhetorical stance. Yassin's successor, Abdel Aziz Rantisi, announced that Hamas was now committed to more than the expulsion of Israel from Palestinian lands: "President Bush is an enemy of God, the enemy of Islam and Muslims. America declared war against God . . . and God declared war on America and Bush."[25] Rantisi himself was assassinated shortly afterward by the Israelis. God had now been enlisted by both sides in an unending global war.

DECONSTRUCTING THE "WAR ON TERROR"

In a famous essay, "Politics and the English Language," written in 1946, the English journalist George Orwell (1903-1950) lamented the corruption of language by politicians and their speechwriters. Orwell himself had been employed by the BBC in World War II to counter German propaganda with that of the British government. Totalitarian regimes such as the Nazis and the Soviet Union had manipulated language as a powerful form of collective thought control, and Orwell brilliantly caricatured this in his novel *Nineteen Eighty-Four*, written two years later. But Western democracies were not immune to the abuse of language. "Political language—and with variations this is true of all political parties from Conservatives to Anarchists—is designed to make lies sound truthful and murder respectable, and to give an appearance of solidity to pure wind."[26]

In our time, political speech and writing are largely the defence of the indefensible. Things like the continuance of British rule in India, the Russian purges and deportation, the dropping of the atom bombs on Japan, can indeed be defended, but only by arguments which are too brutal for most people face, and which do not square with the professed aims of political parties. Thus political language has to consist largely of euphemism, question-begging and sheer cloudy vagueness. Defenceless villages are bombarded from the air, the inhabitants driven out into the countryside, the cattle machine-gunned, the huts set on fire with incendiary bullets: this is called pacification. Millions of peasants are robbed of their farms and sent trudging along the roads with no more than they can carry: this is called transfer of population or rectification of frontiers. People are imprisoned for years without trial, or shot in the back of the neck or sent to die of scurvy in Arctic lumber camps: this is called elimination of unreliable elements. Such phraseology is needed if one wants to name things without calling up mental pictures of them.[27]

Language suffers from the general moral and intellectual decay of society. But it also contributes to the latter. Slogans, clichés and well-worn idioms hinder clarity of thought. Rescuing political language from "euphemism, question-begging and sheer cloudy vagueness" is not a matter of sentimental archaism, like those who prefer the King James Bible to modern English translations. It is rather the first step in helping people grasp important political ideas. Language "becomes ugly and inaccurate because our thoughts are foolish, but the slovenliness of our language makes it easier for us to have foolish thoughts."[28]

What would Orwell have made of the neologisms with which the Western media have inundated us in recent years: "smart bombs," "surgical airstrikes," "collateral damage," "Patriot Act," "holy terror," "narco-terrorists"? What about the "axis of evil" and "ridding the world of evil"? And how about that ubiquitous phrase that came into prominence all over the world after September 11, 2001, the "war on terror"?

Seven weeks after the World Trade Center attacks, the U.S. State Department spokesman, Richard Boucher, declared that, "The President has made it clear that the United States is engaged in a war against the scourge of terrorism. . . . [W]e will not rest until every terrorist group has been removed as a threat to the United States, our citizens, our interests, and our friends and allies."[29]

The State Department announced that twenty-two names of "foreign terrorist individuals, entities and groups" would be added to a list established under Executive Order 13224, signed by President Bush on September 23, 2001. The list included the Basque independent movement, ETA; Sri Lanka's Tamil Tigers, who had been fighting for a separate homeland for the northern Tamils of that island from the late 1970s; the Kurdish separatist party, PKK; Colombia's Marxist guerrillas, the FARC; and Islamic radicals in Lebanon and the West Bank fighting against the Israeli occupation. All had their assets in American banks frozen. None of these organizations had any links to the perpetrators of the September 11 carnage. President Bush declared, "Our war on terror begins with al-Qa'ida but does not stop there. It will not end until every terrorist group of global reach has been found, stopped, and defeated."[30] The list continued to grow to include hundreds of seemingly random individuals and organizations from Islamic countries as well as Protestant military groups in Northern Ireland, leftist groups in the Philippines and movements pursuing an independent Sikh homeland in the Punjab, northern India.

What did all these groups have in common that they should be singled out as "terrorists" with a "global reach"? It mattered little whether they posed a military threat to the American public or government, or enjoyed widespread popular support in their own countries, or were more the victims rather than the perpetrators of political violence. The people of the United States, represented by their government, had unilaterally declared a global war on all nonstate actors who were committed to violent struggle.

America's war on terror led to the creation of a coalition of armed forces, from states as wide apart politically as Australia and Uzbekistan, several of whom needed little further inducement to crack down on their own irritating dissidents. America's first allies in the war on terror were the old Northern Alliance warlords in Afghanistan, whose fanatical, internecine violence had plunged Afghanistan into violent chaos and paved the way for the Taliban

tyranny. They were transformed overnight in the American media into freedom fighters committed to a democratic Afghanistan, and were handsomely
bribed by the U.S. government into lending their support in the drive against
the Taliban and the hunt for Osama bin Laden.

Once the United States had declared a "global war on terror," it was difficult for Western nations to criticize the Russian army's brutal suppression
of the secessionist movement in Chechnya or Beijing's crackdown on Muslim Ugher separatists in western China. Israel's prime Minister Ariel Sharon
seized the moment to label Yasser Arafat "our bin Laden" and threatened
to assassinate him. Autocratic regimes from Uzbekistan to Burma relished
the opportunity to justify their own vicious suppression of opposition critics.
Even Robert Mugabe leaped on the bandwagon. He aligned himself with the
Bush administration and claimed that independent journalists whom he had
thrown into jail were "supporters of terrorism."

In a speech to the nation reporting on the progress of the war in Afghanistan, President Bush ratcheted up the rhetoric: "We wage a war to save civilization itself. We did not seek it, but we will fight it, and we will prevail. This
is a different war from any our nation has ever faced—a war on many fronts,
against terrorists who operate in over 60 different countries. And this is a war
that must be fought not only overseas, but also at home."[31]

For decades the United Nations has failed to agree on what constitutes
"terrorism," and efforts to draw up a global antiterrorist treaty have been at
an impasse since 1996. The Bush administration could equate Saddam Hussein's regime with global terrorism despite the lack of any evidence linking
Saddam Hussein to 9/11. In his address marking the end of the invasion of
Iraq, President Bush announced: "The battle of Iraq is one victory in a war on
terror that began on September the 11, [sic] 2001, and still goes on." He continued: "The liberation of Iraq is a crucial advance in the campaign against
terror. We've removed an ally of al Qaeda, and cut off a source of terrorist
funding. And this much is certain: No terrorist network will gain weapons of
mass destruction from the Iraqi regime, because the regime is no more. . . .
Any person, organization, or government that supports, protects, or harbors
terrorists is complicit in the murder of the innocent, and equally guilty of
terrorist crimes."[32]

The war continued in Iraq but the coalition was no longer confronting a conventional army. Iraqis opposed to the American-led occupation kidnapped and murdered Western journalists and businessmen. Vast numbers of local Iraqi civilians and policemen suffered indiscriminately as bombs were planted in crowded public places by an enemy that was never properly identified. Their actions, rather than political affiliations, earned them the catch-all label "terrorists." Occasionally they were described as "insurgents" by military spokesmen in order to differentiate antigovernment Iraqis from foreign jihadi fighters, who were called "international terrorists." Usually the coalition used the terms interchangeably. No explanation was offered as to why one attack was labeled "terrorist" and another not. Moreover, in defiance of Orwellian warnings, the abuse of language has continued: the conflict is always a "war," not an invasion, a "liberation," not an occupation, and cities are "secured," not captured.

In an interview with the BBC, the leader of the Mujahedin Council in Solo, Indonesia, is reported to have said, "We don't recognize the word 'terrorist.' It's a word used only by Western countries because they have all the sophisticated weapons. Islam never had a weapon so when it defends itself, it is called 'terrorism.' In the US, 'terrorism' means opposing Western civilization, wishing to establish an Islamic state or having Osama bin Laden as an idol. That means there are millions of terrorists in Indonesia."[33]

Interestingly, the terms *terror* and *terrorist* in a political context first came into English usage in the bloody confusion surrounding the French Revolution (1789-1794). The Jacobin rulers launched a self-styled "Reign of Terror" to instill fear on any groups that challenged the authority of the new republic. In French it was known simply as *la Terreur*. For Robespierre, the leader of the Jacobin party, the French were the first people in the world who had established true democracy, and that victory had to be defended against all who opposed the sovereignty of the People. Terror, said Robespierre, is "merely prompt, severe and inflexible justice. Hence it is itself an emanation of justice, less a particular principle than a consequence of the general principle of democracy applied to the country's most pressing need." In language that perfectly exemplified Orwell's "Newspeak" and has chilling resonances with much of the utterances emerging from the White House in recent years, he described himself and his associates (the revolutionary government) as "a despotism of liberty against tyranny" in which any wavering or restraint would simply increase the strength of the republic's enemies and divide and weaken its friends.[34]

For most of the nineteenth century, however, the word *terrorist* came to refer to all revolutionaries who threatened the monarchies of Europe, such as the Russians who assassinated Tsar Alexander II and the French anarchists who formed the Paris Commune. The Clerkenwell bombing of 1867, carried out by an Irish nationalist group, the Fenians, prompted a wave of hysteria in London reminiscent of July 7, 2005. Paris suffered anarchist bomb attacks no less than eleven times between 1892 and 1894, and seven heads of state were assassinated in Europe between 1881 and 1914. With the rise of state fascism in the 1920s the term reverted to its usage during the French Revolution but with wholly pejorative connotations. Hitler and Mussolini applied a system of state-sanctioned terror to crush internal opposition, and their thugs who roamed the streets of German and Italian cities were labeled "street terrorists" by the British press. Stalin's "Great Terror" sent tens of thousands of Soviet citizens to their death by way of show trials, and sentenced millions of others to lifelong imprisonment in labor camps.

It was after World War II, when the British and French empires found themselves vulnerable to nationalist agitation in their colonies, that *terrorism* came to be used exclusively of acts of political violence committed by nonstate actors. The newly independent states of Asia and Africa took over this definition of terrorism and applied it in subsequent years to all those militant guerrilla organizations that challenged state authority. The use of force for political ends, whether in the context of a declared war or otherwise, is inextricably bound up with terror. In the Palestine of the 1930s and 1940s, Menachem Begin's Irgun organization killed scores of Palestinian civilians and British soldiers using terrorist techniques. The most brutal anticolonial struggle of the twentieth century was probably the Algerian war, in which over a million people perished. The French were savage in the techniques of mass killing, and the new military rulers of independent Algeria deployed the same techniques against supporters of the Islamic movement in the 1990s.

Consider the internal conflict in Sri Lanka, the context in which I am writing. What began as a legitimate struggle for civil rights in the 1950s and later developed into a violent demand for a separate state for Tamils quickly descended into a protracted "tit for tat" spiral of revenge. There is little doubt that the Tamil Tigers are a ruthless organization who developed the use of the suicide bomber long before New Yorkers and Londoners experienced its savagery in the hands of Islamic groups.[35] But while the atrocities committed by the Tamil Tigers are well known around the world, war crimes and other human rights abuses by the Sri Lankan armed forces have never been seriously investigated by the government or the international justice agencies (despite being frequently highlighted by human rights activists and church leaders, local and foreign). The typical government response to any suicide bombing is to order aerial attacks on areas in the north or east of the island controlled by the Tamil Tigers. Civilian casualties from such attacks are high, but rarely reported in the southern Sinhalese or English press. When a landmine explosion results in the death of soldiers in a Tamil region, local youth are rounded up and either executed on the spot or taken into custody and tortured. Many have simply disappeared. Neither side has taken the safeguarding of civilian lives seriously. State-sponsored paramilitary groups have deliberately executed civilians in Tamil-speaking regions as acts of revenge or in order to terrorize the local population. So, as often happens in such instances, the army becomes the most effective recruiting agency for the rebels.

There has long been an international aspect to the conflict, which is perhaps one reason it has proved so intractable. The main source of funding for the Tamil Tigers has been the affluent Sri Lankan Tamil diaspora in Britain, Australia, Canada, New Zealand and the United States.[36] In the aftermath of the huge refugee influx to India in 1983, the Indian intelligence services began to train Tamil Tiger recruits in secret camps in south India. There is evidence that the Tigers also had links with militant groups operating in other parts of the world, and arms have been smuggled by boats from various ports in southeast Asia. The Sri Lankan army looked to Pakistan, Britain and the Israeli Mossad for its own training and armament needs. Massive corruption over arms deals with foreign governments and mercenary arms brokers on the part of some senior Sri Lankan politicians, bureaucrats and army generals is one major reason the war has continued for so long. Wars and civil conflicts can be very lucrative for some corporations, banks and politicians.

Following 9/11 and the launch of the "war on terror," Western governments, led by the United States and Britain, have proscribed the Tamil Tigers as a terrorist organization and cracked down on their fundraising and propaganda activities in the West. Expatriate Sri Lankan Sinhalese have welcomed these moves, while Tamil cultural organizations in the West (some, though not all, of which are fronts for the Tigers) have lobbied politicians in their countries to lift the bans and to see the Tigers as a legitimate political movement. Sinhalese and Tamil professionals who may have lived and worked side by side in Sri Lanka before they emigrated West, are often more fiercely chauvinist abroad and fan the flames of hatred from a safe distance.

Successive Sri Lankan governments, and the government-controlled sections of the mass media, have always referred to the Tamil Tigers as terrorists and so welcomed the proscription of the organization by the United States and Britain (and later by Canada and the European Union [EU]) with glee. There is little doubt that the move compelled the Tigers toward accepting a ceasefire and the reduction of their demand for separatism to a federal constitution that involved a substantial degree of autonomy. Even such a move, though, was unacceptable to Sinhalese chauvinists in the south and to influential sections within the Sri Lankan political leadership. Both the Tigers and the Sri Lankan government were pressured into a series of (eventually aborted) "peace talks" by Norwegian peace facilitators, various human rights organizations and some Western governments. There was a curious anomaly in this process. The United States and United Kingdom governments, which have repeatedly said that there is "no negotiating with terrorists," have been exerting pressure on the Sri Lankan governments to do just that. Not unreasonably, the Tamil Tigers demanded the withdrawal of all EU "ceasefire monitors" in the regions under their control, saying that as long as they were proscribed as a "terrorist" organization peace talks were impossible.[37]

While the histories of Sri Lanka, Northern Ireland or Spain are all very different, comparisons are inevitable. A sustainable peace was only achieved in Northern Ireland when the British government accepted that the cause of the violence was political and that a solution must also be political. This led to the Good Friday Agreement of 1998 and the subsequent demilitarization of the IRA. The Spanish government, which sent troops to support George Bush's global war on terror, had refused to negotiate with the Basque "terrorist" group ETA and even secured the proscription by the Spanish Supreme Court of the Basque political party, Batasuna, in March 2003. Two months later, the U.S. government added Batasuna to its growing list of "terrorist groups." As long as the Basque problem was defined by the Aznar government as "terrorism," there was only one solution, a military victory. The horrific Madrid train bombings of March 2004 were blamed on the Basque separatists, justifying further crackdowns on Batasuna and the ETA. When popular anger at the deception of the government led to the Socialist Party returning to power after eight years, the mood changed. A demoralized Basque separatist movement and the new socialist government were willing to talk in earnest. One tragedy seems to have given birth to hope for the end of another.

Unless we subscribe to the naive belief that governments do not engage in acts of terror against their own citizens, let alone the civilian populations of other nations, the one-sided use of *terrorism* by the world's media is baffling. Violent actions by the Israeli army or Israeli settlers against Palestinian civilians are never described as "terrorist," but the term is routinely used in large sections of the Western media for violent acts undertaken against Israelis. Surely journalistic integrity requires that the term *terrorism* should either be dropped for its vagueness or be used evenhandedly to embrace all organized acts of terror, including those by governments. The terms *militant, guerrilla* or *insurgent* do not carry the same connotations of evil that *terrorist* does; and hence the hijacking of that term by governments who want to scapegoat those who challenge their legitimacy. "Terrorism" is always what our enemies do.

On September 5, 2006, President Bush released an updated National Strategy for Combating Terrorism (NCST). The rhetoric was unchanged. The United States was still waging "a relentless war against the terrorists using all elements of national power and influence." The enemy the American people face is "a transnational terrorist movement fuelled by a radical ideology of hatred, oppression, and murder." The war on terror is a "different kind of war, involving both a battle of arms and a battle of ideas." Not only is the United States fighting terrorist enemies on the battlefield, it is "promoting freedom and human dignity as alternatives to the terrorists' perverse vision of oppression and totalitarian rule." The report again affirmed, "We make no distinction between those who commit acts of terror and those who support and harbor terrorists. We are working to disrupt the flow of resources from states to terrorists while simultaneously end state sponsorship of terrorism."[38]

That the United States has been the biggest haven in the world for terrorists and corrupt ex-dictators is a well-known fact to those who live south of its border. Fort Benning in Georgia has often been dubbed the world's "university of terrorism" because it has trained Central American military and paramilitary death squads in torture, assassination and mass terror. At the start of the massive U.S. bombing of Afghanistan in response to 9/11, George Monbiot wrote in the British newspaper *The Guardian:*

> Given that the evidence linking the school to continuing atrocities in Latin America is rather stronger than the evidence linking the al-Qa'ida training camps to the attack on New York, what should we do about the "evil-doers" in Fort Benning, Georgia? Well, we could urge our governments to apply full diplomatic pressure and to seek extradition of the school's commanders for trial on charges of complicity in crimes against humanity. Alternatively, we could demand that our governments attack the United States bombing its military installations, cities and airports in the hope of overthrowing its unelected government and replacing it with a new administration administered by the UN. In case this proposal proves unpopular with the American people, we could win their hearts and minds by dropping naan bread and dried curry in plastic bags stamped with the Afghan flag.[39]

APPLYING JUST-WAR REASONING

The just-war tradition is a proposal, strongly shaped by Christian theological reflection, for doing justice even in the context of the horrors of war. Wars are never just, but sometimes necessary. The proposal is best regarded as a tool of practical reasoning, designed to help political leaders and private citizens understand their obligations before God and neighbor in the face of evil. It seeks to discipline both the resort to war *(ius ad bellum)* and the conduct of war *(ius in bello)*, bringing them under the threefold constraint of authority, proportionality and discrimination.

The just-war tradition argues that armed conflict can and must be reconceived as an extraordinary extension of the ordinary acts of judgment by governments. As such, it is subject to the moral restraints of ordinary acts of domestic judgment. While its roots lie in the thought of Cicero, Augustine, Ambrose and Aquinas, the classic just-war thinkers of the early modern period in Europe were the Spanish Catholics Francisco de Vitoria (c. 1485-1546) and Francisco Suárez (1548-1617), and the Dutch Protestant jurist Hugo Grotius (1583-1645). It was their deliberations, in the context of the emerging nation-state system, that led to the formulation of a regime of international law that sets limits on the claims of national sovereignties. Unlike secular versions of the proposal, ancient and modern, which emphasize the legitimacy of self-defense, Christian thinkers have stressed that the protection of the innocent—defenseless victims of aggression—sometimes obliges the Christian to use coercive force, thereby situating the proposal within the context of love of neighbor.

A common way of distinguishing between terrorism and other forms of political violence is in terms of the just-war criteria of discrimination and proportionality. Discrimination has to do with intention in armed combat. A discriminate act of force is one that intends to make a distinction between the innocent and the guilty, between those who materially cooperate with wrongdoing and those who do not (noncombatants). Proportionality also follows from the character of war as judgment, a reactive pronouncement upon an offense. The means undertaken in resorting to war must correspond with the purpose, and the latter must correspond to the offense addressed. The British moral theologian Oliver O'Donovan, who has written extensively on the Christian contribution to the just-war tradition, describes terrorism as "the waging of war by disordered means, in defiance of proportion or (especially) discrimination," and he sums up the difference between terrorists and guerrillas in this way: "The terrorist makes his point by slaughtering the innocent intentionally; the insurgent makes his by forcing his opponent to slaughter the innocent unintentionally. Insurgents may also be terrorists in fact. . . . Yet the difference is not to be dismissed lightly."[40]

O'Donovan also points out that it is the issue of intention that separates "collateral damage" from indiscriminate killing:

> One can test for the intention to harm non-combatants by putting a simple hypothetical question: if it were to chance that by some unexpected intervention of Providence the predicted harm to non-combatants did not ensue, would the point of the attack have been frustrated? If on 6 August 1945 all the citizens of Hiroshima, frightened by a rumour of what was to occur, had fled the city, would the attack have lost its point? If the answer is "yes," then there was an intention to harm them, and their deaths were not collateral. . . . The truly collateral damage in war is that which, if it could have been avoided, would have left the intended attack on a combatant object uncompromised. That is what is meant by calling it a "side effect."[41]

The principles of discriminate and proportionate harm, taken together, rule out the concept of total war. While the economic infrastructure of a country may prima facie be a legitimate object of attack, since it serves military as well as civilian use, the productive capacity of the economy itself is not. O'Donovan argues:

> The traditional scorched-earth campaign, intended to deny the enemy the use of crops, was a common tactic of war; but burning of a crop does nothing to harm productivity, and may even improve it. Poisoning the land or its water-supplies, on the other hand, was categorically prohibited; for that would attack the very possibility of future cultural life in the region. . . . When Iraq deliberately created an oil-slick in the Arabian Gulf in the course of the 1991 war, it was not, strictly speaking, an indiscriminate act, since it was aimed at allied naval operations. But the vast environmental damage incurred was disproportionate to its politico-military purpose.[42]

O'Donovan's arguments are persuasive and helpful. But his own examples highlight the moral inconsistency of limiting the language of terrorism to nongovernmental military (or military-style) organizations. The intentional targeting of noncombatants, to spread maximum terror among the enemy, was what the Allies resorted to under the euphemism of "strategic airwar" in World War II. Robert McNamara's frank but belated revelations, in the film documentary *The Fog of War,* details how he and other defense planners sought to maximize Japanese civilian casualties at minimal cost. Having little in the way of air defenses, Japanese cities provided soft targets to U.S. bombers. Four months before the atomic devastation of Hiroshima and Nagasaki, most of Tokyo was razed to the ground in a hellish firestorm generated by sustained American bombing. More than one hundred thousand people lost their lives. Tokyo was selected as a target precisely because it was very densely populated and made mostly of wood. McNamara quotes General Curtis LeMay, with whom he served during the firebombing of Japanese cities, as saying, "If we'd lost the war, we'd all have been prosecuted as war criminals." McNamara himself admitted, "I think he's right. . . . But what makes it immoral if you lose and not immoral if you win?" The bombing of densely populated urban centers, even when there were no military targets, was removed from the category of war crimes at the Nuremberg and Tokyo trials, simply because the Allies did it much more than the Axis powers.[43]

As O'Donovan himself has noted, strategic airwar became the cornerstone of postwar Western and Soviet defense strategy. The stockpiling of nuclear, chemical and biological weapons is what governments have done and continue to do, not Third World insurgents or terrorists (at least till now). President Kennedy authorized the use of napalm in Vietnam in 1962, and without any declaration of war against that nation. The widespread use of cluster bomblets and similar incendiary devices by Western and Israeli armed forces in recent military operations in Afghanistan and Lebanon were designed to spread maximum terror and turn casualties into fatalities. They are disproportionate in their effects and betray a lack of discriminate intent. The whole purpose of the so-called neutron bomb is to kill civilians by radiation and leave physical structures intact. By contrast, al-Qa'ida's aim in the 9/11 attacks was not primarily to kill as many civilians as possible but to destroy the symbols of American economic and military power.

The number of civilians who have died as a result of aerial bombardment during the twentieth century is far greater than those who have been blown up by bombs planted in public places or airplane hijackings. Supposing, on July 7, 2005, instead of the four bombs that went off in buses and the London underground, which killed fifty-two civilians, an airplane had flown over the city and dropped bombs that killed the same number of people. Would it be morally less intolerable if the perpetrators argued that the intention was to attack police stations and key logistical centers, and that the civilians who died were simply "collateral damage"? Operation Shock and Awe, the illegal Anglo-American invasion of Iraq in 2003, was, as its name suggests, intended to frighten the Iraqi population into turning against Saddam Hussein and supporting the invading ground troops. The missiles and bombs that rained on Iraq in one week killed or injured thousands of civilians just as innocent as those who died in New York and Washington on September 11, 2001, or in London on the July 7, 2005.[44]

In an intriguing discussion of counterinsurgent warfare, O'Donovan identifies two major moral questions that this kind of conflict raises: How can government force operate effectively while respecting the principle of discrimination that an insurgent movement may not share? Can counterinsurgency be conducted in such a way as to persuade insurgents to abide by the principle of discrimination? O'Donovan focuses on the second of the two questions. Prior to the Fourth Hague Convention of 1907 any captured revolutionary fighter was summarily lynched on the nearest tree or lamppost. The offer of prisoner-of-war status for captured fighters was made to irregular militias as an incentive to restrain themselves in battle. Since then the successive Geneva Protocols and international treaties that have developed have had as their aim the steady expansion of the status and conditions governing irregular fighters. The laws have sought to induce such insurgent movements, operating under a wide variety of circumstances, to sign up to international norms of conduct.

O'Donovan invites us to consider the mutual benefits that would accrue if "civilised societies began to think of insurgency movements as their opponents in war rather than as gangs of criminals."[45] If the enemy is to be persuaded to observe the rule of discriminate attack, counterinsurgency forces must be distinguished from ordinary agencies of government, such as the police. Dealing with the IRA as a gang of vicious criminals, for instance, and seeking to pursue and prosecute them through regular police and criminal courts led to all these institutions (and individual judges and senior police officers) becoming legitimate targets for attack in Britain. He states:

> The essential difference between a gang of criminals and an insurgent army is simply that the latter can count upon a wider supportive community, in relation to which it occupies something of a representative role. Where such a community exists, and inter-communal enmity is woven into the fabric of society, it does no good at all to ignore the fact, and to pretend that it is not civil strife but merely criminality that has to be overcome.[46]

Moreover, the tragedy of internal conflicts fought by guerrilla methods is that they are unending. The destructive spiral of revenge and counter-revenge engulfs whole societies and poisons several generations. O'Donovan believes that both insurgents and counterinsurgent forces have a duty "so to act as to bring [the conflict] to an end within a reasonable time-scale, whether by victory or by concession." He argues, "The virtue of taking prisoners of war rather than imprisoning criminals is that it brings to bear upon both parties an increasing pressure to settle generated by a growing colony of exiled prisoners, waiting upon the conclusion of hostilities for the opportunity to resume their normal lives at home."[47]

The relevance of these reflections to, say, the way the Israeli government deals with Hamas or the Sri Lankan government with the Tamil Tigers, is evident. Similarly to many other organizations proscribed by the U.S. government as "terrorists." Even with regard to the hunting down of Islamic militants associated with the attacks in the United States, claiming that this is a "war like no other," and therefore exempt from the moral demands of the just-war proposal and patiently accumulated body of international law (embodied in the Hague Conventions and Geneva Protocols of the last century), will only backfire on Western societies for generations to come. If Western governments, and especially the United States and Israel (which is often treated as a European nation by the Western media rather than as a Middle Eastern one), flout international law with impunity, it will be impossible to convince estranged, embittered local communities that the violent extremists that they harbor should be persuaded to exercise moral restraints (e.g., avoiding "soft targets" or not taking civilian hostages).

Torture, surveillance of private mail, arbitrary arrest and detention without trial, even the abduction of terrorist suspects by CIA-operated "ghost flights" to clandestine prisons where things could be done to them that cannot be done under U.S. law—all these have now become routine practices, much to the dismay and anger of many around the world who have campaigned against such abuses in their own nations.[48] The moral credibility of the West's denunciation of human rights violations in places like Sudan, Russia, China and Burma have been seriously undermined. In the light of Guantánamo Bay, Abu Ghraib, Fallujah and other horrors of the Iraq war, it is impossible for many in the Muslim world to accept that talk about the rule of law and human rights on the part of the United States is anything more than self-serving hypocrisy.

O'Donovan's proposal to distinguish counterinsurgency forces from the normal agencies of government is not without its problems. Armies and wars create more dilemmas than they solve. While military action is sometimes necessary to combat insurgent violence, especially where the conflict is territorial, it is often not very effective. The Peruvian army spent twenty years in a scorched-earth campaign against the Sendero Luminoso (Shining Light) guerrillas, during which about seventy thousand people lost their lives. The group was finally defeated and disbanded after a change of tactics. A seventy-man police team captured its leader after six months of incisive analysis and good intelligence. The kind of painstaking surveillance and intelligence gathering that led British police forces in August 2006 to foil a potentially devastating terrorist plot to blow up several airliners in mid-air across the Atlantic, is an example of effective prevention.

Undoubtedly, the death of Osama bin Laden is not going to end the violence of ragtag networks like al-Qa'ida. But by refusing to demonize "terrorists" and rejecting the use of terror themselves, governments pull the rug from under them. Recognizing that "terrorists" are not madmen, though (like many armies) they often contain sadists and psychopaths in their midst, means addressing the underlying historical grievances and perceptions. This is not to be dismissed as appeasement, nor does it imply justifying evil deeds.

As the recent history of Northern Ireland, Egypt and Nepal have shown, the conversion of "terrorist" groups into peaceful political movements is often possible. Once their rationale for violence has ceased to exist, or they realize that resort to large-scale violence alienates them from their local and global constituencies, exhaustion sets in and tactics change.

O'Donovan has argued that political and military leaders in a time of war are responsible for a "certain articulate precision in the account they give of the wrong they propose to remedy, for the way the situation is described determines the shape of the enactment which may remedy it."[49] But this goes to the heart of the moral dilemmas surrounding war and conflict in an age of political spin doctors, media hype, mass propaganda and what has been called the "manufacture of consent." Weapons of mass deception employed by national governments raise moral questions as challenging as those posed by weapons of mass destruction.

The capacity of citizens to judge the legality and morality of war, especially against states said to be harboring terrorists and sponsoring terror, depends crucially on access to information. Deceit undermines the trust in public discourse that is at the heart of a democratic polity. In the case of deception in order to justify going to war it prevents the accurate assessment of risks and benefits, and forecloses alternative courses of action. Lies beget more lies and tarnish irrevocably the integrity of governments that lie to their citizens. They destroy the self-government of free and equal citizens and reinforce popular feelings of alienation and powerlessness.

Thus the *ius ad bellum* criteria should be strengthened to incorporate a democratic understanding of what constitutes a legitimate authority. There must be a public commitment to truth-seeking and truthful speech on the part of any political authority, which would naturally involve the active encouragement of counterevidence and countervoices to those in government. The counterevidence and countervoices may come from beyond the boundaries of the nation-state. No war in today's world can be prosecuted by a cavalier dismissal of the authority of the United Nations and other global institutions set up precisely to curb the unilateral tendencies of states. A government that failed to fulfill such a requirement would fail the *ius ad bellum* test of legitimate authority.

NEEDED: HUMILITY AND COURAGEOUS IMAGINATION

A large part of this chapter has been taken up with sketching recent history, and for good reason. It is salutary to recall that Menachem Begin and Nelson Mandela were once blacklisted by British and American governments as terrorists, and that Ronald Reagan compared the mujahedin and Afghani Arabs like Osama bin Laden to the Founding Fathers. All totalitarian regimes know that controlling the past by suppressing memories and rewriting the history books is the most effective way of consolidating their power. Without historical awareness, we can never acknowledge the part we play in generating and nurturing terrorism. Antistate terrorism is always a response to acts by sovereign states, and unless political and local community leaders are courageous and humble enough to face this fact, they will perpetually fuel the spirals of violence. A people convinced of their own innocence cannot make peace. It is only if we are willing to take responsibility for our own inhumanities that we can hold others responsible for theirs.

Historical attentiveness also can help us break out of our parochial perspectives and recognize the dark tragedies that have been raging in many parts of the world, as well as how such conflicts are often interconnected. American media pundits have written most of the books hailing globalization; yet those same pundits seem to have never realized that if speculative traders on Wall Street could cripple families in Pakistan, then what occurs in Pakistan could also shut down Wall Street. We have also seen that wars waged by nations, whether by the United States or Israel, are a hundred times more deadly for innocent people than the attacks by "terrorists," vicious as they are. In that perspective, a war on terrorism is a contradiction in terms.

George W. Bush and the German theologian Jürgen Moltmann make strange bedfellows. But in the aftermath of the events of 9/11, Bush spoke of the appearance of "a new kind of evil" and of "evil folks lurking out there." In an essay not long afterward, Moltmann wrote of the world being confronted with "a new type of apocalyptic terrorism." The "suicide-murderers" represent a new "demonic" terrorist who will end up in "what was earlier called hell." What happened on that day, according to Moltmann, has "changed the situation of humankind."[50] Enough has been said in this chapter to show that suicide bombers have been wreaking their carnage long before 9/11. As for changes to the human situation, it was quickly back to "business as usual" where governments and the military-industrial complex were concerned. For the vast majority of people on the planet life has hardly changed since 9/11.

Terrorism, like nuclear weaponry, is not going to disappear. But we can reduce, to some degree, its appeal to the present generation of youth and children. The wretchedness of life in much of the Third World creates conditions in which those with enough rage and despair can be motivated to sympathize with or actively support "terrorist" movements and taken in by propaganda that claims to speak in their name. Addressing local economic and social inequities cannot be divorced from the quest for global justice, which will involve more than sending scraps from the tables of the rich to the poor who occasionally flicker on our TV screens; it calls for a radical overhauling of a global economic system based on corporate greed, waste and exploitation; and the strengthening of international democratic mechanisms and institutions that limit the sovereignty of states and hold corporations as much as governments morally accountable.

The following well-known words of Paulo Freire, the great Brazilian educator and social activist, are still worth remembering in many situations of conflict today: "Never in history has violence been initiated by the oppressed. How could they be the initiators, if they themselves are the result of violence? How could they be the sponsors of something whose objective inauguration called forth their existence as oppressed? There would be no oppressed had there been no prior situation of violence to establish their subjugation."[51]

Many of us who live in societies that have been traumatized by decades of terrorist and counterterrorist violence, slowly become desensitized to it. We are tempted to justify brutal retaliation by the police and military whenever our own security is shattered by a bomb attack. We have seen how "terrorist" suspects in most countries are treated neither as prisoners of war nor as criminals. In either case they would come under protective judicial procedures. The category to which they are reduced is that of the subhuman, and so they can be tortured and executed without qualm. This is an affront to the inherent human dignity that they share with us.

Dialogue with those we call terrorists is inevitable. History gives countless examples of yesterday's terrorists turning into today's statesmen. For

more than two decades Colonel Gaddafi of Libya was regarded as the epit-
ome of terrorism by Western governments and media; at the time of writing
this book, he is one of the West's allies in the war against terror and the
French are even selling Libya a nuclear reactor. Whether out of pragmatic
reasons or genuine moral conversion, terrorist groups (and states that support them) can be persuaded to change tactics. Where these groups enjoy
some degree of legitimacy among a local community (as do Hamas, Hizbullah, the Tamil Tigers or the FARC guerrillas in Colombia) it is suicidal
to exclude them from the negotiating table. However much we feel moral
repugnance at their methods of warfare, Christians refuse to play God by
damning them eternally. Until the final day of judgment we must bear witness to God's own patience in the face of evil and hold out the hope of every
person's redeemability.

All governments sell the myth that the sacrifice of individual liberties is
necessary in the interests of greater security against terrorist attacks. Most
of us would certainly agree that some restrictions on liberty are indeed necessary for greater collective safety in every society. But it is the rare person
who asks the obvious question: *Whose* liberty is sacrificed and for *whose* security? There is all the difference in the world between my putting up with
the trivial inconvenience of taking off my shoes before boarding an aircraft
or my car being stopped and searched at a military checkpoint (a routine oc-
currence in cities such as Colombo or Beirut) and individuals from minority
groups being selectively targeted for harassment and detention simply because they are deemed suspicious by the rest of the population. We all accept
certain constraints in the expectation that we will all enjoy greater security.
But the liberty-versus-security logic has been used to justify mass detention,
routine surveillance of mail and computers, incarceration without trial, and
brutal methods of interrogation. Clearly those individuals who are subjected
to such treatment enjoy neither liberty nor security. Not only are costs and
benefits unfairly apportioned, but, inevitably, such discriminatory practices
sow seeds of resentment and desires for vengeance that will make the next
generation both less safe and less free. When governments squander moral
legitimacy in tit-for-tat counterterrorist tactics, they play into the hands of
terrorist groups.

Furthermore, the methods we use determine the kind of society we become. This raises a deeper moral quandary that is rarely debated publicly. Popular talk of a tradeoff between liberty and security is too simplistic, for security is a collective good. In liberal democracies it concerns the protection of values (such as tolerance) and institutions (such as constitutional government) and is not simply a matter of securing the safety of the majority. If the "counterterrorist" tactics employed end up coarsening and brutalizing our collective life, resulting in greater intolerance and the loss of respect for human rights, is this a way of life really worth protecting?

I have noted that, tragically, undemocratic regimes have used the post-9/11 war on terror to strengthen their own repressive policies, secure in the belief that their excesses would be ignored. New laws and detention practices have been introduced in a significant number of countries, all broadly justified by the new international war on terror. They are used to suppress political dissent and to stifle expression of opinion of many who have no link at all to terrorism. Majority rule by itself, and legality on its own, are insufficient to ensure a civil and just society. Hence the need to strengthen international law and to insist that no state should be allowed to regard itself as an exception to the rule of law.

Wars on terrorism are enormously profitable—for the giant armament manufacturers and their subcontractors, for the arms dealers, for corrupt politicians and military generals. According to the International Action Network on Small Arms, military spending globally is about fifteen times the amount spent on international aid. The figure is higher than the Cold War record of 1987-1988 in today's prices, and in 2006 the United States, Britain, Russia, France and Germany accounted for an estimated 82 percent of all arms transfers. In a combined report of Amnesty and Oxfam, *Arms Without Borders*, the agencies say U.S., EU and Canadian companies can get around regulations by selling components and subcontracting manufacturing to companies overseas.[52] Weapons, including attack helicopters and combat trucks, are being assembled from foreign components and manufactured under licence in countries such as China, Egypt, India, Israel and Turkey. Despite U.S., EU and Canadian arms embargos against China, China's Z-10 attack helicopters (sold to despotic regimes around the world) would not fly without parts and technology from European, Canadian and U.S. firms.

The December 2004 *Report of the UN Secretary-General's High-Level Panel on Threats, Challenges and Change* endorsed what it called "the emerging norm of a responsibility to protect citizens from large-scale violence that is held, first and foremost, by national authorities. When a state fails to protect its citizens, the international community then has a further responsibility to act, through humanitarian operations, monitoring missions and diplomatic pressure—and with force, if necessary, though as a last resort."[53] The threat must be serious, involving "genocide and other large-scale killings, ethnic cleansing or serious violations of international humanitarian law, actual or immediately apprehended."[54]

Who is intended by the term *the international community* if it is not the United Nations and its agencies? Those of us who favor humanitarian interventions in principle, and yet were opposed from the outset (through the application of *ius ad bellum* thinking) to the American-led invasion of Iraq in 2003, cannot evade the thorny dilemmas of the new world order. While we are wary of the unilateral exercise of power, would we not have been grateful to see anyone intervening unilaterally in Rwanda in 1994 to stop the slaughter of Tutsis, just as we welcomed the Vietnamese intervention in Cambodia to depose Pol Pot and the Indian army's support for East Pakistan (now Bangladesh) against a ravaging Pakistani army? These actions were roundly condemned in the West at the time, yet they were genuine humanitarian interventions, and both Vietnam and India were also directly affected by what was happening in their neighbors.

The UN has its failings and critics, but its modest achievements must not be ignored.[55] Without its machinery and the powers given to it by international consent in its charter, the world would find it harder to avert, control and limit war than it is. The main problem with the UN is neither corruption nor lack of legitimacy, but the fact that it was conceived in a world of sovereign states, a world where the overriding concern of the post-World War II settlement was the guarantee of the inviolability of national borders and sovereignty. But in today's world, entire populations, or minorities within populations, need assistance against the terror of their own despotic governments. Thus the UN Charter's emphasis on the inviolability of sovereign states poses a conundrum. Moreover, lacking an armed police force of its own and often hamstrung by the chronic lack of funds and use of the veto by the permanent members of its Security Council, its peace-making and peace-keeping abilities have been severely curtailed.

The political health of the United States is of great importance to the well-being of the rest of the world. However, the United States seems to have lost all credibility as an influence for good. Despite the touching faith in its institutions that many American Christians still show, the fact is that the United States today is a poor example of democratic values for the rest of the world. Its newspapers and television, with very rare exceptions, have been bullied into acquiescence and have allowed the executive to ride roughshod over the law and violate human rights with impunity. It has been left to groups like Human Rights Watch and Amnesty International to do what the church and investigative journalism in the United States should have been doing. But there is no substitute superpower on the horizon. Japan, the European Union and China may come to rival the United States in economic power, and the United States in turn is heavily dependent on Japan and China for the strength of the U.S. dollar and the financial undergirding of its military adventures abroad; but they cannot provide what sometimes only the United States can. China, with its growing energy demands, is wooing the worst regimes around the world and is more deaf than the United States to human rights concerns at home and abroad.

In the same essay quoted previously, Jürgen Moltmann wrote, "There is no personal life any longer without danger. Personal life has no meaning without political engagement in the necessary resistance against public terror and death, as well as the no-less necessary work of justice world-wide."[56] Again, this is not a new truth. It is the experience of many of us, whether living and working in the midst of war, civil conflict, repressive regimes or among the downtrodden in inner-city ghettos. Suffering, conflict and violence form the usual contexts in which the covenant people of God are called to witness to the power of redemptive love.

The experienced Mennonite peace campaigner Jean Paul Lederach suggests that, whether in local or international conflicts, we are unable to overcome cycles of violent patterns precisely because "our imagination has been corralled and shackled by the very parameters and sources that create and perpetrate violence." The challenge we face is one of moral imagination: "how to invoke, set free, and sustain innovative responses to the roots of violence while rising above it."[57] Lederach sums up four aspects of the moral response needed for peacemaking: Reach out to those you fear. Face the complexity at the heart of every conflict. Imagine beyond what is seen. Risk vulnerability one step at a time.[58]

The prospect of endless acts of terror creates a sense that the future is closed, inevitable, hopeless. Christians abide in a hope that is not based on the conditions of world history. It is rooted, nevertheless, in a conviction that God has not abandoned God's world to usurping "principalities and powers," but has acted decisively in Christ for its healing and re-creation. The Christian hope that energizes a passionate and sustained engagement with this world, in the face of violence and terror, is a hope that looks forward to the coming One whose life began with the slaughter of the innocents, who fled as a refugee with his family to Egypt, who suffered torture and terrorism at the hands of the imperial power of his day, died so that both victims and victimizers may find forgiveness and new beginnings, descended into hell to show solidarity with all who have experienced its destructive power, and finally defeated death, fatalism and terror by his bodily resurrection. To be baptized into that death and resurrection is to be both free from the fear of dying and also fearful of dying in the service of the wrong cause.

"Show us, good Lord, the peace we should seek, the peace we must give, the peace we can keep, the peace we must forego, and the peace you have given in Jesus our Lord."[59]

2

MYTHS OF RELIGIOUS VIOLENCE

In 1603, Ahmad al-Mansur, the king of Morocco, presented his English ally, Queen Elizabeth I, with a simple proposal: England would help the Moors colonize America. The king proposed that Moroccan and English troops, using English ships, should attack the Spanish colonies in America, expel their hated Spanish enemies, and then "possesse" the land and keep it "under our dominion for ever, and—by the help of God—to joyne it to our estate and yours." There was a catch, however. Might it not be more sensible, suggested the king, that most of the future colonists should be Moroccan rather than English? For "in respect of the great heat of the clymat, where those of your countrie doe not fynde themselfes fitt to endure the extremetie of heat there and of the cold of your partes, where our men endure it very well by reason that the heat hurtes them not."[1] After due consideration, the Moroccan offer was not taken up by Her Majesty.

What is noteworthy is that such a proposal, remarkable to us today, raised few eyebrows at the time. After all, the English were close allies of both the Moroccans and their Ottoman overlords. Rivalry among Christians was always a powerful factor leading to alliances and arrangements between Muslims and so-called Christian states. The English might have their reservations about Islam, but these were nothing compared to their hatred and fear of "popery." On the global principle that the enemy of my enemy is my friend, Elizabeth sold weapons to the Moroccans to use against the Portuguese, Charles I sought Moroccan aid against Spain, and from 1704 onward Britain looked to Algiers and Morocco to provision Gibraltar and Minorca, and so protect them from the Spanish.[2]

It was not only reasons of state that led to such alliances. Many Protestants saw affinities with Islam in the latter's ban on icons from places of worship, in the rejection of monastic orders and in not seeing marriage as a sacrament. When Elizabeth sought an alliance with the Turks the argument she employed was that Protestants and Muslims were alike in hating the "idolatries" practiced by the Catholic king of Spain. As well as treaties of trade and friendship there were several joint expeditions, such as an Anglo-Moroccan attack on Cadiz in 1596. It also led to a great movement of people between the two worlds, as the Palestinian scholar Nabil Matar's work has shown us. Elizabethan London had a burgeoning Muslim community, which encompassed a large party of Turkish ex-prisoners, some Moorish craftsmen and a number of wealthy Turkish merchants.[3]

ESCAPING PAROCHIALISM

Throughout history Muslims, Jews and Christians have traded, studied and negotiated with each other across the frontiers of religious differences. The neat civilizational blocs imagined by writers such as Samuel Huntington have always been more porous than the mere textual study of religions suggests. As Richard Bulliet argues, *"The past and future of the West cannot be fully comprehended without appreciation of the twinned relationship it has had with Islam over some fourteen centuries. The same is true of the Islamic world."*[4] Even the Crusades (c. 1095-c. 1291), which marked the nadir of Christendom-Muslim relations, were important conduits for the transmission of ideas and technologies into Europe. The Italian city-states of Venice and Genoa that developed into global mercantile powers assimilated various financial practices and institutions that first emerged in the Middle East.

The late Palestinian-American scholar Edward Said reminded us, in the introduction to his best-known work *Orientalism*, that

the Orient is not only adjacent to Europe; it is also the place of Europe's greatest and richest and oldest colonies, the source of its civilisations and languages, its cultural contestant, and one of its deepest and most recurring images of the Other. In addition the Orient has helped to define Europe (or the West) as its contrasting image, idea, personality, experience. Yet none of this Orient is merely imaginative. The Orient is an integral part of European material civilization and culture.[5]

But Islam was never simply the Other, in a geographical or cultural sense, connected (as Said suggests) through European colonization. It penetrated, indeed colonized, parts of Europe not too long after its emergence in the Arabian peninsula and helped to shape European science, technology, art and literature over the next several hundred years, in the Mediterranean, the Balkans, Cyprus and Russia.[6] The great Islamic cities were not only Damascus or Baghdad but, depending on the historical moment, Cordoba, Grenada, Palermo, Athens, Tirana, Budapest or Kiev.

All cultures and civilizations that live in close proximity borrow from each other. Throughout history the colonizers learn from the colonized as much as the other way round. The Arabs were impressed by Persian and Byzantine architectural styles in the lands of their conquest and readily incorporated them into the design of their mosques, especially the domes and arches. What is rarely acknowledged by secularist and Muslim historians alike is the influence of non-Western Christians and Jews on the development of both Islamic civilization and of European civilization via the Arabs. Persian Christians and Jews lived in the new Arab empire in tax-paying religious ghettos (dhimmis) and provided the administrators, secretaries, scholars, craftsmen and peasants, teaching their nomadic conquerors the skills of governance and urban planning. The best-known and most far-reaching influences came through the translation of Greek works of philosophy, science and medicine into Arabic. These translations were, at the beginning, almost exclusively the work of Christian priests and physicians employed in the courts of Muslim rulers. The first translations from Greek to Arabic were via Syriac, the language of the Persian Christian churches. The first known scientific work in Arabic was a treatise on medicine, written in Greek by Ahrun, a Christian priest from Alexandria, and translated from Syriac into Arabic in 683 by a Jewish doctor from Basrah (Iraq).[7]

The Egyptian-born Jewish scholar Bat Ye'or points out that Islamic civilization "glowed in the full blaze of its glory" not in Mecca or Medina, but "in the lands of dhimmitude, in periods when the dhimmis still formed majorities subject to the conquering Muslim minorities. Under the Arabs, it reached its apogee in the Christian East and in Spain. Similarly, it was not in their Central Asian homeland that the Seljuks and Ottomans founded a prestigious empire, but in Anatolia and the Balkans, through the subjection of its Christian Orthodox populations."[8] She adds:

> Zoroastrians, Jacobites (Copts and Syrians), Nestorians, Melchites, and Jews translated into Arabic treatises on astronomy, medicine, alchemy, and philosophy, as well as literary narratives and stories. This work necessitated the invention of new words and the forging of the Arabic language and grammar into new conceptual moulds, not only philosophic, scientific, and literary, but also administrative, economic, political, and diplomatic.[9]

The classical heritage was preserved by Christians and Jews who had integrated the Hellenistic culture with biblical spirituality and then fled to Europe as refugees from Muslim lands. The elites who fled to Europe took with them their scholarship and cultural cosmopolitanism. "Thenceforth, in the Christian lands of refuge-Spain, Provence, Sicily, Italy—cultural centers developed where Christians and Jews from Islamized lands taught to the young Europe the knowledge of the old pre-Islamic Orient, formerly translated into Arabic by their ancestors."[10]

Many of us who have studied or taught for any considerable time in either Western Europe or the United States are struck by how ignorant of their own history many university students, and even their professors, are. The ignorance extends both to what the Christian faith (both in its Western and non-Western forms) has contributed to the culture, institutions and political values that are simply taken for granted today, as well as the huge debt that the West owes to Arab, Indian and Chinese civilizations over the course of the past millennium. Europe benefited from a global economic order created by the Chinese, Arabs, Africans and Indians.* For instance, when the Portuguese explorer Vasco da Gama, circumnavigated the Cape of Good Hope in 1498, he was guided by a Gujarati Muslim pilot and almost all his nautical and navigational instruments and techniques had been developed either by the Chinese or the Arabs. Indian, Javanese and Chinese traders had made it across to the Cape centuries before da Gama, and the Sassanid Persians had been sailing to India and China from the early centuries of the first millennium A.D. The Portuguese did not need to "discover" Asia and Africa. The peoples of Asia and Africa had been in contact with Europeans for centuries.

Moreover, once the Portuguese began to explore the Indian coastal regions, they were astonished to find more than 100,000 indigenous Christians who traced their heritage to an era before the creation of Europe itself. Europe's identity after 1453, when Constantinople was lost to the Ottoman Turks, was constructed along imperialistic lines, leading to the appropriation of Eastern land, labor and markets. Much of this violence was committed in the name of a "Christian civilization" that was largely ignorant of its own history, let alone the fact that far more Christians had lived outside the jurisdiction of Rome (and the Latin West) than within, ever since the first century A.D. If not for the Muslim conquest of Persia and the later Mongol devastation across Central Asia, Christianity would have been predominantly an Asian religion at the dawn of European colonialism. There were also ancient and thriving Christian societies across Africa prior to the arrival of Portuguese and later British missionaries. However, even the negative story of Africa's contribution in terms of slavery and plunder to the industrialization of Europe and the United States, and its continuing economic exploitation at the hands of Western governments and corporations, rarely impinges on modern Western consciousness.

This widespread parochialism was revealed in the aftermath to 9/11 and subsequent bombings in European cities. Numerous articles and bestselling

---

*We shall return to this theme in chap. 6. Europe has always been an ideal, never a self-enclosed geopolitical reality. Hence attempts by the Vatican and some Protestant Christian groups to oppose entry of Turkey into the EU are historically misguided. They also perpetuate the myth of a "Christian" Europe that is insensitive to the experiences of non-European Christians as well as non-Christians in Europe.

books exploring the ubiquity of "religious violence" appeared all over news-papers, the Internet and bookshops. Old Euro-colonial prejudices resur-faced: Western liberal democracy was contrasted with Muslim (and gener-ally Eastern) political immaturity, secular rationalism (which was European and humanist) with "oriental" religious bigotry. No matter that not a single Western state was a democracy (by today's definitions) before the twentieth century. No matter that, compared to the few thousand who lost their lives in these major Western cities, there have been hundreds of millions of poor people who have been slaughtered, imprisoned and impoverished all over the world in the name, not of any traditional religious god but of the modern secular religions of nationalism, fascism, globalizing capitalism, revolution-ary Marxism, and state socialism. No matter that, as we saw in chapter one, Iraq's Ba'athist regime and the vast majority of similarly repressive states from Algeria to Indonesia have been aggressively secularist, not religious, oligarchies. Secular deities are ignored, and the potential for destructive fa-naticism is laid at the door of the religious gods, and in particular the three Abrahamic faiths that in one way or another converge in the conflicts that affect the Western world.

THE COMPLEXITIES OF "RELIGIOUS VIOLENCE"

Religious violence—whether directed by one religious group against the state or against another religious group, or by a religious state against national minorities—is a notoriously ambivalent term. It is usually used within a post-Enlightenment Western mindset that draws neat categorical distinc-tions between religion, politics, culture and so on. Consequently, it deeply obscures the way that violence perpetrated on a massive scale for the sake of such commonplace notions as, say, progress, national security, promoting democracy or economic development may be profoundly religious acts. They call for the sacrifice of human life in the service of a transcendent ideal, and they embody a particular definition of "reality" (albeit often concealed) and a particular, normative understanding of what makes for humanness and hu-man flourishing.

For all orthodox Christians, the profession that "Jesus Christ is Lord" has always had a politically subversive dimension. It has meant, among other things, that loyalty to the teaching and example of Jesus supersedes submission to any social or political authority. It has brought Christians into conflict with the state in which they live as responsible citizens. (That many Christians have, in the past as well as today, surrendered to nationalist, tribal or other collective loyalties is a tragedy that does not change the central convictions of the Christian tradition.)

Indeed, the very notion of the "secular," it has often been pointed out, originated in Christianity. The opposite of secular is not the spiritual or the sacred, but the eternal. The *saeculum* denotes the temporal order that, while incapable of itself to deliver the kingdom of God, is hallowed by creation and incarnation, and called to anticipate God's reign in the ordering of human life. It represents a realm in which submission to human authorities, even those that do not explicitly acknowledge the sovereignty of God, is valid but always conditional.

Moreover, in most Asian societies, political, religious, ethnic and cultural identities overlap and interpenetrate each other. Religious conversion was central to the debates in pre-independence India, and the religious categories used to classify people in official censuses were strongly contested right up to the drawing up of the Indian Constitution in 1951. When dalit communities convert en masse to Buddhism or Christianity in protest at their oppression at the hands of higher-caste Hindus, it is self-evidently a political act. But every personal religious conversion implies also a reorientation of political loyalties. (The same ambivalence is found in post Reformation Britain, say, right until the mid-nineteenth century. Locke's famous treatise on religious toleration excluded Roman Catholics from the purview of toleration because they were seen as fundamentally a political community whose final loyalty lay with the pope and not with the British crown.)

Moreover, in an Asian context, where religious identities are still strong, all modernizing as well as countermodernizing movements express themselves in religious terminology. Christian minorities in Asia have often suffered at the hands of religious extremists for promoting secular government, "secularism" understood (as the Indian Constitution defines it) not as hostility to religious truth claims or the marginalization of religiously committed peoples but as evenhanded treatment by the state of all religious and cultural communities. Unfortunately, Christians, when in positions of relative numerical strength (as in the Philippines or South Korea), have tended to slip into the tendency to use the state apparatus to secure privileged treatment for themselves.

Since 9/11 there has been an avalanche of books and articles designed to give Americans and Europeans a crash course in, as the phrase goes, "understanding Islam." Handbook introductions to the Qur'an, the life of Muhammad, Islamic values, the fast and pilgrimage or the meaning of the veil are suddenly on offer. Self-styled authorities on Islam have arisen overnight explaining difficult concepts such as jihad, dar-al-Islam versus dar-al harb, and so on. It is surely an occasion for great rejoicing if Americans and Europeans, apart from scholars in religious studies departments, are actually beginning to read the Qur'an and Islamic theology. One hopes that they will also move on from there to the Bible and the best of Christian theology, including that arising from the Third World! But, alas, it will not help them to make sense of 9/11 or any of the other tragedies unfolding in the Middle East or anywhere else in the Islamic world, as chapter one sought to explain.

While it is hugely important for politicians, economists and international relations theorists to attend to the religious beliefs and values of peoples more carefully than they have hitherto, we need to remember that all cultures, religious or secular, are complex, dynamic networks which are not sealed into water-tight compartments but interact constantly with others. There are conservatives and reformists within all cultures, and often what is invoked as "our traditional beliefs or values" by conservatives may be quite recent, as well as being a site of contention within that culture.[11] Selected interpretations of religious texts reflect a given political context and ideological purpose. Extratextual concerns always affect our approach to texts, whether "sacred" or ordinary. Therefore, all attempts to reduce conflict between peoples to "irreconcilable religious differences" ends up masking the real interests at work and the power struggles that are taking place in a particular society or region of the world. It diverts attention from what states and groups are actually doing to each other. We have seen that it is historical amnesia, more than theological incomprehension, that needs to be addressed today in the United States and Western Europe.

The causes of religious violence vary so greatly from one context to another that we dare not make facile generalizations. It is very rarely that violent conflict breaks out simply because of doctrinal disputes or competing worldviews. Even the so-called wars of religion in sixteenth-century Europe were not straightforward sectarian conflicts between Roman Catholics and Protestants, but rather struggles for dominance among rival political dynasties, kings and nobles, who were often willing to change church allegiances if they served their secular interests. As William Cavanaugh has pointed out, these wars were "the birthpangs of the modern state":

> What is at issue behind these wars is the creation of "religion" as a set of beliefs which is defined as personal conviction and which can exist separately from one's loyalty to the State. The creation of religion, and thus the privatization of the Church, is correlative to the rise of the State. It is important therefore to see that the principal promoters of the wars in France and Germany were in fact not pastors and peasants, but kings and nobles with a stake in the outcome of the movement toward the centralized, hegemonic state.[12]

It is common for political manipulation to disguise itself in religious garb. For instance, one of the principal acts which instigated the second Palestinian intifada in September 2000 was the Israeli prime minister Ariel Sharon's visit to the Al Aqsa mosque in Jerusalem. There is little doubt that such an act was politically motivated. With the full awareness that most devout Muslims would interpret as an outrageous act such a violation of their "sacred space" by someone who was their sworn enemy, Sharon was determined to demonstrate the overwhelming superiority of Israel's military might. The Indian subcontinent has witnessed many similar events in recent decades, such as the notorious destruction of a Muslim mosque in Ayodhya in 1992 by Hindu nationalists on the specious grounds that it was the birthplace of the god Rama, an action that was in open defiance of the Congress government of the day. Similarly, the Gama'a Islamiyah, a militant Egyptian Islamic movement, has used unprovoked violence against Coptic Christians and Western tourists to weaken and destabilize the Mubarak regime.

Furthermore, religious ideas often lend an ideological clarity to what in many cases have been real experiences of personal humiliation, social oppression, political corruption or the frustrated aspirations of modern life. Images of cosmic struggle (good versus evil) can give these bitter experiences meaning. As Mark Juergensmeyer has argued, the act of being involved in violence in the name of a great cosmic cause provides a sense of "symbolic empowerment" greater than what the act of violence may actually achieve politically. Militant supporters of the Bharatiya Janata Party in India frequently evoke images of the great wars of the Hindu epics, the Mahabharata and the Ramayana. When the Sikh leader Jarnail Singh Bhindranwale exhorted his followers to violent action against the Indian government, he called for "a struggle . . . for our faith, for the Sikh nation, for the oppressed."[13]

Violence and political marginality often go hand-in-hand. Militant groups that have espoused violence and justified it in the name of their religion have been marginal to their own religious societies. The nineteen Muslim activists who participated in the suicide assaults of September 11, 2001, were mostly men without countries. They were middle-class professionals in their thirties who had been trained in scientific and technical subjects in Western colleges and spoke a Western language. Alienated from their native lands in Egypt and Saudi Arabia, they had formed sleeper cells in European cities, communicating with each other via the Internet and the occasional clandestine rendezvous. Juergensmeyer has dubbed this phenomenon "e-mail ethnicities": transnational networks of people whose ethnicities,

> united by Web sites and the Internet, are extensions of traditional societies whose adherents and cultures are dispersed throughout the world. Among these expatriate groups have been some notoriously politically active ones—Sikhs, Sri Lankans, and Arabs—including the followers of Osama bin Laden, who moved from Saudi Arabia to Sudan, to Afghanistan, and Sheik Omar Abdul Rahman, who lived variously in Egypt, the Sudan, and New Jersey.[14]

During the 1990s London was a haven for Islamist clerics and lay activists who had fled imprisonment and certain torture in their native lands. The British security services were content because they could keep these asylum seekers under observation and monitor their actions. Muslims respected the

British tradition of providing a home to political refugees from despotic nations. The clash of cultures seems to have been more violent in their relatively homogenous countries than in cosmopolitan London. London's cosmopolitan nature still stands in marked contrast to the rest of the country. All this changed, however, with the British government's decision to send troops to Iraq in 2003. The Iraqi war generated an intense debate within the Muslim communities around Britain, with the more radicalized elements arguing that the Anglo-American war on terror was an assault on Islam and so justified attacks by Muslims on British targets.

As I have written elsewhere, drawing on a prominent theme in Ian Buruma and Avishai Margalit's work *Occidentalism:*

> To see the conflicts of the present world as a clash of Western rational
> ist ideals and oriental religious zeal is profoundly misleading. If Euro-
> pean powers justified their imperial conquests with claims of progress
> and enlightenment, Asian rulers translated those same ethnocentric
> claims into brutal nationalist projects, murdering millions of their own
> countrymen in doing so. In the twentieth century they resulted in the
> mass graves of the Gulag and the killing fields of China, Indonesia
> and Cambodia. The Taliban's destruction of the unique Buddhist rock-
> carved statues in Afghanistan in 2000 was foreshadowed by the Meiji
> samurai who, in their modernist reformation of the Japanese state in
> 1867, changed their kimonos for tailcoats and top hats, and set about
> smashing Buddhist temples and transforming their country in the name
> of progress, science, and enlightenment. Most revolts against Western
> imperialism, and its local offshoots, have borrowed heavily from West-
> ern ideas.[15]

The modern Japanese emperor cult (which produced the notorious kamikaze suicide bombers of World War II) was based partly on a misunderstanding of religion in the West. Accustomed to Confucian codes of obedience to authority, Japanese scholars in the Meiji reform era assumed that Christianity was the social cement that held European nations together as disciplined communities. They concluded that the answer to European power lay in Japan having its own state religion, and this was to be state Shinto, a politicized

version of ancient rites, mostly to do with nature and fertility. "The alternative to the Christian God was to be Amaterasu, the Sun Goddess; and the
emperor, hitherto a remote and politically powerless figure in the old capital
of Kyoto, was moved to Tokyo as a combination of kaiser, generalissimo,
Shinto pope, and the highest living deity."[16]

Thus we need a more nuanced understanding of religious transformations
and of religious conflict if we are to respond to these with integrity. No one
who has seriously studied Christian and Muslim theology can deny that there
are fundamental differences between, say, Christian and Islamic understandings of God or of salvation, differences that translate into different ways of
perceiving and acting in the world. (One does not have to be a philosophical
idealist to believe that how we see the world informs the way we act in it.) It is
these differences, as well as much that is shared in common, that are explored
in the normal course of living together and communicating with each other
in meaningful conversation. But does stressing the differences between faiths
necessarily lead to violent conflict, as some Western theologians and religious
commentators seem to assume? If it is rival concepts of God or salvation that
always occasion violent conflict, why have the most bitter wars in history
(and right up to the present day) been waged between coreligionists and not
between adherents of rival religious communities?

Fred Halliday of the London School of Economics observes of Muslim-
majority nations:

> Islam may, in some contexts, be the prime form of political and so-
> cial identity, but it is never the sole form and is often not the primary
> one. Within Muslim societies divisions of ethnicity matter much, often
> more than a shared religious identity; this is equally so in emigration.
> . . . No one can understand the politics of, say, Turkey, Pakistan or
> Indonesia on the basis of Islam alone. Despite rhetoric, Islam explains
> little of what happens in these societies.[17]

Halliday, like many secularist sociologists and political commentators,
tends to underestimate the religious factors behind social systems and political change because their skeptical presuppositions prevent them from understanding how social actors invest so much religious significance to their

actions. But, nevertheless, his caveats in the other direction are important re-
minders of how religious motivations and practices are always situated within
secular contexts.

Violent conflict between religious communities is often provoked by
insidious stereotyping and caricaturizing of the other's practices, beliefs
and aims. Stereotyping is compounded, ironically, by those liberal politicians and local community leaders who gloss over deep-seated differences
in the mistaken notion that this is what tolerance demands. In this context
Anantanand Rambachan, a Hindu scholar from Trinidad who teaches at a
Christian college in the United States, makes the interesting observation
that "Communities where differences are real, but where they are mini-
mized or downplayed, are more likely to suffer violence and traumatic up-
heavals when, in times of tension and conflict, such differences become
prominent." Rambachan continues:

> Communities, on the other hand, which engage each other in a deep
> search for mutual understanding and which honestly acknowledge dif-
> ferences and cultivate respect are less likely to explode in times of con-
> flict. Such communities are less likely to cite difference as a basis for
> hostility towards the other. I often wonder about this matter when we
> witness neighbours, in many recent conflicts, suddenly turning upon
> each other with ferocity and violence, shattering the veneer of civility
> and harmony.[18]

TWO ASIAN CASE STUDIES

Sri Lanka. Ever since the civil conflict in Sri Lanka first came to the attention of the global media in July 1983, it has been routinely described as an
ethnic conflict and even at times a religious conflict (as most of the majority
ethnic group known as Sinhalese are Buddhists, and most of the minority
Tamils are Hindus). But conflicts in the complex societies of Asia are rarely
this simple. Sinhalese Buddhism in Sri Lanka has always had a dominant political role, given that historically Buddhist sects and monasteries flourished
on the island and sent missionaries to southeast Asia long after Buddhism's
decline in India. Sinhalese kings have battled invading armies from south

India, often urged on by Buddhist monks who invoked the favors of celestial deities on them even as they, in turn, depended on the kings for temple lands and patronage.[19] British colonialism changed all that and gave birth, as a counter-reaction, to a virulent form of Buddhist nationalism in the early twentieth century.

In recent decades Buddhist monks and militant Sinhalese-Buddhist lay organizations have from time to time been at the forefront of mobs attacking Tamil or Christian communities, and have engaged in violent street fighting with peace activists (much to the confusion of Western observers who have been brought up to believe that Buddhists were all benign, otherworldly mystics). A prime minister, S. W. R. D. Bandaranaike, was assassinated by a Buddhist monk in 1959, and violent antigovernment insurgency of youth in the south of the island, first in 1971-1972 and later in 1986-1989, stemmed from a peculiar mix of Buddhist nationalism, unemployment, Maoist indoctrination, Che Guevaran romanticism and populist revolution. Both insurgencies were brutally suppressed by the army with heavy loss of lives. Like their counterparts in all religious traditions, Buddhists in Sri Lanka have justified the resort to violence on moral grounds, either as self-defense against foreign aggression or to protect Buddhist religion against its subversion by evil rulers. Monks officiate at all government and military ceremonies, often preaching sermons extolling the meritorious deeds of soldiers in protecting the Buddhist nation from Tamil Tiger aggressors. But there have also been a few monks and several lay Buddhists who have been vigorous defenders of the Tamil people and their civic rights, as well as being actively involved in the peace movement.[20]

Postcolonial Tamil nationalism was, in turn, a reaction to Sinhalese-Buddhist attempts to demote the status of the Tamil language and to assert their sovereignty over the northern and eastern provinces that Tamils regarded as their traditional homelands. Tamil nationalism, unlike its Sinhalese counterpart, has rarely evoked religious myths to back up its claims. Its understanding of Tamil nationhood owed more to Leninist ideas than the Hindu epics. The movement for a separate state became more popular among Tamils as well as more violent after the anti-Tamil pogrom in the south in July 1983. It splintered over the next decade into several factions warring with each other over strategy, as well as deep-seated differences based on caste, region and personalities. The Tamil Tigers emerged as the most powerful and best-known internationally among the various Tamil factions. As mentioned in chapter one, they perfected the art of suicide bombings and have assassinated several prominent Tamil public figures who dared to question their methods or political agenda.

A high proportion of those fighting in the ranks of the Tamil Tigers are young women and teenage boys conscripted, indoctrinated, and brutalized by military training. Many join out of revenge for army killings or because there is no schooling or employment available for them. A large number of suicide bombers are young women, and their radicalization in this way has been attributed to the thirst for revenge at being viciously raped at army checkpoints in the north or for the loss of close family members in the war. It is unlikely, though, that these atrocities in themselves would occasion such an extreme and spectacular reaction as suicide bombings.

A Hindu social scientist, Rajmohan Ramanathapillai, from Jaffna in northern Sri Lanka, has argued that one of the reasons for the effectiveness of the Tiger guerrillas in gaining the support of the majority of Hindu Tamils in the 1980s lay in their manipulation of religious symbols and themes drawn from the medieval Puranas and epics.[21] These stories are disseminated widely through school textbooks, cinemas and songs, as well through ritual enactments and recitations at public festivals. A dominant theme in all the myths and epics is that coercion and violence are necessary for the protection of cosmic and social dharma. In the politically volatile atmosphere of northern Sri Lanka, the Puranic association of evildoers with "heretics" *(nastikas)* and "barbarians" *(mlecchas)* has easily lent itself to the extermination by the Tamil Tigers of all those Tamils who publicly express disagreement with their methods and ideology. Ramanathapillai points out that there is no Hindu tradition of nonviolent resistance to evil which has taken root in Tamil society. He writes: "The LTTE's success would not have been possible had the sacred symbols of Tamil religion not already shaped the people's ethos and worldview toward accepting and legitimizing coercion and violence as norms for the protection of society during times of chaos."[22]

At the time of this writing, a vicious splinter group of the LTTE in the eastern part of the island is working hand-in-glove with the Sri Lankan army (which is almost exclusively Sinhalese) against the Tigers. It seems that they have been given immunity by the army to abduct Tamil businessmen and hold them for ransom as a way of acquiring funds for purchasing weapons. The government also turns a blind eye to their forced conscription of young Tamil men and women in the areas of the east where they currently are in control. In the meantime there is a third group that is becoming increasingly radicalized as a result of infringement by both Sinhalese and Tamils on their towns and villages, namely, Muslims who define themselves both as a religious and an ethnic category depending on which proves more advantageous in which context.[23] They have been receiving funds from Middle Eastern governments and Islamic organizations, some of which are deployed in providing military training to Muslim youth in villages bordering on LTTE-controlled enclaves.

Indonesia. I noted in chapter one how Egyptian, Yemeni and Saudi Arabian salafist Muslims have spread their particular brand of militant Islam in all those parts of Asia and Africa where Muslim communities have lived relatively peaceably with their non-Muslim neighbors. Mention was made of the struggle between Islamists and cosmopolitan (as well as nominal) Muslims in Indonesia, a struggle that has heightened after the fall of the dictator General Suharto. Despite having the largest Muslim population in the world, the Indonesian constitution has not been based on Islamic shari'a but on the pluralist concept of Pancasila (five binding principles, the first of which is belief in God almighty, which form a kind of civic religion).

In only five out of twenty-six provinces in Indonesia is there a non-Muslim majority: Bali, East Nusa Tenggara, Irian Jaya, North Sulawesi and Maluku. The latter is better known in English as the Moluccas, the original Spice Islands, which drew the Dutch East India Company in the seventeenth century and eventually led to the colonization of the whole country by the Dutch.[24] With the exception of Bali, which is mainly Hindu, all the provinces have substantial Christian populations. Irian Jaya, rich in gold, uranium and other mineral deposits, has been colonized by Australian and American mining companies, and has seen very little of its wealth translated into human development by the central government. Naturally an independence movement has been spawned, and this has been brutally attacked by government troops and foreign Islamist jihadis whose propaganda portrays the secessionist struggle as a "Christian rebellion" against the government.

Religiously motivated attacks in various parts of Indonesia against Christian churches and the business premises of ethnic Chinese (the majority of whom are Christians) grew during the last few years of Suharto's rule. The Chinese were the main entrepreneurs in the country and, owing to their prosperity, became easy scapegoats for the nation's economic woes. The Suharto family's massive corruption, siphoning off vast fortunes from the nation's resources and depositing them in European and American banks, was well known internationally, but the United States, British and Dutch governments had not only supported Suharto's bloody coup in 1965 but regarded him and the Philippine dictator Ferdinand Marcos as their principal allies in Asia during the Cold War.

Suharto, like many Western-backed dictators, first used Islamist groups against the alleged "communist threat" and then viciously turned against them. As his popularity in the West declined after the end of the Cold War, he started wooing extremist Islamist organizations. Christians were side-lined in government, the civil service, the military and higher education. The loyalty of army generals was bought by granting them the exploitation rights to large tracts of tropical rainforest. An Indonesian Islamic Intellectuals Association was set up, spearheaded by Suharto's eventual successor, B. J. Habibie, to advise the government on policy and to win over Islamist factions.

Following the Asian financial crisis of 1997, which precipitated Suharto's downfall and saw widespread social unrest in the country, anti-Christian activity increased as part of a growing Islamization of political and educational institutions. Many key positions in the Moluccas, in the government, police and military were taken away from Christians and handed over to Muslims. The traditional relationship between Christians and Muslims in the Moluccas has been relatively harmonious, the two groups sharing many similarities in culture, including common animist beliefs. According to a recent study by the anthropologist Farsijana Risakotta-Adeney, the bloody violence that erupted in the period 1999 to 2002, depicted in the international media as Muslim-Christian conflict, had more complex roots. Her interviews with

tribal kings revealed that almost all of them saw the conflicts not primarily
as religious but as multifaceted, involving history, ethnicity, land ownership,
local custom and so on. For example, on one island agricultural land which
traditionally belonged to a Muslim-animist tribe was bought by a banana
export company in Jakarta. The tribal people became indentured laborers
on the banana plantations that were managed by ethnic Chinese managers
of the company. When a labor dispute turned violent, the local media kept
referring to the Chinese managers as "Christians." This is like a red flag to
a bull. Immediately Islamist organizations from elsewhere got embroiled in
the dispute, which quickly escalated into a "religious conflict."[25] Labeling
a conflict religious is to indulge in self-fulfilling prophecy. It immediately
sucks in co-religionists from all over the country and, in the case of Islam,
even from all over the world.

Al-Qa'ida made its most successful inroads into Indonesian militant
groups during the conflict in the Moluccas. Camps were built around Ambon, and money provided by Saudi charities financed the arming and training of the militias. These private armies also had links to powerful politicians
and sections of the Indonesian army and police. A violent vigilante group,
Lashkar Jihad, set up with assistance from local politicians, was responsible
not only for horrific massacres, such as that which took place in the village
of Soya at Ambon in the Moluccas on April 28, 2002, but also the forced
conversions of Christians. These involved forcible circumcisions of males and
females.[26] The leader of Lashkar Jihad, the Yemeni-born Jafar Umar Thalib,
was charged with inciting hatred in the Moluccas. He was acquitted a few
months after his organization voluntarily disbanded in October 2002. Violence has continued to flare up sporadically ever since.[27]

ATHEIST POLEMICS AND COLLECTIVE DECEPTION

The events of September 11, 2001, and the subsequent "terrorist" attacks in
European cities by individuals and groups with strong religious identities
have been seized upon by those academics and journalists who have long been
cynical toward any religious truth claims and worldviews. They have been
used to discredit religion in general by drawing attention to the particularly
destructive nature of "religious violence." In the case of violence committed

by Muslim suicide bombers, statements made by them or their families about attaining paradise for their acts of self-sacrifice have provided extra fuel for the ire of polemical secularists such as Richard Dawkins and Polly Toynbee in Britain, and Sam Harris in the United States. It is not too difficult to find divinely authorized violence in the sacred texts and rites of most religious traditions, and to point to repression, brutality, even genocide, committed in the name of some deity or other. When asked what he thought was the real axis of evil, the journalist Christopher Hitchens replied, "Christianity, Judaism, and Islam."[28] Dawkins's response to 9/11 was typical: "To fill the world with religion, or religions of the Abrahamic kind, is like littering the streets with loaded guns. Do not be surprised if they are used."[29] Religion is the problem, not the solution, and the only hope for us all lies in its demise.

There are many ironies here. To begin with, it is strange to find religious evolutionists (those, like Dawkins, who subscribe to evolution as an all-embracing worldview rather than as a biological paradigm) regarding violence as an aberration rather than a natural aspect of existence. Second, it was the academic fashion, not too long ago and among those on what is sometimes called the cultural left, to dismiss all religious claims and behavior as mere epiphenomena—byproducts of political, economic and social changes—that would eventually disappear with the progress of modernity. In Hegelian fashion, they believed that all societies would converge toward the secularist ideal of Western Europe. Religions, if they persisted, could be tolerated in the realm of the private as essentially benign (because intellectually vacuous) practices. Today the mood has swung to the other extreme: religions are powerful and dangerous because they are the underlying motivation behind all violent resistance to progressive change.

After interviewing many violent activists, Professor Jessica Stern of the Kennedy School of Government at Harvard University writes, "I've noticed that one thing that distinguishes religious terrorists from other people is that they know with absolute certainty that they're doing good. They seem more confident and less susceptible to self-doubt than most other people."[30] But why is such absolute certainty confined to religious militants? What Walter Wink has called the "Myth of Redemptive Violence" ("that violence saves, that war brings peace, that might makes right") is present in many societies, and is not necessarily tied to religious worldviews.[31]

Indeed, the most terrible violence of the twentieth century was inflicted by officially atheistic regimes, such as in the Soviet Union, Mao's China and North Korea, or those like Nazi Germany which combined German paganism and racist theories (promulgated by anti-Christian and anti-Jewish scientists) into a new state religion. The bloodletting of the last century, the most secularized in human history, exceeds by far all that preceded it.[32] Even today, most dictatorial regimes are not Islamic or "religious" in any traditional sense. Whether in North Korea, Burma or Zimbabwe, Buddhist and Christian dissidents have been deprived of civic rights, imprisoned or killed. Moreover, it is not devout Muslims who have been developing and amassing weapons of mass destruction but "enlightened" secular states. The idea that promoting secular democracies will automatically put an end to violent conflict and war flies in the face of history.

A further reason for bemusement is that such militantly atheistic critics who issue apocalyptic warnings of a new "dark age" of religious superstition and obscurantism that is about to overrun the world, simply echo the rhetoric of people like George W. Bush who announced "a war to defend civilization" and in the wake of 9/11 told the American Congress: "Americans are asking, why do they hate us? They hate what we see right here in this chamber—a democratically elected government. Their leaders are self-appointed. They hate our freedoms—our freedom of religion, our freedom of speech, our freedom to vote and assemble and disagree with each other."[33] If Western secular freedoms were what incensed al-Qa'ida, and religiously inspired hatred of Western democracy is what inspires Muslim radicals around the world, why were Sweden or Norway not the targets of Muslim militants, instead of the Pentagon and the Twin Towers?

Interestingly, most of the hardcore of the "neocons" who planned the invasion of Iraq long before 9/11 (men such as Richard Perle, Paul Wolfowitz, Donald Rumsfeld, Kenneth Adelman and Douglas Feith) had no pretensions to Christian or Jewish faith. But their atheism/agnosticism was never an issue for the left-leaning liberal media that made Bush's faith profession an object of incessant ridicule, even blaming U.S. foreign policy on an evangelical worldview. One cannot but wonder: are all of America's wars to be called religious wars since "in God we trust" is inscribed on all the dollar bills that finance those wars? Does the obligatory "God bless you" with which most U.S. presidents, Democrat and Republican alike, end their speeches to the nation signify religious sincerity and devotion? Is the mere invocation of God in a speech peppered with lies or half-truths sufficient to label it Christian or Jewish? Does the content that goes into the name God not matter at all? If we can accept that patriotic fervor or scientific knowledge can be manipulated for self-serving interests, why not sacred scriptures and religious sentiment?

On February 5, 2003, a month before the Anglo-American invasion of Iraq, General Colin Powell, a man not given to open religious sentiment, claimed before the UN Security Council and a live global audience—and with an absolute certainty that would have made most religious people around the world squirm—that the U.S. possessed "incontrovertible" evidence that Iraq had not only produced chemical and biological weapons but was planning their imminent deployment against the United States. Powell showed impressive satellite photographs of weapons movements, an unmanned Iraqi airplane capable of delivering chemical weapons, and confidently rattled off other "evidence" of war preparation culled from leaked documents, interviews with recent Iraqi exiles, and reports from informants within the Iraqi armed forces. The next day's *Washington Post* carried an editorial fulsome in its praise for Powell's "compelling detail" and thanking the Secretary of State and his spies for having assembled "as powerful a case as the most exacting critic could expect and backed it up impressively yesterday."[31] Other national editorials were also genuflecting in admiration. The lack of susceptibility to self-doubt that Jessica Stern identified as being at the root of religiously inspired terrorism was clearly in evidence in these hallowed secular journals, as well as many intellectual clubs in Boston and Washington.

How do we account for the gullibility, indeed obsequiousness, of the liberal secular media in the United States? It is only after the evidence of deliberate deception became overwhelming that the liberal media came to express righteous indignation. One can understand the naive trust that Christian fundamentalists in the United States show toward any president claiming to be "born again," a trust based largely on ignorance of American history and a childish faith in the divine origin of the American form of government.

But when normally cynical, atheistic liberals only register moral indignation when presidential falsehoods become too obvious to deny, something deeper is at work in the collective American psyche that fills many non-American observers with alarm.

There were indeed many Americans of every color and creed who registered their protest against going to war on such flimsy evidence. Many Christian churches and parachurch organizations in the United States, covering a wide theological and social spectrum, officially denounced the preparation for war, but their voices were largely muted in the secular, liberal media. I think it is significant that many of the early antiwar voices, Christian and otherwise, stemmed from people who either had a sense of historical perspective or had experienced long periods of living and working outside the United States. Those Christian denominations and organizations that were part of larger, international networks were more likely than their more home-grown sister churches to distance themselves from the jingoistic patriotism that pervaded American society.

As for Islamist organizations, the majority of their leaders and sympathizers have eschewed violence. However, we have seen that the violent overreaction of states (and the suppression of traditional religious authorities) led to the radicalization of many youth. In countries such as Algeria, Egypt, Saudi Arabia and Indonesia, thousands of men and women have been tortured in jails or executed by state-sponsored death squads. I noted in chapter one that state-sanctioned "terrorist" violence has killed far more people than Islamist "terrorism."

Moreover, the thirst for heroic sacrifice in a higher cause is not found only in some radicalized Islamic or Hindu groups. Buruma and Margalit recall that European fascism in the 1920s and 1930s "appealed precisely to mediocre men, because it gave them a glimpse of glory by association, by feeling part of a supernation, and in Nazism a superrace, supposedly endowed with superior virtues and spiritual qualities."[35] Such men saw the West as part of an "old world, effete, money-grubbing, selfish and shallow." The seductions of this old world were corrupting and enervating German youth who should be fighting for a more glorious future. "Only their sacrifices in a storm of steel would save them from being ruined by the banality of the West."[36]

Consider the following analogy. Given the universality of sexual experience, it is hardly surprising that this powerful human drive should also be the site of rape, pedophilia, bestiality, genital mutilation and other grotesque acts. Most of us would regard these acts as twisted perversions of a healthy and important component of our human identity and flourishing. (Indeed, we have been taught by feminists that rape is primarily about power, not sexual pleasure.) Why not apply the same reasoning to religious faiths? Given the universality of religious experience, it is hardly surprising that certain acts of grotesque violence should not only occur in religious communities but be imbued with religious meanings and justification. As a specialist in religious studies from New Zealand, Chris Marshall points out, "If history teaches us anything, then, it is that humanity's irrepressible religiosity is exceeded only by its incessant and unbearable cruelty."[37]

Marshall quotes with approval from a 2004 Bradford University (U.K.) study on war and religion which demonstrated that "armed conflict is rarely, if ever, solely about religion or religious differences. Although armed conflicts may take on religious overtones, their genesis is found in a complex matrix of crisscrossing and mutually exacerbating factors, such as economics, politics, resources, ethnicity and identity, power struggles, inequality, oppression, and other historical grievances."[38] Marshall himself concludes, "Religion always *contributes* to conflicts because it conditions and informs all other significant cultural activities. But religious belief or practice is never *solely* to blame (nor is it wholly *free* of blame) simply because religion is, by definition, interconnected with all the rest of social reality."[39]

The British theologian Alister McGrath, writing in a very different context, rebuts the charge, common in Western academic circles since Auschwitz, that belief in God is discredited by the massive scale of violence in the world:

It is only fair to point out that those who planned the Holocaust, and those who slammed shut the doors of the Auschwitz gas chambers, were human beings—precisely those whom Ludwig Feuerbach declared to be the 'new gods' of the modern era, free from any divine prohibitions or sanctions, or any fear of future divine judgment. . . . While some continue to argue that Auschwitz disproves the existence of God, many more would argue that it demonstrates the depths to which humanity, unrestrained by any thought or fear of God, will sink. There are many today who affirm a belief in humanity in preference to a belief in God. Yet this humanity has been responsible for a series of moral, social, and political catastrophes, some inspired by a belief in God, others by a belief that God must be eliminated, by all means and at all costs. The common denominator here is *humanity*, not divinity.[40]

Furthermore, the advocates of nondefensive violence in most religious communities remain a very small minority precisely because the majority of believers perceive that such violence transgresses against "core" precepts of their religious tradition. If religions have legitimated certain acts of violence, they have also prevented or limited the frequency and scope of violence. All over the world we will find local churches and organizations as well as international agencies, such as the Mennonite Central Committee, the World Conference on Religion and Peace, the Society of Engaged Buddhists, Catholic Relief Services or the three hundred-odd evangelical Christian organizations that comprise the Micah Network, that are deeply engaged in societies torn apart by violent conflict. They conduct workshops and training courses in conflict transformation, drawing explicitly on religious resources for facilitating communication and dialogue between communities at enmity with each other.

Such "religious militants for peace," in the words of Scott Appleby, "plumb their respective religious traditions for spiritual and theological insights and practices useful in preventing deadly conflict or limiting its spread."[41] He argues further:

> In an era when so many violent conflicts occur among people living in close proximity to one another, such virtues give local religious actors a decided advantage in conflict management over most governments and their remote bureaucracies. Operating from within religious communities or as members of transnational social movements, religious actors offer irreplaceable and effective remedies to the ills that beset societies mired in social inequalities and vulnerable to systematic or random violence.[42]

RECOVERING CHRISTIAN INTEGRITY

Whatever the underlying causes, religious intolerance and persecution are on the rise and have been implicated in many tragic conflicts around the world. Many Western observers forget that non-Western Christians often bear the brunt of such violence. A great majority of the seventy-six worst Christian martyrdom situations of the past two millennia, including eight of the fifteen with over a million martyrs each, occurred in the twentieth century.[43] Moreover, "The parochialism of Western public opinion is striking," notes Philip Jenkins. "When a single racial or religiously-motivated murder takes place in Europe or North America, the event occasions widespread soul-searching, but when thousands are massacred on the grounds of their faith in Nigeria, Indonesia, or the Sudan, the story rarely registers. Some lives are worth more than others."[44]

However, Christians betray the very core of their faith whenever they only highlight anti-Christian violence without at the same time speaking up for others unjustly persecuted for their respective faiths (whether religious or secularist) and also acknowledging with shame the violence directed in the name of Christianity at others (as happened in Serbia, Bosnia, Indonesia and elsewhere in recent history). It is time for all Christian churches and organizations, across the entire theological spectrum, to take stock of such blind spots in their narrations of violence.

All Christian traditions, even those mainstream traditions that have justified violence in carefully defined and limited circumstances, have always declared violence to be evil. Violence and war arise from the breakdown of human relations, usually prompted either by greed for resources or perceived threats to one's identity (involving language, culture or religion). Although the global media tend to focus exclusively on those parts of the world where American or British troops are involved in combat, the vast majority of conflicts in recent decades have been within states rather than between them. Very rarely do ethnic, cultural or religious differences per se lead to conflict. It is when such differences are practiced within a wider matrix of social, political or economic discrimination that cultural and religious traditions provide powerful resources for militant struggle. The "other" now becomes an enemy, and differences are absolutized.

Christians, of all people, should be least surprised by the phenomenon of religious violence. At the heart of Christian faith stands a cross, an instrument of torture, degradation and mass execution. Orthodox Christian theology has always insisted that the one who was crucified at the instigation of the religious leaders of his society was no less than the incarnate Son of God. A God who has chosen to be vulnerable to suffering and death cuts away the ground from beneath an atheism of protest, because protest atheism envisages God as a cruel tyrant who manipulates people and moves them around like pieces on a chessboard. It also cuts away the ground from beneath every form of religious theism that seeks to co-opt God in the service of a political ideology. The God of Christian belief is not an ahistorical deity conceived of in abstract, metaphysical categories (Supreme Being, Absolute, World Spirit) beloved of religiously inclined philosophers, East and West. God denotes a form of uncreated life, lived in three eternally self-giving and self-responsive movements, in which all things participate and in which all things find their true value. If this God suffers in solidarity with the victims of crucifixion, then God cannot be on the side of the torturers, oppressors and the advocates of violence.

The fourth-century "conversion" of the Roman emperor Constantine altered the relationship to violence of large sections of the Western church, hitherto a frequently persecuted and oppressed social movement. Christianity changed its self-understanding once it became a state religion. The church became more and more institutionalized and was eventually identified territorially (Christendom). The persecution that had been directed against it was now redirected against its pagan neighbors and their environment. That the church has so often betrayed the basic evangelical truth that the reign of God is spread through self-giving, suffering love, and allowed itself to be seduced by geopolitical ambitions, is perhaps the chief cause of its loss of credibility in our (post)modern world.[45]

The inability to think outside the boundaries of nationalism leads to idolatry. When Christians identify the kingdom of God with the kingdom of America, for example, believing that America's wealth and prominence on the world stage is the reward of a divine providence for its exceptional virtue, they have already been co-opted into the war machine. As long as secularist Democrats and Republicans alike believe that whenever their presidents talk of America's "national interests" and "national security" they are thinking of poor inner-city ghettos and the one in five children living below the poverty line, and not of the interests and security of IBM or Halliburton, they will continue to be fooled by talk of "promoting democracy and liberty" around the world. Moreover, an uncritical Christian Zionism, based on dispensationalist readings of the Old Testament, found in large pockets of Midwestern America and spread abroad by some missionary organizations, is the religious counterpart to the powerful pro-Israel lobbies in New York and Washington.

Some of this uncritical Christian support for Israel is, no doubt, a reaction motivated by the memory of violence inflicted by Christians on the Jews. The Western Christian treatment of Jews over the centuries is indeed a deep scar on global Christian witness and an abiding source of shame. To many non-Christians as well as Jews, it exposed Christian claims of love and reconciliation as hollow. Jews were prohibited from most professions and education, and they were enclosed in ghettos for centuries. They entered banking in the Middle Ages because this was forbidden to Christians. In the nineteenth and early twentieth centuries Jews apostasized for the sake of social advancement, and were looked on by other Jews as traitors. The Christian theologian Ellen Charry reminds us that patristic theologians wrote at least twenty-six separate treatises "against the Jews." One cannot help but wonder, as Charry herself does, as to what a difference it would have made if the historic creeds of Christianity had not moved directly from the doctrine of creation to the incarnation, thereby bypassing God's election of ancient Israel for the sake of the nations.

"To speak of Christ in relation to Judaism is painful," observes Charry, "for it is impossible to do so without evoking centuries of vituperation, violence and counter-violence, and reciprocal hostility, fear, and contempt." She continues:

> Jews have said NO to Christ for two millennia, enduring humiliation, persecution, oppressions, degradation, and death in order to act upon their integrity as the people of God. While a few said yes out of true

faith in him, others were baptized under threat of banishment, death, torture, or other forms of coercion of adults and children. This was especially the case during the Counter-Reformation in Spain.[46]

Once the Christian theological critique of Judaism expanded into angry polemic against Jews and the latter began to suffer legally and physically simply because they were Jews, they came to despise the church.

At root, violence derives from the attempt to replace God with ourselves, as individuals and as nations, and to force others and the world to conform to our desires. What are called religions are frequently an idolatrous sanction for that rebellion. In the New Testament the writer of the epistle to the Hebrews reminds his readers that Jesus "suffered outside the city gate" on the municipal rubbish site where the carcasses of the animal sacrifice of the Jerusalem temple were burned. The religious system and the religious leadership discarded him. The writer warns his readers, who are themselves facing religious persecution because of their obedience to this Jesus, that religious violence is what they must expect because "here we have no lasting city, but we are looking for the city that is to come" (Hebrews 13:11-14). The religious violence associated with sacred spaces and holy territories as well as the attempt to domesticate God within one's cultural traditions has long been the object of prophetic denunciation.

Christians do not have a naively optimistic view of religions, including Christianity insofar as it has come to share in all the trappings of religion. They recognize that religious practices, like everything else we do, reflect the ambivalence of our human condition. Hence the just-war tradition as it was developed by Christian theologians since Augustine and Ambrose grew precisely out of the profound conviction of our own innate self-centeredness and propensity for self-deception and self-justification, so that we need to set up restraints in both directions, against evil and against the evil with which we restrain evil. The pervasiveness and self-deceptiveness of sin, even among the victims, deconstructs all linguistic binaries such as "innocent us" and "evil them." Reconciliation with the enemy or peaceful coexistence is the ultimate goal of any use of armed force. By contrast, religious and secularist extremists seek victory over the enemy, and the means they use are subservient to that end.

The just-war tradition that we discussed in chapter one is more than a proposal about waging war. It is a way of thinking about politics that puts justice at the heart of political responsibility. Justice stands opposed to every form of tyranny. Tyrants recognize no restraints, whether in peace or in war. They are a law to themselves. Human beings, whether combatants or innocent noncombatants, are merely means to private ends. "Religious" tyrants may be personally devout but they manipulate scriptural traditions or communal folklore to deflect all criticism of their actions.

Those voices within the worldwide Christian church that have long been critical of the just-war tradition have argued that events such as the Anglo-American invasion of Iraq in March 2003 show how the tradition is either ignored by powerful nations or manipulated by their spin doctors. The "legitimate authority" who alone can authorize a just war, even in liberal democracies, lie to their electorates and conceal contrary evidence. In Britain, all church leaders openly condemned the buildup to the invasion as an unprovoked act of aggression. Nevertheless, Prime Minister Tony Blair and the British Parliament, on the basis of "doctored" intelligence information, chose to defy not only the Church of England but also the UN Security Council and the advice of UN weapons inspectors working in Iraq. It committed British troops to support the ill-conceived adventure.

No doubt the just-war tradition, like every other body of accumulated wisdom, needs to be critically reconceived and freshly articulated in every new context of violence. As a living tradition it must address the new challenges that new forms of warfare and new experiences of political chicanery bring. However, the gratuitous violence inflicted by insurgents and state-sponsored death squads in many parts of the world also poses hard questions to the "just peace" (or peace church) tradition among Christians. Is it not inconsistency bordering on hypocrisy to expect non-Christian police and intelligence services to apprehend those who threaten our lives and so ensure our well-being, while we shun any recourse to armed force on the grounds that it is evil?

MUTUAL CRITICISM

"Never before have we needed so much the criticism of religion," wrote Douglas Meeks soon after 9/11, and immediately added, "But the most historically effective criticism of religion comes from within the religion itself."[47] A cursory acquaintance with any of the major world faiths will quickly show that they all contain self-correcting elements to overcome fanaticism and violence. The critique of religious bigotry and hypocrisy did not begin with the eighteenth-century European "Enlightenment." "You shall not use God's name in vain" is the second commandment in the Torah (the Mosaic law). In the eighth century B.C., the prophet Isaiah of Jerusalem announces Yahweh's verdict on the religion of his day:

> Bringing offerings is futile;
>   incense is an abomination to me. . . .
>   I cannot endure solemn assemblies with iniquity.
> Your new moons and your appointed festivals
>   my soul hates. . . .
> When you stretch out your hands,
>   I will hide my eyes from you;
> even though you make many prayers,
>   I will not listen;
>   your hands are full of blood.
> Wash yourselves; make yourselves clean;
>   remove the evil of your doings
>   from before my eyes;
> cease to do evil,
>   learn to do good;
> seek justice,
>   rescue the oppressed,
> defend the orphan,
>   plead for the widow. (Isaiah 1:13-17)

While, in the middle of the first century A.D., the apostle Paul writes of those who shared his ancestral religious heritage: "You that boast in the law, do you dishonor God by breaking the law? . . . The name of God is blasphemed among the Gentiles because of you" (Romans 2:23-24); and, elsewhere, "I can testify that they have a zeal for God, but it is not enlightened" (Romans 10:2).

Indeed, we know from the historical record that Christians are every bit as culpable as any other kind of fanatic of reducing other people to instruments in the service of their cause, and have often proved incapable of distinguishing what is genuinely Christian from what is nationalist or cultural chauvinism. The church, called to be the covenant people of God and a sign of God's intention to heal the nations, is a flawed and fallible human institution, and in every age struggles to free itself from those idolatries that compromise its message to the world.

If Muslims rightly resent the negative stereotyping of a monolithic Islam by Western writers, then they need to look with equal dismay at the identical stereotyping that is widespread in the Muslim world. Anti-Western polemic often blends with anti-Christian sentiments, even in the more serious Muslim literature. Moreover, Kate Zebiri, a lecturer in Arabic and Islamic Studies at the University of London, has noted that "the study of Christianity by modern Muslims does not, on the whole, compare favourably with that of the medieval scholars," many of whom considered it important to understand the arguments and doctrines of Christianity on their own terms before seeking to refute them.[48] Ironically, "Christianity is sometimes portrayed in the very same terms that have been used of Islam in both earlier Orientalist scholarship and the contemporary media: as power-seeking and war-mongering on the one hand, and irrational, obscurantist, backward-looking, and in need of reformation on the other."[49]

Writing in the context of interfaith dialogue, Anthony O'Mahony criticizes the false objectivity of those who choose a vacuous, post-Enlightenment "religion" in a superficial quest for harmony, thereby sidelining specific religious commitments:

> Those who adopt a theoretical, privileged position outside of every specific faith community, and elaborate a general structure of religious "truth" that can provide a space for every religious tradition, but which nobody believes in, will not satisfy. Lack of commitment under the pretext of openness leads to no real dialogue, or to sham agreements. We cannot put *our* faith in parentheses to connect with another's faith.[50]

From time to time newspapers in Western countries and mobile-phone pollsters conduct inane surveys concerning religion. A popular question, ever since Islamist attacks in Western cities, has been "Do you think religion is good for society?" Given the pervasive lack of historical awareness, mentioned at the start of this chapter, and the typical vagueness with which the subject of religion is approached, such questions only reinforce ignorance. They reflect and bolster a therapeutic culture in which feeling good or being healthy is the summum bonum of life. Questions of truth are sidestepped. Lifting my body from my couch in front of the TV to start exploring the evidence for the truth claims of Christianity or Islam is too discomfiting and intellectually demanding.

All the longest-standing religious traditions call people to commitment, sacrifice and solidarity with others. They put us out of step with prevailing opinion. All prophets experience anguish, angst and loneliness, not bonhomie or detached observation. The moral question of the legitimacy of violence in some transcendent or "sacred" cause presupposes a prior epistemological judgment on the content of the sacred. Should we be pleased or dismayed at the sight of religious believers inspired by "sacred rage" against unjust economic policies, corruption and hypocrisy in government, the despoliation of nature or endemic violence against certain groups of people that is embedded in social structures? How we answer that depends on our worldview. Discussing religious violence in isolation from the violence in which we all participate, overtly or tacitly, and from deeper debates about societal worldviews is rather like discussing an issue such as capital punishment in isolation from the deeper issues of crime and effective law enforcement, judicial sentencing, penal conditions, the meaning of punishment and restorative justice.

The question is raised increasingly by right-wing politicians in European and North American nations, with regard to Muslim migrants: Are they Muslims first or citizens of our nation first? It is clear what answer is expected. Interestingly, the same question is never asked of Christians or Jews who support the state of Israel. Perhaps it should be asked; the answers will be very revealing. All scripture-based faith communities understand themselves as transcending national borders and historical epochs. Any state that refuses to acknowledge such multiple allegiances is sowing the seeds of future violence. We shall explore more fully the idolization of the modern state in chapter four.

Finally, Scott Appleby, who has devoted decades of study to the impact of secularization on religious groups, argues that contrary to widespread misconception, religious people play a positive role in the world of human conflicts and contribute to peace—not when they "moderate their religion or marginalize their deeply held, vividly symbolized and often highly particular beliefs" but rather "when they remain *religious actors*."[51] We have seen that the view of the modern secular state as the benign peacemaker between inherently violent religious factions is part of the mythology of European modernity.

In similar vein, Miroslav Volf, the Croatian theologian now teaching in the United States, observes that it is easy to show that "the majority of Christians—and the majority of religious folks in general—are nonviolent citizens, peace lovers, peacemakers and peace activists, not in spite of their religion but out of religious reasons." Since the purveyors of violence who seek religious legitimation are statistically a small minority, why is the contrary opinion so widespread? Volf points to the "tendency of the evil to loom larger than the comparatively much larger good," a tendency that is strengthened by the dominance of the mass media. Volf invites us to consider the following contrast:

> The Serbian paramilitary who rapes Muslim women with a cross around his neck has made it into the headlines and is immortalized in books on religious violence. But Katarina Kruhonja, a medical doctor from Osijek, Croatia, and a recipient of the alternative Nobel Prize for her peace initiatives, remains relatively unknown, as does the motivation for her work, which is thoroughly religious. While it's true that the success of such work depends on low visibility, our unawareness of it also has to do with the character of mass-media communication in a market-driven world. Violence sells, so viewers get to see violence.

Volf's bold challenge to those who would replace full-blooded historic Christianity with a tepid, vague, liberal religiosity is important:

> If we strip Christian convictions of their original and historic cognitive

and moral content, and reduce faith to a cultural resource endowed with a diffuse aura of the sacred, we are likely to get religiously legitimized and inspired violence in situations of conflict. If, on the other hand, we nurture people in historic Christian convictions that are rooted in sacred texts, we will likely get militants for peace.[52]

A remarkable meeting took place in Solo, Central Java (Indonesia), in February 2007.[53] The Hizbullah command center in the city hosted an international group of about thirty Christian leaders. Solo had been the scene of bloody conflict between Chinese and Javanese, Muslims and Christians, in 1998. The meeting was the result of the resourcefulness of a young Christian pastor, himself a former prayer leader in a local mosque, who heads up an interreligious peacemaking committee. The pastor had invited the Hizbullah commander and his officers to work alongside Christian teams in Banda Aceh in post-tsunami reconstruction. Prior to the December 26, 2004, tsunami that devastated the region, Banda Aceh had been a hotbed of Islamist militancy. Much of the reconstruction, however, came from Christian philanthropy. Amazingly, the invitation was accepted and Hizbullah and Christian leaders worked together in rebuilding projects. The commander and the pastor slept in the same room and quickly became friends. One evening, he began to weep and confided: "When I think of what we have done to you, and how you reciprocate with love, my heart has melted within me!" As a further step toward reconciliation, the Christian leadership in Solo working with Hizbullah is developing relations with Jamaah Islamiah, the radical movement responsible for the Bali bombings of October 2002. The strategy is to build bridges with peace-loving Muslims and then together woo some of the militant Muslims who, in turn, open the door to the terrorist groups.

Such stories, common in many situations of violent conflict around the world, will not normally be found on the BBC or in the *New York Times*.

3

MYTHS OF HUMAN RIGHTS

In a remote Punjabi village in Pakistan in June 2002, Mukhtaran Bibi, an illiterate rural woman was gang-raped on the orders of a panchayat, or tribal council of elders. This was an "honor" punishment meted out against her to avenge a higher-caste woman of the village who had allegedly had an affair with Mukhtaran's twelve-year old brother. Pakistan's shari'a legal system requires four male adult eyewitnesses to testify to rape, otherwise the victim can be convicted of fornication and adultery. So most women keep silent. In the days that followed the rape, Mukhtaran resisted the impulse to commit suicide out of her public shame, but took the men to court. Her tearful testimony helped convict the men, and she was catapulted into international fame, becoming a symbol for women's rights in Pakistan and elsewhere. With the compensation money and contributions from people who read about her struggle, she created a school for girls. In October 2005, the American woman's magazine *Glamour* honored her with their "woman of the year" award. A year later the Pakistani parliament changed its legal code concerning rape, despite opposition from some Islamist organizations.

THE LANGUAGE OF RIGHTS

Such stories are important for at least two reasons.[1] They remind us that the struggle against social injustice should be the concern not only of politicians, lawyers and legal scholars, but rather of every citizen. They also tell us that civic or political rights is a matter of ordinary men and women standing up and claiming what belongs to them. A right is a claim to some good to which one is legitimately entitled. When we use the language of rights we are not appealing to the generosity of governments, civil institutions or other individuals. Rather, we are making a claim as a matter of justice: to receive what is owed to us. We do not beg for rights, we claim them.

Most societies recognize different kinds of rights (or legitimate entitlements). There are some entitlements which are based on achievement: if I were to win the marathon at the Olympic Games, then I have a right to the gold medal. No one else enjoys that right apart from myself. If the judges were to refuse me the medal, simply on account of my skin color, say, or because of personal dislike, my rights would be violated. There are other rights based on contract: if you were to promise me payment for some work I do for you, and then refuse to pay me even though the work has been done to your satisfaction, you have broken your promise. I am morally injured as my right to payment has been violated. There are other rights that society recognizes based on status (a parent has rights with respect to his or her children which others do not, a magistrate has the right to punish me which others do not, etc.) or ability (an employer has the right to refuse me employment if I am not suitably qualified for a vacant post), and legal statute (a policemen has the right to fine me for a traffic offense). Some rights are natural: parents' rights with respect to their children are not grounded in contract or ability or systems of law. In many ancient societies it was believed that certain royal families were naturally entitled to govern, being equipped by nature or the gods for such a role.

There is a special class of natural rights which has come to be called human rights. These are rights that are ascribed to human beings simply because they belong to the human species. They are not based on achievement, contract or social status. Nor are they conferred on human beings by governments or legal systems. The latter only recognize and articulate them. Natural human rights are grounded in the nature of human beings. In principle we could have human rights that are not natural; that would be the case if we had a world government that could promulgate laws that applied to all human beings on the planet earth. But that is currently not the case.

1. Do rights and duties always go together? Some philosophers have criticized the language of rights as being too individual-centered, and prefer for

us to use instead the language of duties or responsibilities. Behind this sug-
gestion is the assumption that the language of rights can be translated exactly
into a language of corresponding duties, without remainder. But this assumption is incorrect. While some duties entail corresponding rights, others do
not. For example, consider two men trapped in a building that is on fire.
Suppose that the firemen only have time to reach one of them. It is the duty
of the firemen to try to save the one they can reach, but neither man can claim
that he has a right to be saved.

It is, therefore, better to think of duties and rights as forming two different moral languages, both of which are necessary for human moral action but
which do not neatly overlap. When I fail to fulfill my moral obligation to another, I am morally guilty. If, however, my rights have been violated, I am morally injured. While we do and should feel grateful when people go out of their
way to help us, or when we are loved and wanted, gratitude for goods that we
are otherwise entitled to harms our self-respect and erodes our dignity.

2. Are rights claims empty demands? Some argue that rights are claims
made against specific individuals or institutions, and are therefore only meaningful if we can identify who is responsible for granting those rights. So, one
common objection to the idea that all men and women have the right to free
choice of employment (article 23 of the UN Declaration of Human Rights)
or adequate living standards (article 25) is that it makes a demand on governments that they are incapable of realizing in practice.

But not all rights claims are made against governments or any specific
individuals. It is better to think of them as a general claim made on society,
namely, that society should be structured in such a way that enables all those
who live in that society to enjoy the rights in question. So, in the case of
economic rights such as previously mentioned, whether such arrangements
are best secured by state-directed action or by market forces in a capitalist economy is something to be discussed and debated in the public realm.
Whoever is capable of social and political influence in such matters carries a
correspondingly greater degree of responsibility than others.

QUESTIONING THE STANDARD LIBERAL STORY

Now the story regularly told in political science textbooks about the emergence of those remarkable entities we call human rights goes something like this. In tribal societies, sharp distinctions are drawn between those within and those outside the group and this militates against any recognition of natural human rights. Similarly in feudal societies, tightly structured on the basis of social class, those who are born as lords and those who are serfs (or in the Indian context, higher and lower caste) are knit together in a complex bundle of rights and duties which attach to them in different ways. For hierarchical thought, human beings are fundamentally unequal, so that some are entitled to power and privilege while others are not. Some humans are determined, either by nature or divine decree, to be inherently superior to others and thus designed to rule others. This is how Plato and Aristotle justified inequality, explaining why some people should rule and others obey, why some people are natural slaves and others are free by nature. On the Indian subcontinent, similar arguments were used by Hindu Brahmans to justify their superiority in Indian society, and by many nineteenth century British aristocrats to justify their empire.

In Western Europe and the American colonies, following the disappearance of both tribal and feudal societies, a clear recognition arose among "enlightened" thinkers of the natural rights that attach to every human being. In this early modern world, the recognition of a broad array of human rights, whose status the thinkers of the time found to be self-evident, came into being, namely, the right to freedom of religion, the right to free speech, the right to private property, the right to freedom of assembly and association, the right to freedom from arbitrary arrest, the right to have a voice in one's civil governance and so on. What united all these rights was a concept of freedom understood as the right of the individual to be freed from all social restrictions that hinder him from being a fully self-determining agent. We are free insofar as we are left alone to pursue our own intentions (projects) in our own way, provided that a like freedom is accorded to others. Thus human rights are grounded not in legal contract or achievement but in the capacity or ability which human beings exhibit of being intentional agents. It is this capacity that human rights language respects. It emphasizes the supreme value of human will.

This standard narrative, however plausible in some respects, fails to convince. For a start, as Nicholas Wolterstorff astutely observes, not all the items in the traditional schedule of human rights (which have now acquired canonical status in modern human rights documents) can be construed as the right to be left alone so as to be a self-directing agent. Having a voice in one's own governance, for instance, cannot mean each of us having the right to govern ourselves as we see fit. Even religious liberty, unlike freedom of speech, is rarely construed as the right of an individual to say and do as he pleases, but rather protects both individuals and religious communities from state coercion. But, more importantly, the right to be a self-determining individual involves more than the right to be left alone. Consider freedom from assault or theft of one's property. In a sinful world this entails more than a right to be left alone. It entails the right to receive aid from our fellows, in the form of judicial systems and police forces — in other words, the right to certain benefits that follow from social structures and arrangements that require contributions from the community for their maintenance. So, we all acknowledge that the right to freedom from assault is more than a right to be left alone; it presupposes cooperation and support from many others.

Thus, if freedom rights are construed as the right to be left alone, then all along Western societies have implicitly recognized that (negative) freedom rights must be supplemented by (positive) benefit rights that are connected with them. If freedom rights are construed as rights to function as self-determining agents, then such freedom rights necessarily incorporate benefit rights and have done so historically. In the twentieth century the range of human rights has considerably widened to include education and social welfare. The 1948 UN Declaration on Human Rights spoke of the rights to work, education and adequate health care. Such economic and social rights have been incorporated into some prominent liberal theories of human rights in recent decades, but the underlying conception of human will as the basis for all rights has rarely been challenged.

What is often forgotten in the standard liberal story of the emergence of human rights in the West is that the philosophers of the early modern period who framed the schedule of rights that we now call human rights did not think of them as the rights of all human beings. Nor do we today, despite the widespread rhetoric. We do not recognize a right of children, for instance, to own property or have a voice in their governance. The traditional schedule of human rights was, until well into the twentieth century in most Western societies, construed as the rights of white, adult, nonindentured males of sound mind and noncriminal practice. The application of all of them has since been expanded, but even today we do not extend them to children or those of unsound mind. Moreover, as the political theorist John Dunn wryly observes, "If ancient [Athenian] democracy was the citizens choosing freely and immediately for themselves, modern democracy, it seems, is principally the citizens very intermittently, choosing under highly constrained circumstances, the relatively small number of their fellows who will from then on choose for them."[2]

Most liberal theories of the modern Western state, from John Locke to John Rawls, are based on a mythology known as a social contract: the parties to the social contract are all independent, equal and self-determining individuals who choose to cooperate together in forming an ordered society and political arrangements that will ensure security, liberty and fairness. The partnership envisaged in this fictional hypothesis is for the mutual advantage of the contracting parties. For instance, Rawls's account of what he calls the "primary goods," the things every society must arrange to distribute fairly to its citizens, is explicitly connected to his account of citizens who possess the "two moral powers" (a capacity for a sense of justice and for a conception of the good) as well as the capacity for instrumental reasoning. Their possession of these powers makes them "free," "equal" and "fully cooperating."[3] Those people who lack the capacities of such independent citizens (children, the destitute, the elderly, the mentally and physically handicapped, political refugees and poor migrants) do not figure in the design of the basic institutions of society. Not surprisingly, such vulnerable groups of human beings have only entered contemporary political thinking as an afterthought.

How then are we to interpret what happened in early modern Western Europe? Wolterstorff suggests that we see it as the emergence of the recognition of the rights that attach to the full-fledged citizen.

> What was new at the time was the rise of wide-spread dissatisfaction with merely being subjects in state and church and the wish instead to

be citizens. The inevitable corollary of that desire was a new schedule of rights—the rights of the citizen. And nobody supposed, either then or now, that every human being is to be treated as a full-fledged citizen. . . . The seventeenth century does not differ from the Middle Ages, as some have suggested, in fully recognizing that among our natural ascriptive rights are human rights, and recognizing, in addition to those, only rights of achievement and of compact. It differs in replacing ascriptive rights of lords, serf, etc., with those of citizens.[4]

Citizen rights are immensely important, but they are not identical to what we mean by human rights. For not every human being is capable of carrying out the functions guarded by such rights as freedom of speech or political association: for instance, young children, the infirm or severely mentally disabled adults. What then secures the rights of those other human beings?

It is very doubtful if any secularist account of human beings can provide a foundation for human dignity and therefore of human rights, as Wolterstorff goes on to argue:

> The natural move of the secularist is to try grounding human rights in respect of certain capacities. But always a dilemma threatens: To insure that all human beings have the rights in question, the capacities singled out must be elementary; but then it proves to be the case that animals have them as well, so that we have not so much grounded human rights as animal rights. Alternatively, to insure the distinctiveness of human rights, the capacities singled out must be sophisticated; but then it proves to be the case that not all human beings have them, so that we have grounded something narrower than human rights.[5]

Similarly Michael Perry, an American law professor, has argued cogently that "there is, finally, no intelligible secular version of the idea of human rights, that the conviction that human beings are sacred is inescapably religious."[6] This is not to deny that many who do take human rights very seriously are agnostics and atheists where religious convictions are concerned. But it does raise serious doubts whether a vision of human rights can be argued for coherently and sustained effectively in societies which lack an appropriate theological understanding of the human person.

If we have no reason to believe that the world has a normative order that is transgressed by violations of human rights . . . and if we nonetheless coerce others, and perhaps even, at the limit, kill others, in the name of prosecuting human rights, then are we coercing and killing in the name of nothing but our sentiments, our preferences, our "inclination of the heart"?[7]

Western libertarian movements have bequeathed to secular modernity a bizarre notion of the human individual: an independent, solitary will, lodged in an unsatisfactory body not of its choosing and entering into voluntary, contractual relations with other wills based on mutual benefit. This rational, independent, self-legislating will was always identified with the male, while the fickle passions associated with the body with the female. The "rights of man" was no empty slogan. And "one man, one vote" simply meant that those who owned property and were thus relieved of manual labor by their slaving minions were entitled to choose their rulers from among themselves. Neither women nor the poor mattered.

"Woman is made to submit to man and to endure even injustice at his hands," wrote Jean-Jacques Rousseau (1712-1778), champion of modern freedom and social-contract theories of the state.[8] For Rousseau, who like many of his fellow Enlightenment thinkers, was dependent on the patronage of rich, intelligent and devoted women, argued in his book *Émile* (whose main theme is complete freedom in the education of boys) that

girls should early be accustomed to restraint, because all their life long they will have to submit to the most enduring restraints, those of propriety. . . . They have, or ought to have, little freedom. . . . As a woman's conduct is controlled by public opinion, so is her religion ruled by authority. . . . Unable to judge for themselves, they should accept the judgment of father and husband as that of the church.[9]

A woman's contribution to the well-being of the state was vital, but it was exercised in the sphere of the family. "Her dignity depends on remaining unknown; her glory lies in her husband's esteem, her greatest pleasure in the happiness of her family."

That some Enlightenment philosophers and the Taliban have more in common than we think is a disconcerting thought for those who believe that the biggest political challenge today is to "drag Islamic societies into the modern age." In the standard secular liberal account of the development of rights discourse, the villain of the piece is usually "religious bigotry." But contrast Rousseau with the apostle Paul, for instance, who is regarded with disdain by feminists and liberals alike as the archetypal male chauvinist. Faced with the strict constraints of patriarchy in the first-century Jewish-Roman world, he nevertheless insisted that "the husband should give to his wife her conjugal rights. . . . For . . . the husband does not have authority over his own body, but his wife does" (1 Corinthians 7:3-4). No comparable statement can be found in any literature prior to the late twentieth century.[10] The equality of women with men has rarely been accepted in societies untouched by a Christian missionary presence.

TOWARD AN ALTERNATIVE STORY

It is the biblical concept of *imago Dei* (humans as the "image of God") that more than any other provides the ontological grounding of human rights which purely secular accounts lack. Medical historians have pointed out, for instance, that the care of defective newborns simply was not a medical concern in classical antiquity. The morality of the killing of sickly or deformed newborns appears not to have been questioned until the birth of the Christian church. No pagan writer—whether Greek, Roman, Indian or Chinese—appears to have raised the question whether human beings have inherent value ontologically, irrespective of social value, legal status, age, sex and so forth. "The first espousal of an idea of inherent human value in Western civilization depended on a belief that every human being was formed in the image of God."[11]

This is not merely of academic interest. When there is no public understanding of why human beings as such carry intrinsic worth, then either every political claim will be dressed up in the emotive language of rights (thus stripping the language of human rights of its unique power) or the public expenditure of scarce resources on the "unproductive" members of society by insuring to all of them certain goods—their "natural human rights"—will make no sense and will be resisted.

Modern political theory takes equality for granted, however hypocritical has been its practice. For many thinkers in the Western political and intellectual tradition, human equality is a fundamental moral axiom. It needs no defense, for it is the starting point rather than the conclusion of a train of moral reasoning. They would agree with the compilers of the American Declaration of Independence (1776) who stated, "We hold these truths to be self-evident, that all men are created equal" (even if they would—crucially—dispense with the language of creation). Even if the American Founding Fathers did not envisage women and blacks as falling within their definition of "all men," most Americans and Europeans simply take it for granted that the equality of all men and all women is so obviously true, although they would be vague, if pressed, to explain what that equality entails. Inequality is always a problem, an anomaly, something that calls for explanation and sometimes for remedy.

Ronald Dworkin famously argues that equality is a foundational principle inasmuch as it needs no justification. The principle of equality, he writes, is "too fundamental, I think, to admit of any defence in the usual form. It seems unlikely it can be derived for many more general and basic principle of political morality that is more widely accepted. Nor can it be established through one or another of the methods of argument popular in political theory for these already presuppose some particular conception of equality."[12] Consequently, the proposition that governments should treat everyone with equal concern and respect is self-evident.

However, if one were to look at other ages and other cultures it is certainly not the case that human equality was regarded everywhere and always as a good thing. Indeed this has always been a minority view. If inequality is held to be an unacceptable, even repugnant, state of affairs that needs to be remedied, this is a cultural presumption that only makes sense if we remember the deep penetration of Western societies over many centuries by the biblical tradition. Nietzsche saw this connection with his customary clarity, denouncing equality as immoral and harmful (the "herd morality") and linking it to the "ressentiment" of weak and ineffectual Christians who aspire to, but cannot attain, the status of the master class. "The poison of the doctrine of 'equal rights for all'—it was Christianity that spread it most fundamentally. Out of the most secret nooks of bad instincts, Christianity has waged war unto death against all sense of respect and feeling of distance between man and man."[13] And elsewhere: "Life itself recognizes no solidarity, no 'equal rights,' between the healthy and the degenerate parts of an organism: one must excise the latter—or the whole will perish."[14]

Historically, in the background of the West's recognition of citizenship rights was an inherited tradition of a wide range of genuine human rights that stemmed from the theological vision of Judaism and Christianity. The preamble to the American Declaration of Independence is self-evident only to those exposed to a biblical Christian tradition that speaks of the equality and intrinsic worth of all human beings because they are created in the image of God. It would have been incomprehensible to someone brought up, say, within Indian or Chinese civilizations. The political theologian Duncan Forrester reminds us that if the theological language in the American Declaration of Independence were removed, the argument of the Declaration at this crucial point would fall apart. We have not simply been born equal; we have been created equal by the Creator God who has also endowed us with rights. The language, as in so many Enlightenment documents, is universal and theological: it is parasitic on the very Christian discourse that it wants to marginalize. As Forrester observes, "It has meaning that its original framers did not recognize. A theological ghost has got into the machine. And it is to this, as well as directly to the Bible, that Martin Luther King appealed successfully two centuries later in the course of the civil rights movement."[15]

This argument goes further than Michael Perry's, mentioned earlier. It is not enough to speak of a vaguely religious view of persons in an abstract sense as if there was some universal genus called religion, but rather a specific religious view, namely, a biblical understanding of human personhood. The dominant schools of Hindu practice, for example, do not recognize the fundamental equality of human beings. Those who lie outside the caste system, the dalits (or "untouchables"), have no moral claim at all on the higher castes and are frequently considered less than human. Moreover, different moral duties and values attach to different caste groups and their occupations.

The notion that human beings, while part and parcel of God's animal kingdom, occupy a special place among all God's creatures because they alone constitute God's image on earth (Genesis 1:26-27) runs through all the biblical literature. The stone or metal image that an ancient king set up was the physical symbol of his sovereignty over a particular territory. It represented him to his subject peoples. If anyone defaced or damaged an image of the king, that person was rebelling against the king's authority. But here, it is men and women who represent God on the planet earth. It follows that the way we treat our fellow human being is a reflection of our attitude to the Creator. To despise the former is to insult the latter (cf. Proverbs 14:31; James 3:9).

Babylonian society, like both other Mesopotamian and Egyptian civilizations, was hierarchically structured. At the top of the social pyramid was the king, who was believed to represent the power of the divine world. Just below him came the priests who shared his mediatorial function, but to a lesser degree. Below them were the bureaucracy, the merchants and the military, while the base of the pyramid was formed by the peasants and slaves. Thus the sociopolitical order was given religious legitimation by the creation mythologies of these societies. The lower classes of human beings were created as slaves for the gods, to relieve them of manual labor. And, since the king represented the gods on earth, to serve the king was to serve the gods. Consequently, the Genesis counter-myth undermines this widespread royal ideology. It radically democratizes the political order. All human beings are called to represent God's kingdom through the whole range of human life on earth.

The image of God, which is the basis for human dignity, is not defined by specific capacities that distinguish us from other animals, though this is entailed. It is God's action, not human agency, that confers inherent dignity on human beings. God graciously enters into relationship with humanity, and despite our alienation from God through sin, God remains faithful and discloses his true image in humanity through Christ. Just as ancient Israel was uniquely chosen, for the sake of all other peoples, so the human is uniquely beloved for the sake of the rest of God's creation.

The biblical narrative reveals a God who is deeply entangled with his world, who immerses himself in our tragic history, who embraces our humanity with all its vulnerability, pain and confusion, including our evil and our death. Here is a God who comes to us not as master but as a servant, who stoops to wash the feet of his disciples and to suffer brutalization and dehumanization at the hands of his creatures. On the cross, God in Christ bears the indignity of all whose human dignity has been violated. In identifying with us in our broken humanity he draws the human into his own divine life. So what this means is that the closer we get to God, the more human we become, not less. This is a unique vision, there is nothing comparable in any of the world's literature or philosophies.

It is these great biblical themes of creation, incarnation, redemption and resurrection that have empowered human beings in the face of suffering and oppression in many and varied situations. When an indigenous Christian leader from northern Argentina was once asked what the gospel had done for his people, he replied that it had enabled them to look the white person fully in the eye.[16] The first Indian Anglican bishop was the remarkable evangelist V. S. Azariah, whose grandfather had belonged to a dalit community in south India, and he himself was of humble origins. In 1936, during the agitation for independence and the nationalist criticism of Christianity as a colonial institution, Azariah and fifty dalit Christians issued this open letter to their fellow "countrymen":

Christianity has brought us fellowship and brotherhood. It has treated us with respect, and it has given us self-respect. It has never despised us because of our lowly origin, but on the contrary has held us as individuals who are valuable before God and man as any man of any origin. . . . Best of all, Christianity has given us happiness and joy that can come only by the knowledge that the Lord has forgiven our sins and has made us His children in Christ. . . . All this was not accomplished through any magic, or done in a day. It has been the result of years of service, patiently and with love poured out for us by thousands of consecrated men and women, both Indian and foreign who have laboured to improve our lot. It has been the result of constant teaching, care and instruction. It has been accomplished, moreover, because we ourselves, freed by Christ from chains of ignorance and fear, have found within ourselves new courage, new hope, new strength to struggle upward.[17]

It is an important aspect of Christian mission to narrate this unique vision of humanness in the teeth of all the other definitions of humanness that abound in the mass media, the academy and the business world. Human beings are to be treated as having an inherent value that is neither given by the state nor can it be taken away by other human beings; it can only be recognized. They are not useful commodities whose value depends on what they can command in the marketplace. Human beings are entitled to be treated with equal respect because they are of equal worth. In G. K. Chesterton's vivid image: people are equal in the same way pennies are equal. Some are bright, others are dull; some are worn smooth, others are sharp and fresh. But all are equal in value for each penny bears the image of the sovereign, each person bears the image of the King of kings.

Duncan Forrester argues that "that is the bottom line, the essential affirmation if we are to have an adequate justification and motive for generous and respectful treatment of people with severe disabilities, of the senile, and of the unemployable. But it is difficult to see how this core affirmation can be justified without theological reference."[18] This is because we do not derive our belief in human equality from either observation or introspection. "The ideal of equality," notes Forrester, "haunts any culture that has been shaped or influenced by Christianity."[19]

Of course there is much in the Bible that is seemingly contradictory and has lent itself in Western history to the buttressing of hierarchical attitudes and oppressive hierarchical structures. However, the dominant narrative stream in the biblical traditions encourages a strongly egalitarian direction of thought, which functions especially to critique relationships of privilege. The tendency of biblical thought, Richard Bauckham argues, "is not in support of but away from hierarchical structures in human society, and biblical images of God's rule function not to legitimate human hierarchy, but to relativize and delegitimize it."[20]

Thus, even when the Bible depicts God in images of hierarchical, masculine power and authority—Lord, King, Father—the way the language is used is subversive of all human hierarchies. To call God King is to say that all human beings are equally God's subjects. To call God Father is to say that all human beings are equally God's children. When we stand before another person, however destitute, disabled, diseased or degraded, we stand before something which is the vehicle of the divine, something which is, in Martin Buber's well-known way of expressing it, a Thou and not an It. The radical implications of this straightforward truth have been grasped more often by peasants in revolt against entrenched tyrannies than by clerics in the service of the state.[21]

If we regard our fellow citizens as only contracting parties to a mutually advantageous bargain, we will not be able to see any value in the elderly, the very young or the permanently disabled. If we are only able to value such people by thinking of them as either potentially or formerly productive, inde-pendent folk, it is unlikely that we will be able to see dignity in the work of dressing, feeding or washing them. Also this work will not receive the social and financial recognition it deserves. We will instead be persuaded by the logic of Nietzsche's counter-Christian "moral code for physicians"—the phy-sician, Nietzsche urged, should encourage in him- or herself active contempt for the invalid, regarding the invalid as a parasite on society when he or she comes to a certain stage of degeneration.[22] The "death of God" does not lead to the glorification of humans but rather takes from men and women any claim they may have to be treated with reverence by their fellows.

INDIVIDUAL RIGHTS

What would a biblically informed schedule of human rights look like? Fun-damental would be the right to life of all human beings, a right that neces-sarily entails access to all the resources that sustain life. From conception to death our life is a gift from God. We do not choose our existence. It is given to us as gift, mediated by nature and history, by culture and society, by parents, friends, teachers, and so on. Throughout our lives we remain utterly dependent on the conditions that make life possible at all. Thus life and the conditions that make life possible are to be respected and nurtured by others in the human community. This right is threatened by policies and commer-cial practices that threaten whole communities with starvation and ecological degradation, as well as by public pressure to abort fetuses with congenital deformities and to kill men and women suffering from incurable diseases.

Unlike the Western republican tradition that puts the citizen (historically, male and property-owning) at the center of the polis, the Christian biblical tradition, especially as it has been recovered in our day in Latin American liberation theology, gives ultimacy to the poor. This follows naturally from the recognition that life is our most basic right. The poor are all those whose lives are vulnerable, threatened and denied. And this ultimacy of the poor appears in God's declared partiality toward them. Thus there is a rich vein of thought in the biblical writings that champions the rights of the poor. For instance:

> Speak out for those who cannot speak,
>   for the rights of all the destitute.
> Speak out, judge righteously,
>   defend the rights of the poor and needy. (Proverbs 31:8-9)

The right to life implies access to the resources that sustain life. To speak of the poor as having rights to sustenance implies that what we owe them is not simply charity but justice.

The Mosaic law made special provisions for specific groups of poor people (e.g., Exodus 23:2-9; Leviticus 19:9-10; Deuteronomy 15:1-18; 24:19-22). The solidarity of the people was a basic assumption in these provisions: they were to relate to one another in a way that reflected Yahweh's love for them. So poverty was not the concern of individuals alone; the social structures enshrined in the law were intended to protect the vulnerable sections of the community and to reveal to the surrounding nations that Yahweh, the covenant name by which God was known in ancient Israel, was a God who defended the rights of the poor. In premonarchical Israel this entailed the economic equality of family households. However strange this is to modern ears, it was simply the recognition that since power and privilege often come from the accumulation of wealth, genuine equality requires an economic base. In the agrarian society of early Israel, individual economic self-sufficiency was out of the question. The economic unit was the family group, and it was essential that each family should have its own portion of land, sufficient for subsistence and inalienable. Israelite land law was designed to ensure that the land could not pass permanently out of the kinship group in which it passed down by inheritance. If people were compelled, through debt, to sell land, there were provisions for the redemption of land by relatives, while in the Jubilee year all land should revert to its original family.

This theme was prominent also in the Christian tradition long before the United Nations Universal Declaration of Human Rights of 1948.* Christian theologians challenged the absolutist and exclusivist understandings of wealth and property that undergirded Roman law. Here are some representative quotations from some of the great leaders of the church:

John Chrysostom (c. 347-407):

This also is theft, not to share one's possessions. Perhaps this statement seems surprising to you, but do not be surprised. I shall bring you testimony from the divine Scriptures, saying that not only the theft of others' goods but also the failure to share one's own goods with others is theft and swindle and defraudation. . . . Need alone is the poor man's worthiness; if anyone at all ever comes to us with this recommendation, let us not meddle any further. . . . I beg you remember this without fail, that not to share our own wealth with the poor is theft from the poor and deprivation of their means of life; we do not possess our own wealth but theirs.[23]

Basil of Caesarea (c. 329-c. 379):

Will not one be called a thief who steals the garment of one already clothed, and is one deserving of any other title who will not clothe the naked if he is able to do so? That bread which you keep belongs to the hungry; that coat which you preserve in your wardrobe, to the naked; those shoes which are rotting in your possession, to the shoeless; that gold which you have hidden in the ground, to the needy. Wherefore, as often as you were able to help others, and refused, so often did you do them wrong.[24]

---

*Frederick Nolde, a Christian seminary professor who was one of the principal architects of the UNUDHR in 1948, reminds us that "an international Christian influence played a determining part in achieving the more extensive provisions for human rights and fundamental freedoms which ultimately found their way into the Charter" (*Free and Equal* [Geneva: World Council of Churches, 1968], p. 25). It is another irony that this declaration is regarded as a secular document by bureaucrats and academics alike, its Christian roots willfully forgotten. See further John Nurser, *For All Peoples and All Nations: The Ecumenical Church & Human Rights* (Washington, D.C.: Georgetown University Press, 2005).

Thomas Aquinas (c. 1225-1274):

In cases of need all things are common property, so that there would seem to be no sin in taking another's property, for need has made it common. . . . Now according to the natural order established by Divine providence, inferior things are ordained for the purpose of succouring man's needs by their means. Wherefore the division and appropriation of things which are based on human law do not preclude the fact that man's needs have to be remedied by means of these very things. Hence whatever certain people have in superabundance is due, by natural law, to the purpose of succouring the poor.[25]

Aquinas continues:

Nevertheless, if the need be so manifest and urgent, that it is evident that the present need must be remedied by whatever means be at hand (for instance when a person is in some imminent danger, and there is no other possible remedy), then it is lawful for a man to succour his own need by means of another's property, by taking it either openly or secretly: nor is this properly speaking theft or robbery.

Aquinas doesn't specify how best to succour the poor nor how to secure their economic rights without infringing on other rights; but the point I wish to underscore here is his clear conviction that all human beings have a natural right to fair access to the means of sustenance.

To say that need alone constitutes the poor man's right to food or medical treatment has profound personal and political implications. If I have food in my house that I do not need for my survival, but my neighbor is starving, then the food in my house belongs to my neighbour and his family, not to me. I commit theft as long as I refuse to share it with them. The right to life trumps the right to private property.[26]

Similarly, if a few farmers own all the arable land in an area and are using it not to grow food for the hungry but cash crops for wealthy businessmen, then the starving rural poor have a God-given right to take over those farms in order to grow food necessary for their survival. In Africa, where out of thirty million people infected with the HIV or AIDS virus only thirty thousand can afford the drugs sold by pharmaceutical companies, the early church theologians would have told the poor, "It is your right to go in those pharmaceutical companies and take the drugs for yourselves." No doubt this would not be wise because it would not be sustainable, but that is a different issue. Simply claiming their right to available medical care would put enormous pressure on corporations and governments to come up with a fairer system of affordable medical treatment as well as shift the focus of medical research toward the needs of the majority of the world's population.

Along with the rights to life and the means to sustain life, the biblical authors recognize the right to freedom from oppression. "To treat unjustly one of these human earthlings in whom God delights is to bring sorrow to God. To wound his beloved is to wound him. Conversely, to treat such an earthling with justice is to delight God. . . . The demands of justice are grounded in the fact that to commit injustice is to inflict suffering on God."[27] As the ancient book of Lamentations reminds us:

> When all the prisoners of the land
>   are crushed under foot,
> when human rights are perverted
>   in the presence of the Most High,
> when one's case is subverted
>   —does the Lord not see it? (Lamentations 3:34-36)

"Where the spirit of the Lord is, there is freedom" (2 Corinthians 3:17). "You will know the truth," said Jesus to those who followed him, "and the truth will make you free" (John 8:32). This is an evangelical liberty, a freedom not of arbitrary choice and uninhibited self-expression but of emancipation from illusions and caprice. Freedom of speech is bound inextricably to the will to truth. However, until the full and final revelation of God's truth "we see in a mirror, dimly" (1 Corinthians 13:12) and so all our formulations of truth remain partial, fragmentary and provisional. This does not mean that there is no such thing as evidently erroneous beliefs or immoral practices. Rather, some judgments need to be withheld because they are outside the authority of the civil authority. St. Paul, writing about the "weaker brother," asks, "Who are you to pass judgment on servants of another? It is before their own lord that they stand or fall" (Romans 14:4).

Recognizing the limits of government, and also on which matters the public good is not imperiled, is not always easy. But that there are limits to state encroachment, which we imply by the language of "freedom of expression" and "freedom of religious belief and practice," is theologically well-founded. No religious commitments that are coerced can be authentic, and they represent perhaps the most basic violation of an individual's dignity. It is why, for the dissenting Christians who fled persecution in Europe for America, the right to religious worship was the foundational liberty from which all others emerged. Alexis de Tocqueville perceived that "Religion in America takes no direct part in the government of society, but it must be regarded as the first of their political institutions."[28] Without being uncritical of American democracy or holding it up as a model for all societies, he still observed that in New England "education and liberty were the daughters of morality and religion."[29]

Freedom of expression, if it is seen as indivisible from the pursuit of truth, will entail both right of access to education and the right to be accurately informed about political decisions that affect our lives and those of our off-spring.† This challenges not only most governments in the so-called Third World but also most Western democracies. In an age of political spin doctors, media hype, mass propaganda and what has been called the "manufacture of consent," it is increasingly difficult to heed politicians' appeals to trust their good intentions and integrity. The weapons of mass deception employed by national governments raise moral questions as challenging as those posed by weapons of mass destruction. Sometimes, no doubt, governments need to exercise prudence on security issues, but the more governments withhold information from their fellow citizens and control what they know, the less accountable they are to the people who elected them. They thus forfeit the right to be called representative democracies.

---

†Whether such a right of access to educational opportunities is best provided by state-supported schools, state scholarships to private schools or a combination of state and private schools is a matter for full and wide-ranging public debate. But, once again, insisting that it is a human right, and not an act of charity, places it high on the political agenda of every society.

Although it would be anachronous to read back into the biblical writings those citizenship rights which are referred to today as human rights in international law and many national constitutions, it could easily be shown as consistent with the thrust of biblical teaching that torture, slavery and arbitrary punishment are universally wrong, that freedom of dissent and political assembly must be safeguarded, and that all national laws and institutions are subject to a higher moral law. Indeed the concept of the rule of law and the development of international law in the late medieval era and beyond are the direct legacy of the Christendom ideal: to curb arbitrary rule and remind kings and governors that they were subject to a universal moral authority not of their own making.

Another remarkable aspect of ancient Israelite legislation was a sensitivity to the rights of strangers. "You shall also love the stranger, for you were strangers in the land of Egypt" (Deuteronomy 10:19). The argument proceeds as follows. It is Yahweh's character to take delight in loving the "other," especially those who are economically and socially vulnerable (v. 18). Israel was a nation of "others" in Egypt, scapegoated in acts of xenophobic violence when national fortunes declined. So Yahweh, true to his character, loved them and rescued them from their oppression. Having experienced Yahweh's love for the alien, they now reflect Yahweh's character by loving the aliens among them. To this is added a further argument in Leviticus 25:23: the land they occupy is owned by Yahweh, so even they, the Israelites, stand before him only as guests and tenants. Israelites were under an obligation to show to "others" hospitality as fellow guests in the land.

The word *gerim*, usually translated "sojourners" or "resident aliens," is the Hebrew equivalent of today's "immigrants." This is because *ger* refers to someone from another ethnic background who has taken up long-term residence in Israel. Nonassimilating *gerim* (those who did not pledge loyalty to Yahweh) were barred from participation in cultic events, such as eating the Passover meal. However, all *gerim*, whether they had assimilated or not, were to be treated before the law in exactly the same way as native Israelites. They received the same economic protection (e.g., Exodus 20:8-11; Deuteronomy 24:14-15) and shared the same welfare benefits (e.g., Deuteronomy 14:28-29; 24:19-22; 26:12-13; Leviticus 19:9-10) that were made available to the most vulnerable members of society. In the New Testament we see Jesus expanding this command to "love the stranger" to loving one's enemies, national as well as personal, and the early church understanding its own calling as one of being "resident aliens" (Greek *paroikoi*) among the cities and nations of the earth.

In the Pauline literature, the theme of hospitality to the stranger is given a christological basis and takes on a fresh political significance in the light of the messianic event: "Welcome one another, therefore, just as Christ has welcomed you, for the glory of God. For I tell you that Christ has become a servant of the circumcised on behalf of the truth of God in order that he might confirm the promises given to the patriarchs, and in order that the Gentiles might glorify God for his mercy" (Romans 15:7-9). The gathering of the nations into the Messiah event is spelled out in passages such as Ephesians 2:11-22 which reaches its climax in the universal affirmation: "So then you are no longer strangers and aliens, but you are citizens with the saints and also members of the household of God" (v. 19). Little wonder then that the practice of "hospitality to strangers" (Romans 12:13), which category included prisoners of war, was a characteristic of the early church in the Roman world.

According to the United Nations, the number of people who have left their home countries in order to settle elsewhere has doubled in the period from 1980 to 2005. In addition, the global refugee population at the end of 2005 stood at 8.4 million, with a further 2 million persons designated as "stateless."[30] Refugees are men, women and children compelled to move across political borders because of war, famine, natural disasters, ethnic cleansing, genocide, religious persecution or the prospect of imprisonment or death at the hands of despotic regimes. In the case of migration, escaping widespread poverty and the lure of better jobs or education for one's children are the principal motivating factors. The now-common sight of bodies of Africans washed up on European beaches after trying to make a hazardous crossing shows the lengths to which people will go to try and move to a new life. Such people are easily exploited by international criminal networks and also by unscrupulous local landlords and employers if their status is that of "undocumented" workers.

Migration flows are not solely from poor to rich countries; about a third of international migrants move from one developing country to another. The fifty Least Developed Countries (LDCs) provided asylum to 15 percent of the world's refugees, with Pakistan and Iran being the biggest recipients of refugees. Even where migrants live and work legally, the poorer ones among them are extremely vulnerable to xenophobia, economic downturns and sudden military or natural disasters. For instance, while European countries were sending warships to bring their citizens out of Beirut when Israel attacked Lebanon in August 2006, eleven thousand migrant workers, mainly domestic servants, were left stranded, abandoned by their home governments. They needed emergency evacuation by the UN. This was despite the fact that cash earned overseas and sent home by such migrant workers represents a substantial proportion of these countries' earnings. In the oil-rich Gulf states, migrant workers are a large and economically important sector of society. Yet those involved in low-paid work as cleaners and builders are vulnerable to physical abuse and overcrowded living conditions, and enjoy relatively little legal protection.

The irony of current technological and economic changes is that, while globalization and the idea of a global village are being constantly touted, national borders in rich nations have been vigorously reasserted and fortified to keep out refugees and undesirable immigrants. It has often been noted that the right to leave one's country does not carry a corresponding right of entry to another. Intergovernmental agreements on asylum have focused on the status and rights of refugees in the receiving state and have not conferred rights of admission on those seeking refuge. Thus article 13 of the Universal Declaration of Human Rights refers to "a right to seek and to enjoy in other countries asylum from persecution" but fails to impose an obligation on states to grant asylum. Freedom of movement is posited as occurring within the borders of a state and as the right to leave and return to one's "own country."

Whether in the affluent West or in the poorer nations, refugees are treated as if they were quasi-criminal elements. Often confined to segregated housing blocks in rural or urban centers, and denied the right to seek employment, refugees and asylum seekers become easy targets for xenophobic hatred. They cannot appeal against the decisions concerning their status and may raise no claims against deportation orders. Thus refugees and asylum-seekers have revealed the shortcomings in the system of rights, while the ease with which the United States and some European governments have connived post-9/11 in transporting "noncitizens" suspected of "terrorist activities" to secret prisons or deporting them to countries where they face being tortured and even executed, has exposed the huge gulf between official Western human rights rhetoric and practice.

Immanuel Kant (1724-1804) famously argued (against the backdrop of European mercantilist pressures on China and Japan to receive European merchants) for a "cosmopolitan right of sojourn." In the third definitive article of his 1795 essay "Perpetual Peace," he wrote:

> The law of world citizenship shall be limited to conditions of universal hospitality. . . . Hospitality means the right of a stranger not to be treated as an enemy when he arrives in the land of another. . . . It is not the right to be a permanent visitor. . . . It is only a right of temporary sojourn, a right to associate. They have it by virtue of their common possession of the surface of the earth, where, as a globe, they cannot infinitely disperse.[31]

Kant's argument is quite remarkable. Since we happen to live in a finite space (the earth is a globe) we have to tolerate one another and so allow people to go anywhere they please. Kant insists that it is not a matter of philanthropy but of right. "Hospitality means the right of a stranger not to be treated as an enemy." Kant is clearly reflecting a biblical influence here. But note that for Kant there is no moral claim to permanent residency. This remains the sole prerogative of the republican sovereign. Temporary sojourn carries no necessary trajectory toward full incorporation.

For Hannah Arendt, writing in the aftermath of the breakdown of the old empires in Europe after the First World War, the forced expulsion of national minorities (turning them into stateless peoples almost overnight) and the rise of anti-Semitism and fascist movements culminating in the Nazi Holocaust, the "right to have rights" is the most basic right of all, and this necessarily entails the right to membership in a republic. Refugees, displaced and stateless persons are categories of human beings created by the actions of nation-states. In a state-centered international order, one's legal status is dependent on the highest authority in the territory in which one resides.

We became aware of the existence of a right to have rights (and that means to live in a framework where one is judged by one's actions and opinions) and a right to belong to some kind of organized community, only when millions of people emerge who had lost and could not regain these rights because of the new global political situation. . . . [T]he right to have rights, or the right for every individual to belong to humanity, should be guaranteed by humanity itself. It is by no means certain whether this is possible.[32]

Since, as Arendt envisioned things, this right to have rights cannot be guaranteed by a world state or any world organization, but only by the collective will of republican polities which in turn perpetrate their own regimes of exclusion, there is a tension similar to that which we find in Kant between a moral cosmopolitanism and a civic particularism. Republican equality (the equality of fellow citizens) always triumphs over human equality. The paradox of democratic legitimation is that the self-constituting, self-determining acts of popular sovereignty are, simultaneously, also acts of exclusion. The statement "We, the people" is made in the name of a putative universal equality, yet draws a rigid distinction between "we" and "aliens." And when the "we" concerned are rich and powerful, the national border is experienced by outsiders as no different from a medieval fortress, guarding unjust privileges. Ironically, the universal equality which is central to the liberal argument for democracy is undermined by the practices of democracy. We shall return to such tensions in chapter four.

RELATIONALITY AND RIGHTS

Taking freedom from oppression seriously will lead us beyond discussion of individual rights, for the theological understanding of human personhood is that we image God in relationality. Just as God's being is dynamic relationality, so we are constituted as persons through webs of interconnectedness. We become the occasion for each other's self-fulfillment. Those who love us make us what we become; we only learn love by being loved.

While we share with others a common nature as human beings, that nature is always mediated through a specific cultural community. We live among others sufficiently like us to be able to communicate with them. Language is a social phenomenon, as is all thought. All intelligent animals are social creatures. Anyone who is able to say "I think, therefore, I am" is heir to a rich, widely shared linguistic tradition and is therefore a member of a company of similar beings. To think of myself in isolation from others, even to doubt the "reality" of their minds, has been one of the most incoherent aberrations of post-seventeenth-century European philosophy. Our lives are woven with each others' in families, neighborhoods, ethnic and religious communities.‡ Which of these groups is considered the primary source of one's identity will vary from place to place and from time to time. However, the individual cannot be conceptualized in an abstract, atomistic, timeless manner as has been done in most liberal political thinking until very recently.

We can hardly be said to respect a person if we treat with contempt or abstract away all that gives meaning to that person's life and makes him or her the kind of person he or she is. For an individual is defenseless and unprotected if the community with whom he or she is identified is subjected to assimilation by another, vilification or perverse stereotyping. Just as under colonial conditions, the discourse of individual rights is meaningless without the prior right of the political community to self-government, so individual rights in many situations simply require as a precondition the rights of a community to maintain and reproduce itself. Thus if human rights charters are not to be perceived as instruments of subjugation on the part of the powerful but rather as (what they are intended to be) instruments to empower the weak and vulnerable members of the human species, then we must recognize that rights attach to groups as well as to individuals. Indeed, article 16 of the UN Declaration of Human Rights clearly states that "the family is the natural and fundamental group unit of society and is entitled to protection by society and the state," while article 29 states that "everyone has duties to the community in which alone the free and full development of his personality is possible."

---

‡The moral community to which we belong also includes parts of the nonhuman world, but exploration of this theme would be to digress. Stressing human rights need not entail any diminution of our moral obligations toward nonhuman animals and the biosphere. Indeed many of the rights to sustenance previously outlined cannot be fulfilled without a concomitant respect for ecological habitats and life cycles. We are also constituted as humans by natural processes whose integrity needs to be protected. See further chap. 5.

Thus individual human rights need to be accompanied by other rights that attach to certain communities. It is not a matter of which has priority but rather of treating them together as equally important components of justice in pluralist societies. This has profound consequences for the way we understand the role of the modern state. The latter cannot limit its role to protecting individual civil and political rights. The enforcement of individual rights can sometimes lead to grave injustices against historic communities: as, for instance, in the case of individual mobility (migration/land settlement) into the traditional homelands of indigenous peoples trying to preserve a premodern way of life against the encroachment of "developers." We shall explore this a little further in chapter four.

It is impossible (and undesirable, in any case) to codify such group rights into a universal charter similar to those protecting the rights of individuals. This is because every individual belongs simultaneously to several overlapping communities (family, religious community, culture, language group, ethnic minority and so on), and the rights that attach to each community will differ from place to place. Every multicultural society needs to devise its own appropriate political structure to suit its history, traditions and range and depth of its diversity. It is not the case (as many liberals argue) that individual rights always have priority over collective rights. It depends on the particular rights in question and the history of the group relations in that particular context. It is understandable, for instance, that Germany and Austria have curbed individual rights to free speech by banning anti-Semitic propaganda.[33] All rights can be misused. If collective rights can be used to oppress individuals, individual rights can be used to damage and destroy communities. Some collective rights threaten individual rights: for example, the right of a group to enforce moral conformity or expel its members or deny them the right of exit. Some collective rights, on the other hand, protect individual rights and empower their bearers because organized groups and communities are better able to defend the rights of their members than the latter can do individually; for example, recognizing a community's right to its language in the public realm makes it easier for its members than if it were solely a matter of an individual's freedom of speech.

Whether we believe that specific collective rights (language rights, self-government rights, migrant representation rights, federalism and so on) need to supplement the conventional list of individual civil and political liberties that go by the term *human rights*, or whether we believe (as I have argued) that a theologically informed notion of human rights includes individual and collective rights that interact in complex ways in different situations, we need to hold both together.

We do not have to choose between an idea of equality that is purely ideal and abstract, an equality before God without social implications, on the one hand, and a totalizing egalitarianism that is destructive of all forms of society on the other. No human society, from a family to a nation, can function without differentiations of labor. But what matters is how such differences are regarded and in particular whether they serve to construct a social hierarchy in which some people are made to feel inferior to others. As Oliver O'Donovan argues, what is required is neither of these choices but "a coordination of our understanding of equality with our understanding of the humane forms of community." He continues, "To have any substance a claim for equality must reflect decisions about what differentiations are constructive and healthy for human existence and what are not. But those decisions in turn reflect a judgment about which differentiations help, and which hinder the meeting of person with person on a basis of equality, with neither of them slave or lord."[34]

The God who expresses his solidarity with us by taking human flesh, relativizes all differences of ethnicity, education, class, gender or citizenship. There is a sense in which humankind is one family. In societies where wealth is the determinant of value and opportunity, restricting equality to "equality before the law" or "equal opportunity" effectively nullifies it. Gross social and economic inequalities, especially where the majority of citizens are poor, destroys solidarity and any notion of a common good.

Moreover, while all nations must necessarily differ from one another in important ways, we can nevertheless dream of a common world founded on equality of respect for all persons. Every society in such a world would be, among things, one where no one has to be deprived of or beg for the basic necessities of life, where women can walk the streets of cities without fear of molestation, where the views of employees are welcomed and listened to by their employers, where mistress and maid can eat at table together, where immigrants and refugees are not shunned and exploited, where the disabled and the elderly have a voice in the affairs of the community, and where the janitor's name is remembered by the college professor.

Every social movement or political experiment began with a vision that others ridiculed as utopian. The vision, to be compelling, has to be expressed in vivid poetic imagery or in the simple, dignified and evocative phraseology of great political documents. "A common social vision or ideal is something people aspire to, are exhilarated by, and are willing to make sacrifices for," writes Mary Jo Leddy. "It transforms present action and interprets it in terms of future possibilities."[35]

LEGISLATING FOR RIGHTS

We have seen that human beings are so situated before God as to possess certain foundational rights to life and freedom from oppression, and those of us who are intentional agents also possess responsibilities toward others.[36] We have also seen that rights are moral claims on the behavior of individuals and collectivities, and on the design of social arrangements. Human rights are fulfilled when the persons involved enjoy secure access to the freedom or resource (e.g., adequate health protection or freedom of association) covered by that right.

In poor countries, economic constraints force the identification of priorities in human rights enforcement. A general affirmation of equality stipulates in very broad terms the kind of society we should strive for, the general direction that social policy should take. Although some inequalities may be justifiable or even necessary, they still require explanation as deviations from the norm. An integrated approach to the different, interlocking forms of inequality— economic, political, cultural, gender and so on—is needed. Moreover, the way that rights are enforced and the ranking we give them depend on cultural and social contexts. Constitutions and laws are important, but these in themselves do not ensure a society where human rights are respected and realized. As a UN report once put it, "In many contexts, establishing legal rights may be the best means of furthering the fulfilment of human rights. Nevertheless, legal rights should not be confused with human rights—nor should it be supposed that legal rights are sufficient for the fulfilment of human rights."[37] It is a challenge to our resourcefulness to seek nonlegalistic, as well as legalistic, ways of promoting human rights.

Just as there is a reciprocal relationship between civil society and the state, each depending upon the other for its effective functioning, so there is an integral connection between the law and the moral ethos of society. Governments can make wonderful laws, but whether and how they are enforced depends on the general temper of the country. The Indian constitution made "caste" an illegal category and gender discrimination a punishable offense. But discrimination and violence against women and low-caste groups is widespread fifty years later. If large numbers of people are interested in freedom of speech, there will be freedom of speech, even if the law forbids it; if there is general apathy, inconvenient minorities will be persecuted, even if laws exist to protect them.

There will always be tension in the enforcement of human rights, both individual and collective, as well as in the way rights conflict with each other in many situations. Human rights are objective and universal, but they are not absolute. International human rights regimes recognize this. Article 4 of the United Nations International Covenant on Civil and Political Rights explicitly allows for short-term curbs on rights "in time of public emergency which threatens the life of the nation." Not anything goes, however; the article states that such emergency measures cannot involve discrimination solely on the grounds of race, sex, language, religion or social origin, and that derogation of rights against murder, torture, and slavery, among others, may not be made under this provision. If governments try to persuade us that particular rights need to be curbed for particular economic or political purposes, they must guarantee that it is a short-term measure and publicly demonstrate how it secures a more important right or secures that same right in the long term. Such civil vigilance is sadly lacking and therefore all the more essential in many Asian societies. And we have seen how, even in the country that presents itself as the model of democracy for the rest of the world, constitutional liberties and safeguards against arbitrary power, patiently built up over two centuries, can so easily be shredded or simply ignored by a powerful executive and a gullible public.

Daniel Bell of Hong Kong University states the challenge wisely:

When countering plausible government justifications for rights violations of this sort, one can question either the premise that the society
under question is actually facing a social crisis requiring immediate political action or the political implication that curbing a political right is
the best means of overcoming that crisis. But whatever the response,
the social critic must be armed with detailed and historically informed
knowledge of that society.[38]

Rights language is often abused in our contemporary world, as when the
abortion of unwanted babies is defended as the exercise of "reproductive rights,"
or forms of commercial sexual exploitation and degradation promoted as
"rights to free expression." In late modern societies a pervasive victim mentality has undermined any sense of moral obligations, and human rights talk has
assumed the status of a secular religion: every misfortune or disappointment is
now responded to with litigation and every grievance couched in the language
of rights. Hence the suspicion with which some Christians regard the latter. It
also seems arrogant and aggressive, especially in the light of the gospel's call to
give our lives away in the service of others. But this is seriously misleading. If
we lay aside some right to a benefit, for the sake of others, it must always be a
voluntary act. Jesus invites us, he does not coerce us, to be his disciples. Moreover, however inadequate the discourse of human rights, its theological justification has nothing to do with individualism as such but rests on the recognition
of an intrinsic human dignity in the name of which we protest the treatment of
some individuals and groups as effectively subhuman.

Therefore, we can agree with the Indian political scientist Neera Chandhoke when she declares:

Rather than feel grateful for things that are our due, or feel diminished
because we are forced to be grateful for things that we are entitled to,
we gain in self-respect and assurance because we are in a position to
demand these things by right. Therefore, no matter how beneficial or
charitable a world that does not speak this language of rights may be, a
world in which people do not relate to each other via rights will be sadly
deficient in moral terms.[39]

Joan Lockwood O'Donovan has argued that because there exist public and private goods which cannot be conceived of in a rights-based way, the emphasis on a rights-based morality to the exclusion of other vocabularies will soon undermine a proper understanding of these other goods and transform public discourse into the assertion of moral individualism:

> The public realm suffers from moral monism, being enslaved to one universally acclaimed good, that of individual self-determination. The public hegemony of this good is both disclosed and maintained in the public hegemony of the language of individual rights. Increasingly, in liberal democratic politics, all communal and institutional aims, aspirations, and claims must be articulated in the individualist language in order to be heard. But this language is unsuited to express the purposes and structural laws of diverse communities. It is equally unsuited to express the goods and laws of marriage—personal commitment and sexual fidelity, or the bonds and duties of family life—parental care and filial obedience, or the purpose and normative structure of economic activity—production to fill material needs and stewardship of natural resources, or of education—the communication of truth under conditions of openness and sincerity. . . . [T]heir various norms cannot be comprehended by the language of moral individualism.[40]

The language of rights is only one part of the wide repertoire of moral vocabulary that we have at our disposal. It is more appropriate (and often necessary) in political situations than in personal transactions. Nothing compels us to use it in places where it clashes with other moral insights that seem more important. My right to freedom of speech (a right usually enshrined in civil law) does not necessarily prevail over your desire for silence, let alone not to be assaulted by obscenities (a valid desire not usually so enshrined). Freedom of expression, I have noted, is not an end in itself; its value lies in the service of the will to truth. It has instead come to be equated in the minds of many libertarians with unbridled indecency or narcissistic self-expression. "Being true to oneself" (whatever that means) seems more important than simply being truthful.

Legislation about rights, Archbishop Rowan Williams affirms, "is a worthy attempt to secure social presence for those whose voices have been stifled."

But he goes on to declare that what it cannot achieve is "the felt recognition of a common humanity granted and welcomed, which is the fruit of events of charity and shared conversation." Williams continues:

> No claim, whether we put rights or responsibilities in the driving seat, will make sense without the prior underpinning of recognition. And recognition entails a move beyond the idea that my good, my interest, has a substantial integrity by itself: no project is just mine, wholly unique to me. I have learned from others how to think and speak my desires; I need to be heard—but that means I must speak into, not across, the flow of another's speech.[41]

RECOVERING A TRADITION

In a fascinating study of the humble origins of the American civil rights movement among the black churches of the American South, Charles Marsh points out that Martin Luther King's vision of equality went beyond confronting racial injustice to the creation of what he called "the beloved community." This vision was grounded in a specific theological tradition. "I am many things to many people," King said of himself in 1965, "but in the quiet recesses of my heart, I am fundamentally a clergyman, a Baptist preacher. This is my being and my heritage, for I am also the son of a Baptist preacher, the grandson of a Baptist preacher and the great-grandson of a Baptist preacher."[42] The black churches did not hide their specific theological commitments when the student volunteers arrived, many of whom were not Christian, but they found ways of working alongside them without erasing the real differences between them.

When the movement lost its anchor in the church, it began to splinter into militant groups whose visions did not progress beyond their own flourishing. The search for beloved community, detached from its theological origins, "produced first spiritual frenzy and then a certain torpor of spirit resembling malaise." The message that all life, "including that of a malnourished or un-born baby or an incarcerated man," is inherently valuable "may not get one speaking invitations in plush conference settings, as they remain theological convictions about the dignity of life." Still, Marsh writes, tongue-in-cheek:

"Academic secularists should be interested to discover—as they will discover when they leave the university campuses and engage their towns and inner cities—that transcendence empowers rather than diminishes the love of life, animates the protest against cruelty, and focuses the moral energies of compassion and mercy."[43]

Archbishop Desmond Tutu also testified, in the context of a different but related protest against oppression, that "our own struggle for justice, peace and equity would have floundered badly had we not been inspired by our Christian faith and assured of the ultimate victory of goodness and truth, compassion and love, against their ghastly counterparts."[44]

A dominant strand in post-Enlightenment thought in the West, also argued by militant secularists elsewhere, is the claim that emancipation from belief in God is a necessary condition for human freedom. The reality of the twentieth century proved otherwise. All those societies that heroically cast off the yoke of divine accountability ended up in new forms of servitude and domination: totalitarian tyrannies of the right and the left, the banal pursuit of self-gratification, a suffocating consumerism and the cynical manipulation of the young by business magnates. It should be clear by now that respect for the dignity and freedom of the individual, especially those most threatened by the political and technological forces unleashed in recent times, requires that a wider matrix of social practices and moral beliefs be in place than the mere assertion of a fictitious "autonomy."

As the legal philosopher Jeremy Waldron suggests, "in a number of ways the Christian conceptions out of which modern liberalism originated remain richer and deeper than their secular offspring."[45] It is the task of contemporary theology to articulate and offer this tradition in public debate. Waldron's words are worth pondering by Christians: "We might reasonably expect to find further clues to a rich and adequate conception of persons, equality, justice, and rights in what is currently being made of the Christ-centred tradition by those who remain centred in Christ."[46]

It is also important to heed Christoph Schwöbel's warning that the church does not uphold human dignity as an ideal principle but has to speak the good news of Christ, in word and action, into those situations where human dignity is violated:

If the cross and resurrection of Christ point to the fact that God re-creates human dignity where it has been violated and abused, the church which claims to be the church of Christ is committed to sharing the situation of those who have lost their dignity in human eyes and to communicating to them the message that their dignity is re-created by the one who first bestowed it upon them.[47]

Finally, a rigorous argument for human rights (as in a Christian theological perspective) will radically expose the hypocrisies and double standards of those powerful nations whose domestic and foreign policies run counter to their lip service to universal norms. In the following chapter we will explore some of the ways that, in the light of both internal pluralism and economic globalization, all democratic nation-states are challenged to renegotiate and rearticulate (through creative public dialogues) the unfolding dialectic between human rights and civic rights, between rights and obligations, and between collective self-determination and international moral norms.

4

MYTHS OF MULTICULTURALISM

A well-known Indian psychologist, Pittu Laungani, now living in England and teaching at Manchester University, recounts his experiences when he first came to that country in the late 1960s:

> England, to me was a shock! There were as many accents there as there are dialects in India—or almost. . . . It was difficult to distinguish between levity and seriousness, between jest and truth, between praise and censure, between affection and affectation, between acceptance and rejection. I found it exasperating not being able to read correctly their feelings and emotions on the rare occasions they chose to express them. . . . I could not always work out what was expected of me in different situations and of different people. Living in a foreign country, I soon realized was like fighting a lone battle on several fronts. . . . Although we spoke the same language, although we had past historical associations, although I had read the books, which I had assumed they would have also read, and although I dressed the way they did, I could tell that a vast ocean of differences separated me from them. . . . Despite our historical associations, I found that we were divided more by our differences than united by our similarities.[1]

What surprised and exasperated Laungani most, however, was the lack of curiosity about his world that even his academic colleagues in psychology showed:

[They] seldom or hardly ever took any genuine, deep-rooted interest in my cultural background, nor did they show a great deal of interest in my religious, social and philosophical beliefs and values. They didn't know. They didn't want to know. Nor were they interested. But they expected me to "meet up" to their own standards. There was an expectation that I would be knowledgeable about western values, including music, art, poetry, drama and literature. But they did not see it as part of their obligation to learn something about my culture and the culture of eastern societies as a whole. There are times when I feel that I am awarded the dubious status of honorary white British person.[2]

■ ■ ■

The Bushmen—or Sana people—of the Kalahari desert are probably the oldest inhabitants of sub-Saharan Africa, and they have a unique culture, language, and lifestyle. Their hardiness has enabled them to survive as hunter-gatherers in the harsh conditions of the Kalahari. On December 13, 2006, a high court in Botswana issued a landmark ruling in their favor. They had accused the Botswana government of cutting off their water supplies and evicting them in January 2002 from their ancestral homelands in order to make way for diamond mining operations and farming. The Sana people brought their case forward after being moved to functional but bleak settlements outside the Kalahari game reserve, where a new way of life was imposed. The government argued that the Bushmen did not belong to the Kalahari any more because their lifestyle had changed and their presence interfered with conservation. The reserve was a poverty trap that denied them access to health and education, it said, arguing that the Bushmen were better off in the settlements, where they had clinics and schools along with better access to food and water. Crowds of Sana had trekked overland to the court in the town of Lobatse to wait for the verdict, which was translated for them. There were scenes of jubilation as the result was announced. The case was the longest and most expensive in Botswana's history, and has encouraged indigenous peoples in other parts of the world.[3]

■ ■ ■

Roughly half the population of Amsterdam is of foreign origin. On November 2, 2004, the Dutch filmmaker Theo Van Gogh, a provocative, self-styled rebel who had published diatribes against Muslims, Jews and Christians (as well as his former friends) was shot in the stomach while cycling to work in the city. He staggered across the street, where his killer shot him again and then hacked his throat with a machete. Van Gogh had made a film, *Submission*, together with the Somali-Dutch politician Ayaan Hirsi Ali, in which Qur'anic verses were projected on the naked bodies of women in a not-too-subtle portrayal of the oppression of women in Muslim communities. (Hirsi Ali herself had been the victim of genital mutilation in Somalia before her exile in the Netherlands.) Van Gogh's assassin, a second-generation Moroccan immigrant, Muhammad Bouyeri, pinned to the dead man's chest a note, in stilted Dutch, seething with Islamist rhetoric. The brutal murder, coming not too long after the murder (though not by a Muslim) of the Dutch anti-immigration campaigner and politician Pim Fortuyn, shocked the nation and raised furious debates all over Europe about whether a multicultural society was a myth.[1]

Mohammed Bouyeri's story is disturbingly similar to the stories of the London and Madrid bombers, as well as the Hamburg-based al-Qa'ida cell at the center of the 9/11 attacks in New York. There was the same initial attraction to and later rejection of a hedonistic lifestyle: sex and drugs and partying; the same sense of rootlessness, the pain of being torn between two cultures; the same influence of a radical imam and the seeking out of Islamist tracts on the Internet; the same global sense of Muslim victimhood exacerbated by horror stories from Bosnia, Chechnya, Palestine, Afghanistan and Iraq. Bouyeri's radicalization seems to have begun when his sister found a boyfriend. For his sister to have sex was to impugn the family's honor. Bouyeri chose to retreat, to imagine himself overwhelmed by a great force, to conceive of himself as a player in a utopian narrative.

Such suicide killers are obviously not representative of the great majority of Muslims living peacefully in Europe; but they are, without exception, extreme and exceptional symptoms of a much broader alienation of the children of Muslim immigrants to Europe. They display the pathology of what Timothy Garton Ash dubs the "In-Between People": culturally-split person-

alities, speaking in the local European language—Dutch, French, English—
with their brothers and sisters, and inhabiting "dish cities" connected to the
lands of their parents' birth by satellite dishes bringing in Moroccan or Turkish television channels, by the Internet and by mobile phones.[5] Unlike most
Muslim immigrants to the United States, many of them physically go home
every summer to the lands of their parents' birth, sometimes for months at a
time.

UNDERSTANDING CULTURES

Most countries today are culturally diverse. According to recent estimates,
the world's 192 independent states contain about seven thousand living languages and over thirteen thousand ethno-linguistic groups.[6] I can take you to
cities in India where neighboring communities simply cannot speak to each
other in a shared tongue, which makes what is called multiculturalism in the
United States rather tepid by comparison.[7] In many of these countries, there
is a lively debate (sometimes breaking out in tragic and protracted conflict)
over the nature of the national community and its collective identity, over
what we take the word *we* to mean.

For much of human history, the movement of peoples from one territory to
another has been the norm: an endless search for new hunting grounds, new
pastures, new sources of trade, new forms of work. Others have been forced
to move as slaves or to escape wars. In the middle years of the nineteenth
century in Europe, the fear of "terrorists" traveling from abroad who would
destabilize the postrevolutionary French Republic, similar fears of revolt and
anarchy in other European states, and the need for taxation of citizens by
newly emerging nation-state bureaucracies led to a system of passports and
passport offices. The movement of commodities and people were now controlled. Colonial powers such as Britain could still transfer large numbers
of unskilled and semiskilled labor from one colony to another for physical
labor, just as they had lifted by force between ten and twenty million people
out of Africa over a two-hundred-year period—with enormous cruelties—
to man the emerging plantations of sugar and tobacco in North and South
America. From 1840 to 1930, around fifty million Indians and Chinese went
to California, Southeast Asia, the Caribbean and Africa to build railways and

cities, to farm and mine gold. By 1930, there were some thirty million Indians working abroad, of whom approximately twenty-four million ultimately returned to India. In South Africa the great mines of the Rand sucked in thousands of workers from Central and Eastern Africa. And between 1800 and 1930, sixty to seventy million Europeans moved to the Americas, to parts of Africa, to Australia and New Zealand.[8]

Anyone who writes today on culture faces a daunting task, similar to what we encountered when discussing religion and religious violence in chapter two. Definitions of culture are legion. They run the full gamut from anthropological studies that deal typically with the languages, myths, rituals, kinship systems of bounded societies (usually tribal or rural) to postmodern aesthetics (embracing just about everything from architecture through "political spectacle" to lavatory graffiti). If the former is too narrow and the latter too nebulous, they can be—and often are—easily inverted. For instance, many writers speak of a particular "postmodern culture," distinguishing it both from a wider dominant culture and also the social, political and economic practices and institutions within which it flourishes. Indeed it has been a characteristic of modern industrial societies to relegate "culture" to an exotic realm quite separate from politics and economics which were themselves assumed to be universal and normless. On the other hand, an excessively generous definition of culture is that provided by the distinguished postwar sociologist Raymond Williams during his Marxist phase: "the organization of production, the structure of the family, the structure of institutions which express or govern social relationships, the characteristic forms through which members of the society communicate."[9]

Some popular sayings ("that's the way we do things around here") convey the implicit, taken-for-granted, practical knowledge and values that we mean when speaking of other peoples' cultures. Since the culture we inhabit is more than what rises to consciousness, perhaps our understanding of what culture is belongs to that area of tacit knowledge which we struggle to articulate. We know it, without being able to define it. Those academics who valiantly try, come up with ambiguous phrases such as "webs of signification" or "signifying systems" or "lived ideologies." The simple questions baffle us. How many people does it take to constitute a culture? Culture certainly has to do with a way of life, but when does a way of life become too small or too diverse for that term to lose its relevance? Do the currently fashionable idioms of "cafe culture," "corporate culture," "gay culture," "gun culture," "a culture of nonviolence" and so on convey anything more than flag-waving exercises, attempts to draw our attention to the presence of new forms of social behavior, reflecting the fragmentations of modern life? Do terms such as "Islamic/Christian/Buddhist culture" make any sense, when used in the singular? And in which circumstances do we regard Muslims as a cultural group, and when do we relate to them as a religious community? If cultures are human constructions, as opposed to what is transmitted biologically, then why is astrophysics not studied along with astrology in the cultural studies departments of Western universities? And so on.

Since the 1960s *culture* has undergone seismic shifts of meaning. It has spawned both "cultural theory" and "cultural politics." Not too long ago Margaret Archer noted that the concept of culture has displayed "the weakest analytical development of any key concept in sociology and it has played the most wildly vacillating role within sociological theory."[10] That gives amateurs like myself some confidence as I venture tentatively onto complex and disputed terrain. In what follows, I will use *cultural* and *ethnic* mostly interchangeably, craving the indulgence of the sophisticated reader, and referring by these terms to those fairly cohesive and stable groups, sharing some sense of a common history and which exist within a wider human society.[11] These groups may be diffused throughout the wider society, occupy a fixed geographical location or span many political boundaries. We can agree, noncontroversially, that such a cultural community performs a role in life that a voluntary association cannot. Membership of it is neither a matter of individual choice nor can it be easily terminated by choice. Because, for the most part, it is not a matter of conscious human creation, it gives its members a sense of rootedness, existential stability, the feeling of belonging to an enduring community of ancient origins and ease of interpersonal communication.

We need to distinguish such cultures from religious communities and traditions, although many (if not most) cultures around the world are deeply shaped by the latter. One does not belong to a religious tradition the same way one belongs to a cultural tradition and community. There is an element of conscious personal decision involved in the former, particularly in the missionary world faiths, which is not normally the case with cultural identity. Moreover, a religious tradition addresses the fundamental questions of human existence, not only linking individuals with each other in an intersubjective, moral community but also to a cosmic, transcendent order. The reason why the major world religions have been so effective for so long is because they incarnate otherworldly concerns and values with everyday, practical living.[12] The boundaries of text-centered faith communities transcend those of nations as well as ethnic groups and endure across generations. Such a plurality of allegiances has to be accepted in the modern world, and any attempt to eliminate them will only lead to bloody violence.

In many instances, language belongs to the core of what constitutes a cultural identity. (However, it is interesting that English and other major languages span a wide range of cultures, and that "the culture of postmodernism" today bridges a variety of languages.) What has distinguished the Christian movement from, say, the ancient Asian religions or global Islam is the way, from its inception, the church did not sacralize either the language of Jesus nor the place of his origins. The language that Jesus used in his preaching was quickly abandoned in favor of country (Koine) Greek and "vulgar" Latin as the uniting media of communication. The entire New Testament was written in a language other than the one in which Jesus preached. That the eternal counsels of God belonged to the commonplace, everyday speech of ordinary men and women was a view that was, and remains, revolutionary. It resisted the tendency in some parts of the early church to cast the gospel into an elitist gnostic-type discourse. Unlike the widespread "mystery religions" no attempt was made to develop a professional cultic language or make a virtue out of elitist secrecy. Today the church exists as a multicultural, multilingual community, with its center of gravity no longer in Europe and North America, but in Africa, Latin America and Asia.

We saw in chapter three that according to the Christian biblical tradition, human personhood is constituted relationally. Within the human community we are related to one another in gendered and cultural diversity. We are formed as persons through relationships, so we do not find our fulfillment as persons apart from God and one another. We are endowed as human beings with marvelous capacities for social and symbolizing activity, for cooperative agency, to imagine and invent other worlds in the light of which we shape our own and extend its God-given potentialities. Thus it is not in competition with the "other" and in striving to preserve my "independence" that I establish my worth, but rather in recognizing my interdependence in a multiculturally constituted human family. Given the social conditions of human life, none of us can live a truly good, fully human life apart from irreducibly shared, constitutive goods such as friendship, family and civil society.

It is the dignity of physical labor, of cultivating and caring for the earth (Genesis 2:15) that lies at the root of all cultural creation. The God of the biblical revelation wills cultural diversity, even as he wills the ecological diversity that is part and parcel of his physical world. We are all created as social beings with common needs such as food, sleep, shelter, warmth, affection, companionship, sexual fulfillment, meaningful work, self-respect and personal dignity, and the like. As far as we can know, animals other than the human are at home in their material environs. Our bodies, since they are not only of a certain material kind but are immersed in a symbolic order, can extend themselves far beyond their sensory limits. Culture does not supplement our nature, it is part of it. We are not only human beings, we are also human *becomings*.

Cultures give different meanings to those natural needs that all human beings share in common, and also add new ones of their own. Since human beings are culture-creating and capable of creative self-transformation, they do not passively inherit a shared nature in the same way that animals do. Human beings acquire certain tendencies and dispositions from their social relationships and activities, some of which can be as powerful as any acquired by biological instinct. Death, over which we have as little control as any other creature and which unites us with them, can be conceived and experienced in a variety of ways: as heroic sacrifice, union with a cosmic consciousness, final annihilation, the wages of sin, loss of all meaning and relationship, the gateway to rebirth in another life form, and so on. So, while human beings share a common species nature as homo sapiens, common conditions of existence, shared life experiences, needs, wants and so on, they also conceptualize and respond to these in quite different ways. Their identity is a product of a dialectical interplay between the universal and the particular, between what they all share and what is culturally specific. Even the universally shared features do not impinge on human consciousness "raw"; they are mediated through linguistic-cultural symbols and acquire different meanings in different cultures.

This means that human beings need to be understood at three different but interrelated levels: what we share as members of a common species, what we derive from and share as members of a cultural community, and what we create for ourselves as self-conscious persons. We belong to a cultural community by virtue of belonging to a common species. But our belonging to a common species is always culturally mediated. Therefore, we are human in different ways, neither wholly alike nor wholly different. Our similarities and our differences are both important and dialectically related. If nature is molded by culture it is also resistant to it. If culture transgresses nature, it is a project to which nature sets rigorous limits. We are neither disembodied, arbitrary self-creators nor mere products of our environs.

It is a common mistake to view cultures as organic, indivisible wholes. On this view, while it is acknowledged that cultures have indeed developed over a long historical process, each is regarded as bearing an immutable "essence" that distinguishes it from others. This is often combined with the deterministic idea that cultures control and limit their members' moral perceptions and intellectual horizons. Creative innovation is possible, but only to rare persons of genius. However, such holism or essentialism is a fallacy. No culture has a timeless "essence." Its traditions, whether expressed as beliefs, values or customs, operate at varying levels of generality, are internally multistranded and are sites of ongoing contestation. This is especially the case when cultures interact with others, as is true for the vast majority of living cultures in the modern world. Reformers try to recover those voices within a cultural or religious tradition that have been marginalized, suppressed or misconstrued by the dominant interpretation of their tradition. As Bhikhu Parekh observes, "A culture cannot survive unless it addresses the issues and aspirations of the age. While conservatives might be more faithful to its texts or history, they risk losing their alienated followers' allegiance and undermining the viability of their culture. Reformers might be wrong or even disingenuous in their interpretations, but they at least keep their culture alive and vibrant."[13]

Since every culture represents a particular way of looking at the world and structuring human relations, it tends to legitimize and sustain a particular kind of social order. Itself a system of power, it is interlocked with other systems of power. So cultures can never be politically neutral. There are always dominant interests which want to define and shape the direction of a cultural community. Debates over particular human rights are often debates over who within the community should have the authority to interpret the community's traditions and culture. When individual members of the group demand their human rights, they often do so in order to be able to participate in the community's process of interpreting its traditions. At the same time, cultural communities compete against others for political and economic goals. Kathryn Tanner writes, "The anthropologist may present native peoples and Western nations as if they were on a level playing field, the one in principle equal to the other as alternative and independent cultural sets. But occluded thereby are the actual unequal political and unequal relations between them, political and economic relations that would have to be attended to in the interest of genuine cultural equality."[14]

Thus there are no pure, monolithic cultures in today's world. All cultures are involved in one another, hybrid, heterogeneous and internally differentiated. This is especially the case where a culture is identified rather loosely, as for instance when people invoke "Islamic culture" or "European culture." European culture is not a homogeneous heritage without negativity or contradiction. Europe is about slavery, fascism, colonialism and genocide as much as about Chartes Cathedral, Dante, Shakespeare, the Magna Carta and democracy. The darker subtexts cannot be wholly separated from the cultural splendors and political innovations.

Therefore, it follows that not all cultures carry equal moral worth and so are deserving of equal respect. We respect all cultures in the sense that we respect the men and women whose culture it is and defend their right of access to it. We can also endorse Charles Taylor's argument that all cultures are entitled, as a "starting hypothesis," to a "presumption of equal worth": "all human cultures that have animated whose societies over some considerable stretch of time have something important to say to all human beings."[15] But this does not absolve us of the responsibility to critique all cultures, including our own, if—after, of course, a sensitive and sympathetic study of it—we conclude that they embody and perpetuate views of God, human beings, the nonhuman world and so on which are deeply flawed.

However, for any critique to be effective, it needs to resonate with some neglected aspect in the belief systems or history of that culture. A widespread example is the treatment of women in most cultures shaped by strong religious traditions (including historical Christian cultures). Muslim women in Islamic societies mount their campaign for women's equality on a reinterpretation of Islamic tradition. They point out that the Prophet's wives were powerful business women, that his favorite wife, Ayesha, was praised for her intellectual abilities, that there is an egalitarian strain in the Qur'an which overrides the suras that are more negative toward women, that compared to pre-Islamic times the Qur'anic provision of inheritance for women and protection from forced marriage were socially revolutionary, and so on.

Thus, while the original inspiration for change arises from triggers in the wider contemporary social and cultural landscape, the way the critique is grounded and articulated should, as far as possible, be from within. In cultures that are shaped by a religious tradition that has a long history, it is usually possible to find some elements that can be interpreted in such a way as to provide strong critical resources. Whether or not such interpretations are plausible depends on the members of that cultural community. It is easy to demonstrate that practices such as female genital mutilation, sometimes associated with Islam, are not Islamic at all but remnants of local tribal customs. Where a cultural or religious community engages in practices that are harmful to the natural environment or to public hygiene, they can usually be persuaded to change by showing that these are not central to their collective identity, any more than eating turkey at Christmas (or even celebrating Christmas) is central to Christian identity! When what have hitherto been considered the central values and practices are no longer accepted by the majority of its members, a culture dies. Since the authority of a culture lies in the willing allegiance of its members, it can never be imposed by force or artificially preserved.

MULTICULTURAL NATIONHOOD

The modern nation-state is defined by the unity of territory, people and political sovereignty. All those who live within a particular territory are defined as constituting a *nation* and of being *citizens* of a political community. The state understands its role as that of safeguarding its territory from external threat and protecting its citizens from both internal and external aggression. Citizens are expected to relate to the state in an identical manner, possessing an identical basket of rights and obligations. To be a citizen is to abstract away one's ethnic, religious and other particularities, and to act as a member of the political community. The state expects all its citizens to subscribe to an identical way of defining themselves and relating to each other and to the state. The nation-state is thus the prime political form of modernity, and the hyphen signifies the link between culture and politics.

Modern states, including liberal democracies, are suspicious of and feel threatened by well-organized ethnic, religious and other communities lest these become rival centers of loyalty. The tendency of liberal political philosophers, no less than their Marxist or socialist counterparts, has been to think of religious and cultural communities as little more than voluntary associations which people can join and leave at will. Almost all the major theories of the state, such as the liberal, the communitarian and the nationalist, take it for granted that it should be homogeneously constituted and differ only in the kind and degree of homogeneity they prefer. Most liberals insist that all citizens should define themselves in individualist terms, communitarians that they should subscribe to common substantive goals, and nationalists want them to share a common national identity and culture. Indeed the nationalist turns to an (usually) imaginary past in order to move toward an imagined future.

Thus, despite its claim to be more tolerant than premodern polities, the modern state is a deeply homogenizing institution and uses mass education and the state-supported majority culture to ensure that all citizens give it their primary allegiance. In multiethnic societies whose constituent peoples have different histories and cannot therefore be treated in an identical manner, the modern state can easily become an instrument of oppression and even precipitate the very instability and secession it seeks to prevent. The myth that the state can simply be based on democratic principles, without supporting a particular national identity or culture, has made it impossible to see why national minorities are keen on forming or maintaining political units in which they are a majority. Many Western liberals can only see such aspirations as primitive and violent: "The more strongly you feel the bonds of belonging to your own group," writes Michael Ignatieff, "the more hostile, the more violent will your feelings be towards outsiders. You can't have this intensity of belonging without violence, because belonging of this intensity moulds the individual conscience: if a nation gives people a reason to sacrifice themselves, it also gives them a reason to kill."[16]

Some Indian and Western political philosophers have, in recent years, broken out of the liberal mainstream and argued that genuine commitment to human liberty must entail the public recognition of collective political rights as well as individual citizenship rights. One of the best-known advocates in this field is the Canadian political theorist, Will Kymlicka:

> The Enlightenment assumption that the state could simply protect individual liberties, without adopting or advancing any particular national identity, is in any event incoherent. After all, the state must decide on the language of public education and public services, as well as on the drawing of the boundaries of internal political subunits, and the recognition of public holidays—all of which unavoidably express and promote a particular national culture.[17]

The project of nation-building, whether in Europe in the eighteenth and nineteenth centuries or the newly independent nations of postcolonial Asia and Africa, often led to the destruction of minority political and educational institutions, and the marginalization (or, in some instances, brutal suppression) of minority languages. We are not thinking here only of well-known and glaring examples like Tibet, eastern Indonesia or the Kurds. Kymlicka writes:

> French and American nationalisms were not just concerned with political principles; they were also concerned with creating a common identity, in part by imposing a common language. In the French case, this language was quite brutally imposed on the Basques, Bretons, and other linguistic minorities, through prohibitions on publications in mi-

nority languages, as well as legal requirements that the language of all education, army units and government employment be in French. A similar process occurred in the United States.[18]

In precolonial Asian states what held society together was not uniformity of culture or religious belief but a broad recognition of the supremacy of the emperor's cult. Rulers, in their turn, had to accept and make the most of the political forms and religious beliefs of the localities and leave them to their own devices. The stability of state power rested in the long term on the co-optation and honoring of local elites or self-governing local communities. The British imperial power largely followed this pattern but aggravated religious, regional and cultural differences between local groups when it suited their interests ("divide and rule"). By 1815 the English king was ruling over Roman Catholics in Quebec and Malta, Orthodox Christians in the Greek islands, and Hindus, Muslims, and Buddhists in South and Southeast Asia. In North Africa, India and Ceylon, global imperialism and wars of revolution (in Europe and elsewhere) served to strengthen hitherto fluid patriotic identities, sometimes combining them with a sense of religious revival. In Morocco and Algeria, faced with what they saw as a new crusade by Napoleon and his successors, Muslims came to identify their faith with their homeland and to revive jihadist language.

The British historian Christopher Bayly has usefully classified types of nationalism on a spectrum. At one end of the spectrum were the nationalisms that emerged out of "old patriotisms"—that is, relatively homogenous communities of language and religion. At the other end of the spectrum were nationalisms that were created by states, as opposed to states which were created out of old patriotisms.[19] Great Britain from the eighteenth-century onward was superimposed, if only for a while, onto much older alignments and loyalties. Linda Colley, in a masterly study of the rise of British nationalism, writes:

> Time and time again, war with France brought Britons, whether they hailed from Wales or Scotland or England, into confrontation with an obviously hostile Other and encouraged them to define themselves collectively against it. . . . They defined themselves against the French as

they imagined them to be, superstitious, militarist, decadent and un-free. And, increasingly as the wars went on, they defined themselves in contrast to the colonial peoples they conquered, peoples who were manifestly alien in terms of culture, religion and colour. . . . Once confronted with an obviously alien "Them," an otherwise diverse community can become a reassuring or merely desperate "Us." That is how it was with the British after 1707.[20]

Thus, as Bayly and others cogently argue, imperialism and nationalism were part of the same phenomenon. The state, urbanization and print capitalism all played a part, but war was the origin of nationalism, just as nationalisms generated wars.

Much state building across the world remained, as it always had been, a massive act of plunder. Canny entrepreneurs and commission agents followed military invaders, and it was they who often helped root the state. Despite their grandiose claims to be advancing "civilization," the French revolutionary authorities and the British colonial governments in early nineteenth-century India were based on the appropriation of money and land rights. Their British, French, Italian, and Indian collaborators had an interest in obscuring this.[21]

Furthermore, having to administer complex, multicultural societies, colonial government was more modern in many respects than the government in the metropolitan center. In the Indian subcontinent officials of the Raj needed to be trained to study local laws and customs, and oversee the complex systems of taxation and judicial arbitration which had been inherited from the earlier Indo-Muslim governments. The East India Company set up a training school in languages and political economy at Haileybury in 1809, which was far in advance of anything in Britain at the time.

There is a paradox, which Bayly well elaborates, in this picture of the rise of the nation-state and its imperial surrogate. "Statesmen may well have conceived nations as monolithic and authoritative entities," he writes,

but people saw the nation as a guarantor of rights, privileges, and claims on resources. When states failed to deliver on these implicit pledges, especially if they were ruled by foreigners, people came to demand them even more vociferously and aggressively. So it was that the triumph of the nation-state also saw the emergence of a plethora of voluntary associations, reform societies, and moral crusades, now increasingly organized at both a national and an international level. The antislavery associations and clubs of liberal reformers which existed in the early nineteenth century were now joined by thousands of new bodies claiming to speak in the name of, among many others, Indians, Irishmen, socialists, women, and indigenous peoples.[22]

National minorities do not feel secure, no matter how strongly their individual civil and political rights may be protected, unless the state desists from engaging in these sorts of nation-building projects. When a majority community defines itself as a nation and claims the cultural ownership of the state, it provokes its minorities to define themselves too as nations. Minority ethnic nationalism is often a defensive reaction against majority nationalism. This is the bloody postcolonial history of countries such as Sri Lanka and Indonesia. In many other countries (for instance, India, Burma and Russia) there have been separatist struggles raging for many years which only flicker intermittently in the global media.

In his Godkin Lectures at Harvard in 1986, the American senator Daniel Patrick Moynihan observed, "The central conservative truth is that it is culture, not politics, that determines the success of a society. The central liberal truth is that politics can change a culture and save it from itself."[23] Holding both these truths together is important. They also apply to culture in the larger sense, the moral culture of the public realm. Usually it is civil society rather than government that is assumed to be the bearer of that culture. However, "For good or bad, government, law, and the other agencies of the state are as much the repositories, transmitters, even the creators of value as are the culture and institutions of civil society. Legislation, judicial decision, administrative regulations, penal codes, even tax codes are all, to one degree or another, instruments of moral legitimization—or illegitimization."[24] From an American context, the African American law professor Stephen Carter points out that:

The mythology of modern liberalism has been that it merely establishes a set of background rules that are themselves somehow devoid of moral content—and morality is the decisions that we make about how to live our own lives against those rules. . . . [P]ractically all laws, whether they forbid me to take your car, outlaw racial discrimination, or coerce the payment of taxes, impose somebody's morality on somebody else. Every law either prevents me from doing something or forces me to do something. The understandable American tendency is to pretend otherwise, as though laws against car theft are without moral content, whereas laws on abortion are dripping in moral judgement. This tendency assists us in evading moral argument but is, of course, deeply uncivil.[25]

So, a morally and culturally "neutral" state which makes no moral demands on its citizens and is equally hospitable to all cultures and conceptions of the good is logically incoherent and practically impossible. And since every law coerces those not sharing its underlying values, a morally and culturally noncoercive state is a fantasy. Openly recognizing this fact is the first step forward in reconfiguring the nature of politics in any pluralist society. Christians should not respond by demanding a state that makes no controversial moral judgments but rather by demanding a state that is more transparent in its judgments, precisely so that they can be subjected to wide-ranging public scrutiny and debate.

A DEFENSE OF MULTICULTURAL SOCIETY

My argument so far has focused on the inevitability of cultural embeddedness, and the consequent political obligation to protect access to cultural community. But why is cultural diversity of moral worth? Other considerations being equal, why is living in a society where different cultures and different cultural perspectives coexist amicably more beneficial in terms of human well-being than living in a culturally homogeneous society?

A typical liberal argument for cultural diversity points to its importance for human freedom as it expands the cultural options available to us. The individual's right to culture is enhanced if there are many live options from which to choose. For Will Kymlicka, a culture offers a specific model of social life and organization that "we may in time come to endorse." As such, liberals need to realize that only by "having a rich and secure cultural structure, people can become aware, in a vivid way, of the options available to them and intelligibly examine their value."[26] But this argument is weak. It underestimates the emotional and moral weight of cultural attachments, unlike voluntary associations, and it has nothing to counter the view of most people that they are perfectly content with their own cultural habitation and do not see the need to explore other cultures as a necessary good. Crosscultural exposure can, after all, be deeply painful and identity-threatening. More seriously, as Parekh points out, this argument assumes that cultures are only valuable if they are options for us to choose. But what about cultures—say, of many "native" peoples (such as the Australian Aboriginals) or the Amish and other isolationist religious communities—that are not realistic options for most of us? The argument implies that the greater the difference between another culture and ours, the less reason we have to cherish it. I believe that the opposite is true.

There is no doubt that a culturally homogeneous society has its strengths. It enjoys greater social solidarity and ease of interpersonal communication, does not face the tendency to ethnic strife and fragmentation, and can mobilize its citizens relatively easily by drawing on their national loyalty. The downside, however, is that it easily become intolerant, chauvinistic and oppressive, tending to discourage dissent and internal differences. Its paucity of internal resources for resistance means that it can be as easily mobilized by the state for evil purposes as for good. The lack of crosscultural interaction means that such homogenous societies are not places where we can expect the flourishing of such intellectual and moral virtues as tolerance, intellectual curiosity, self-criticism, moral imagination or empathy with those who are different from us. "It is the creator's will," writes Oliver O'Donovan, "not only that human beings should live in communities and cultural homes, but that from their homes they should be able to engage peaceably with those of other communities."[27]

In a culturally pluralistic society, people from different cultures can engage in mutually beneficial friendships and mutual interrogation. In the course of our everyday lives, we encounter and learn from people who challenge our accustomed ways of doing things and our taken-for-granted values and beliefs. We know how, historically, different artistic, literary, musical, moral and other traditions have challenged and probed each other, borrowed and experimented with each other's ideas. Out of that fruitful interchange have arisen novel developments of each tradition that have enriched the lives of its adherents. New sensibilities, embodied in new traditions, have also emerged.

We all have what has come to be called our cultural blind spots. However rich it might be, no single culture embodies all that is valuable in human life and develops the full range of human possibilities. Only when I am deeply exposed to another cultural tradition and community do I become aware of my own; my imagination is stretched as I am forced to rethink my own in the light of another way of life, and I come to cherish what is good and challenge what is bad or ugly. For instance, a native tribal peoples' sense of ecological harmony, their material contentment and simplicity, compel us to question the values and priorities of our own technologically sophisticated societies. They expose the limitations of our own intellectual and moral horizons. The value of other cultures is, therefore, independent of whether or not they are options for us. Indeed they are often valuable precisely because they are not. It is their genuine "otherness" that constitutes the challenge.

This is why the Bible, and Christian theology in general, endorses cultural diversity. There is a tendency for all cultures to absolutize themselves, to replace the living God with cultural substitutes or with the whole culture itself. We need the whole human family to unmask our cultural idols, to free us from our cultural addictions, and to draw us out of our narrow obsessions. O'Donovan argues,

> It is essential to our humanity that there should always be foreigners, human beings from another community who have an alternative way of organizing the task and privilege of being human, so that our imaginations are refreshed and our sense of cultural possibilities renewed. The imperialist argument, that until foreigners are brought into relations of affinity within one cultural home they are enemies, is simply a creation of xenophobia. The act of recognition and welcome, which leaps across the divide between communities and finds on the other side another commu-

nity which offers the distinctive friendship of hospitality, is a fundamental form of human relating. Xenophilia is commanded us: the neighbour whom we are to love is the foreigner whom we encounter on the road.[28]

Similarly, the American theologian Charles West points out that the gospel renews and invigorates the variety of human cultures and "secularizes" them at the same time: "They are blessed as expressions of human creativity and community, in their limited time and purpose. They are called to be open to change through encounter with other cultures and with history."[29]

Contrary to some popular stereotyping of Christian missionaries, the church has often included within its mission the defense of threatened native peoples and the protection of vernacular languages. The New Testament elevates and desacralizes all cultures. It thereby celebrates and critiques them all. Unlike Islamic and Brahmanical Hindu practice, where Arabic and Sanskrit (respectively) have been considered the divine tongues and consequently the culture of origin becomes normative for others, the Christian doctrine of incarnation has shaped Christian mission in a different direction. If God reveals himself in the vernacular speech of ordinary men and women, then the vernacular can become the bridge to the knowledge of God.

The West African scholar Lamin Sanneh has rebutted the popular charge that Christian mission in Africa and Asia has always led to the destruction of other cultures in the form of Western cultural hegemony. Sanneh points out that the major plank in Protestant mission strategy was always Bible translation. This often involved writing down a vernacular for the very first time, and the creation of grammars and local literatures. Translation of the Bible into over two thousand languages has been the chief instrument of indigenous cultural renewal in many parts of the world. By believing that the vernacular was adequate for participation in the Christian movement, the more serious-minded missionaries and translators have preserved a great variety of languages and cultures from extinction, and lifted obscure tribes and ethnic groups into the stream of universal history. "It is one of the great historical truths of our day that otherwise obscure tribes, without a claim to cosmopolitan attainment, should find in indigenous particularity the sole grounds for appeal to international recognition."[30]

Sanneh also notes:

The fact of Christianity being a translated, and translating, religion places God at the center of the universe of cultures, implying free co-equality among cultures and a necessary relativizing of languages vis-à-vis the truth of God. No culture is so advanced and so superior that it can claim exclusive access or advantage to the truth of God, and none so marginal or inferior that it can be excluded. All have merit; none is indispensable. The vernacular was thereby given the kiss of life.[31]

Perhaps it is only Christians who can confidently hope that everything that is true, beautiful, just and pleasing to God in every period of human history and in every human culture has not disappeared forever but will be retrieved, restored and redirected toward the eternal worship of God and the risen Christ. The outpouring of God's Spirit through the manifold languages of the world on the day of Pentecost was a foretaste and anticipation of that apocalyptic vision of a multilingual, multicultural worship around the throne of God (Revelation 7:9-10). The biblical story begins with a picture of a couple in a garden. It ends with that marvellous vision of a city, the New Jerusalem, a place of multicultural cohabitation, where the peoples of the earth will "bring into it the glory and the honor of the nations" (Revelation 21:22-26). Surely the first and easiest step in bearing witness to this vision would be for Christians, wherever they live, to take an active interest in the artistic creations, values and customs of people right on their doorstep in a multicultural society. The eschatological horizon should also keep Christians from presumption: we do not yet know which particular aspects of any cultural or religious tradition, including our own, will contribute to the heavenly polis and which will be judged.

RECONFIGURING THE MULTICULTURAL STATE

Modern nations are highly complex human creations. They comprise millions of strangers about whose well-being one is expected to be concerned and for whose sake one is required to pay taxes and even give up one's life. They also include countless unseen past and future generations, to which one is bound by moral and emotional ties and with which one is supposed to form a historic "community." Modern nations therefore require a great imaginative capacity. Their cohesiveness and strength depend on the shared political imagination of their citizens.

The shared political imagination of a nation centers on the kind of community its members think it is, their understanding of how it came to be what it is, and what they think it should become in the future. Where the moral formation of a people is deficient, where all human relationships are reduced to the contractual and the commercial or where the mass media and educational institutions promote xenophobia and one-sided views of the nation's history, democracy can lead to the deep alienation and oppression of many who live within its territory (the Third Reich springs readily to mind). Democracy, then, is not an end in itself. There is a tension between international human rights claims and particularistic cultural and national identities that plays out in a variety of ways today, and this tension is constitutive of democratic legitimacy.

In many liberal democracies today, authentic crosscultural engagement is very often stifled or circumvented. In the name of the liberal-procedural state or the alleged neutral objectivity of Western science, other ways of life are, at best, reduced to exotic commodities for tourist consumption. They are not allowed to challenge the prevailing political paradigm. Since the public realm in every society generally enjoys a far greater prestige than the private realm, although other cultures are free to flourish in families and local neighborhood associations, they exist in the overpowering shadow of the dominant culture. Subjected to the relentless assimilationist pressure of the latter, their members, especially youth, internalize their inferior status, lead confused lives or retreat into their communal ghettos. In multicultural states, learning to live with the otherness of others whose ways of life may be deeply unsettling to our own therefore involves more than practicing tolerance.

Bhikhu Parekh argues that a multicultural society is likely to be stable, cohesive and vibrant if it meets certain conditions. These include "a consensually grounded structure of authority, a collectively acceptable set of constitutional rights, a just and impartial state, a multiculturally constituted common culture and multicultural education, and a plural and inclusive view of national identity. None of them by itself is enough."[32]

Let us examine his important argument in more detail. For a structure of political authority to be considered legitimate by its citizens and to count on their continuing allegiance, it must be seen to act fairly and to ensure its citizens the basic conditions of the good life. These, however, are not enough. Legal citizenship is about status and rights, but belonging is about being accepted and feeling welcome. This feeling of being citizens and yet outsiders is difficult to analyze, but it can run deep and seriously damage the quality of social and political involvement. Although such individuals are free in principle to participate in public life, they often stay away or ghettoize themselves for fear of rejection and ridicule or out of a deep sense of alienation. That is how, for example, many African Americans in the United States, Pakistanis in Britain, Arabs in Israel, and Muslims and, until recently, Sikhs in India feel about their respective countries.

Thus the modern liberal state is faced with two contradictory demands. On the one hand, how does it foster a sense of unity and common belonging among its citizens, as otherwise its authority is weak and so it cannot enforce collectively binding decisions? Without some shared vocabulary and a certain measure of common interests, individuals and communities will not recognize the political community as theirs and have any sense of loyalty to it. On the other hand, how does it ensure that its nation-building tendencies do not destroy the very pluralism that it claims to protect? Paradoxically, the greater the diversity in a society, the greater the cohesion it requires to hold itself together and nurture its diversity. In a society with weak political structures, communities feel threatened by differences and lack the confidence to cooperate with others and make their own unique contribution to national life.

I suggested in chapter three that every multicultural society needs to devise its own political structure to suit its history, moral traditions and range and depth of cultural diversity. In countries as different as India and the United States, however, we have come to recognize in recent years that equal respect for people does not always mean treating them identically, as this can perpetuate an unequal playing field. Where certain groups (cultural or otherwise) have suffered historically from longstanding abuse and its members demoralized as a result, equal respect translates into nonequal treatment. The community concerned needs to be granted additional rights in order to equalize them with the rest. There may be other worthwhile goals such as social harmony that also call for the granting of collective rights. If some groups lack the confidence and the opportunity to participate as equals in mainstream society, we might need to give them special rights, such as protected representation in government bodies and perhaps the right to a veto over laws relating to them. The purpose of such additional civil rights is to draw the groups involved into the mainstream of society and give substance to the principle of equal citizenship.[33]

But this raises questions such as how we can ensure that such differential treatment does not hurt the weaker members of other groups or does not become entrenched as a self-perpetuating system of reverse discrimination. There are no easy answers to these questions. In the Indian context, positive discrimination in educational and government employment policies in favor of Scheduled Caste groups has had the unwitting effect of consolidating caste-based collective identities.

The burden of justification for nonidentical treatment must surely rest with those who argue for the latter, but their arguments must be listened to with humility and sensitivity. We need to ask, in each context, questions such as, Which cultural or ethnic community sees itself as threatened, and why? What historic injustices need to be remedied, and is a form of affirmative action the best way to restore equality for hitherto disadvantaged and excluded groups? Is the granting of rights the best way of dealing with this problem, and, if so, does the group in question have the institutional resources to enjoy those rights? What is the tradeoff between the protection of individual rights of members in such collectivities and the rights of the collectivity as such?

Ellis Close, in his book *The Rage of a Privileged Class*, tells the story of a young white man in the United States who was "choleric" at the notion that "unqualified minorities" would dare to demand preferential treatment:

> A person of modest intellect, he had gotten to Harvard largely on the basis of family connections. His first summer internship, with the White House, had been arranged by a family member. His second, with the World Bank, had been similarly arranged. Thanks to his nice internships and Harvard degree, he had been promised a coveted slot in

a major company's executive training program. In short, he was already well on his way to a distinguished career—a career made possible by preferential treatment.[34]

Endorsing affirmative action for every visible minority clearly militates against social justice. It seems quite unfair that the child of highly educated and wealthy Chinese immigrants, living amidst the prosperous Asian community in Vancouver, should have preferential access to jobs over the child of poor and uneducated whites living in economically distressed fishing villages in Newfoundland.[35] Insofar as we view affirmative action as a way of helping genuinely disadvantaged minorities and of overcoming the danger of ethnic exclusion and separatism, then it is crucial to make sure that it is not just the group with the loudest voice that is heard. Given the human proclivity to sin, it is hardly surprising that every group feels outrage at the way it has been abused or neglected by others, while either denying or downplaying the evil it has committed against others. In Sri Lanka, for instance, the northern Jaffna Tamils' demand for a separate state has acquired an international voice, owing to the wealth and influence of the Jaffna Tamil diaspora. But the suffering of other regional Tamils and local Muslim communities at the hands of the Jaffna Tamils as well as the dire economic plight of Tamil tea-plantation workers (indentured labor brought over from South India by the British Raj) have been largely silenced.

In countries such as Sri Lanka, where there has been protracted civil conflict between territorially focused ethnic communities, the sovereignty of the state needs to be dispersed among several centers of authority exercising overlapping jurisdictions and reaching decisions through negotiations and compromise. In the multilayered politics of today's world, self-government for such minorities need not be seen as a threat to states, but rather as a precondition for their long-term stability. The legitimacy of federalism depends on the ways that boundaries are drawn in a federal system and on the ways that powers are distributed. It is often difficult to make these decisions in a way that truly satisfies the aspirations of national minorities as well as removing the fears of minorities within their own ranks no less than those of the larger majority culture. Also, even as staunch an advocate of federalism as

Will Kymlicka notes with caution, "Federalism does not provide a magic formula for the resolution of national differences. It provides at best a framework for negotiating these differences, and to make it work requires an enormous degree of ingenuity, goodwill and indeed good luck. And even with all the good fortune in the world, multinational federations will face secessionist movements."[36]

Moreover, when it comes to social policy in multicultural societies, the important question arises as to who represents the view of a minority community as a whole? Whether in India or in Europe, it is often elderly males who perform this role of spokespersons, mediating between the state and their community, much as local elites did in India under the British Raj. In Britain liberal fears of treading on ethnic sensibilities lay behind the slowness in social policy to outlaw child marriages or forced marriages and to intervene in situations of domestic abuse in South Asian families. This, ironically, made the British authorities vulnerable to charges of racism because the attitude implied that underage sex had a less harmful effect on South Asian girls than other girls. In India the bitter experience of partition and recurring Muslim-Hindu tensions made early Congress governments sensitive to the insecurity of a large Muslim minority in a predominantly Hindu society. They gave in to the insistence by conservative Muslim male leaders that their "personal law" dealing with divorce, marriage and inheritance derived from the Qur'an and was therefore unalterable. They allowed Muslims to retain their special marriage laws—to the advantage of Muslim men in India but not Muslim women, whose rights, after a divorce, are limited.[37] The political issues raised by these decisions are still alive and unresolved.

A multicultural society, like any other society, needs a broadly shared "public culture" to sustain it. Since this shared culture needs to be multiculturally constituted, it can only grow out of the vigorous interaction of majority and minority cultures, and not by their relative isolation. If we continue to think of cultures according to the fallacies mentioned earlier, the idea of a multiculturally constituted, shared collective culture may seem incoherent. But a moment's reflection will remind us that this is indeed what happens on a regular basis in our daily interactions with each other in local neighborhoods that are not ethnically segregated. Cultural beliefs and customs develop in a manner that cannot be planned or foreseen. Intercultural communication and evaluation are possible, and no one outside the academy argues for—let alone practices—cultural relativism. So a continually contested but coherent public culture is possible, one that grows out of the conversation between different cultures and does not replace them but respects their diversity, while at the same time providing a shared vocabulary of common interests.

Thus we should reenvision the nation-state not as an aggregate of individuals but as a community of communally embedded citizens. In such a reconfiguration, cultural and religious diversity is not confined to the private realm, as in most Western liberal societies, but permeates all areas of life. The different communities enjoy varying degrees of autonomy, and are encouraged by the state (not least through the media and educational institutions) to enter into a continuous public conversation with one another on issues of mutual concern. All are held together by shared legal bonds and by a dialogically formed common public culture. "Rights, and other principles of the liberal democratic state," as the political philosopher Seyla Benhabib argues, "need to be periodically challenged and rearticulated in the public sphere in order to enrich their original meaning." When new groups emerge who claim that they belong within the circle of addressees of a right from which they have been hitherto excluded, "we come to understand the fundamental limitedness of every rights claim within a constitutional tradition as well as its context-transcending validity."[38]

We need to remind ourselves, from time to time, that it is not the paraphernalia of general elections that make a well-functioning democracy but rather the responsiveness of governments to public deliberations over the common good. The representative parliament, the archetypal symbol of democracy in the West, "constitutes a forum of deliberation before which a government is expected to explain itself and expose itself to critical interrogation. . . . It deliberated not on its own behalf but in response to a wider context of deliberation, open to all, to which it must be attending carefully."[39]

Seyla Benhabib argues persuasively for "democratic iterations" which would lead to a position she calls "cosmopolitan federalism." Democratic iterations refer to "complex processes of public argument, deliberation and exchange through which universalist rights claims and principles are contested and contextualized, invoked and revoked, posited and positioned, throughout legal and political institutions, as well as in the associations of civil society."[40] These can take place in legislatures and the judiciary as well as in the informal publics of civil society associations and the media.

Such a broad-based, deliberative public culture is more likely to enable different individuals and communities to identify with the political community and to encourage democratic participation by all than the mere invocation of "civic nationalism" or "constitutional patriotism." We have observed that a society's legal and political institutions are embedded in and nurtured by the wider public culture. The meaning of political values such as justice, equality, liberty and so on should always be negotiable and new conceptual languages developed through critical dialogue across the whole spectrum of society. This could lead to a richer public culture that is less polarized and confrontational. Not all will approve of it entirely, but all will find some aspects that they recognize as their own and will give it more allegiance than to a public realm dominated by a single, hegemonic discourse.[41] The answer to the naked public square, then, is not a sacred public square envisioned by religious nationalists (whether Muslim, Hindu, Buddhist or Christian) but a civic public square: a place of public moral discourse, which must of necessity draw on the resources of the various religious and other communities that comprise the polity.

SECULARIST FUNDAMENTALISM

There is a militant secularist fundamentalism both in the West and in parts of Asia that is as destructive of authentic pluralism as its religious counterpart. This is seen, for instance, in the French government's ruling against the wearing of the hijab by Muslim schoolgirls or the hysterical vilification in the mass media of any public figure who rejects the liberal rhetoric of reproductive rights or sexual preferences. Secularization is not an inevitable process thrown up by abstract, impersonal forces that are subsumed under the label of modernity. It is often actively promoted by vested interests (whether academics, artists, businessmen or journalists). Intellectuals are especially prone to self-deception, seeing themselves as the standard-bearers of the cult of originality, having emancipated themselves from all the constraints of tradition, community and obligation.

The failure to respect persons is often evident among intellectuals who show more interest in the arcane and esoteric than they do in the beliefs and values of their colleagues from other cultures. Scholarly journals such as the *New York Review* or the *Times Literary Supplement* are more likely to publish essays on the pseudo-Gospels of the second and third century Gnostic cults, which perhaps a handful of American academics in religious studies departments follow, than they do on the living faith traditions followed by billions of Christians throughout the world, not to mention those African and Asian churches which have sprung up in the heart of many Western cities.

A latent paternalism has operated within secular liberalism, which may be somewhat muted after the recent discovery of militancy among second-generation Muslim migrants in Western Europe. It simply took it for granted that any individual who has tasted the autonomy and range of choices made available in a liberal, consumerist society will choose this form of life over any alternative. When, in October 2006, the then British home secretary, Jack Straw, and the prime minister, Tony Blair, publicly expressed not only their "discomfort" at the wearing by Muslim women of the niqab (the black veil that covers all but the eyes) but even suggested that this was a "symbol of separation" from the rest of British society, their comments generated an uproar in the Muslim community as well as hearty cheers from secular intellectuals. The Dutch Parliament, one of the most liberal in the world, passed legislation banning the wearing of the niqab. There is widespread ignorance about Muslim dress and behavior in Europe, an ignorance paralleled only by that concerning Christian beliefs and history. The niqab is worn by recent migrants from Somalia or Yemen as part of their cultural tradition. It is actually a symbol of status in their community. There is another group of Muslim women, usually younger and British-born, who have adopted it as an expression of religious piety in what is perceived to be a promiscuous, sexually charged public space. Most Muslim women in the West do not wear the niqab, but if a minority have chosen to do so and are consequently vilified in the national media, this only exacerbates the sense of social alienation that most migrants experience. It further undermines efforts by community leaders to help integrate the most fearful, usually women, into European society.

When politicians try to tell the general public what "religious" symbols mean and even seek legislation to outlaw them in public, without any attempt to listen to the explanations of the women themselves, the state reveals the hypocrisy of its purported tolerance and impartiality. How, in a supposedly tolerant society, does one express nonviolently one's repugnance at blatant sexually provocative behavior or pornography? Would the British and Dutch governments have reacted the same way to, say, a group of white lesbians who chose to avoid all contact with males in public places? The much-vaunted sexual freedom of British society had led to an epidemic of sexually transmitted diseases, teenage pregnancies, single-parent families and soaring alcohol abuse among young women. Does the fact that many non-Western Christians in Britain, no less than Muslims, reject this widespread myth of sexual freedom in favor of monogamous commitments, mean that they are also "unwilling to integrate" with the rest of society?

Timothy Garton Ash of Oxford University remarks that it is the personal attitudes and behavior of non-Muslim Europeans, "in countless small, everyday interactions," that will determine whether their Muslim fellow citizens begin to feel at home in Europe or not. Together, of course, with the personal choices of individual Muslims and the example they receive from their spiritual and political leaders. However,

> if the message they hear from us is that the necessary condition for being European is to abandon their religion, then they will choose not to be European. For secular Europeans to demand that Muslims adopt their faith—secular humanism—would be almost as intolerant as the Islamist jihadist demand that we should adopt theirs. But, the Enlightenment fundamentalist will protest, our faith is based on reason! Well, they reply, ours is based on truth![42]

Even as Muslim (and Christian) fundamentalists need to be persuaded that learning to restrain their truth claims in a pluralist public domain is not a surrender to religious skepticism, so their dogmatic liberal cousins need to learn just how narrow and culture-bound their view of reason actually is.

RIGHTS OF REFUGEES AND ASYLEES

Immigration is an emotional political issue in many countries, especially in

Europe and the United States. Opposition to immigration is generally far more prominent than support for it, but that is to some extent countered by economic interests. The main argument cited in support of immigration is economic, usually related to the need for both high-skilled labor in the growth sectors of the economy and low-skilled, low-paid employment in restaurants, farms and building maintenance services. The main anti-immigration arguments are straightforward xenophobia, economic (costs of welfare services), environmental (impact of population growth), and the impact on the national identity and the nature of the nation-state itself. The politics of immigration has become increasingly associated with other issues, such as national security, terrorism and in Western Europe especially, with the presence of Islam as a new major religion.

In recent debates over such migrations, especially the influx of refugees and asylees, the contradictions among the discourses of "state sovereignty," "the global village" and "human rights" becomes glaringly apparent. We have seen how the modern nation-state replaced the frontiers of old empires with borders. The border is not simply a geographical location but a political construction, defining the identities of those who live on either side. Those enclosed within the border are citizens and those outside are aliens or foreigners. Within the limits of its borders, a state is said to have exclusive territorial control, and on crossing a state's border all individuals and property fall under the territorial authority of that state. There has, of course, been a growing international consensus that the sovereignty of a state to dispose over the life, liberty and property of its citizens or residents is subject to internationally recognized norms which prohibit genocide, mass expulsions, enslavement, organized rape and forced labor.

At the same time, however, borders are not only being fortified in the rich nations, they are being "globalized" such that a person may experience a foreign border while still within the territory of their country.[43] Africans applying for migration or asylum in France or Spain are moved to transit processing centers in some North African countries. Thus those who have physically entered a European Union state are moved into a non-EU location from where they have to renegotiate entry. The non-European transit center becomes the site at which they experience the borders of the EU. In Australia, certain asylum seekers are detained and their applications processed "offshore" in countries like Nauru and Papua New Guinea, so that they can be resettled in third countries. But the Australian states' borders have been contracted rather than expanded so that detention centers within Australia stand outside the jurisdiction of Australian law. Some senior Australian politicians have sought to argue that international law also does not apply in such no-man's lands.

How may the biblically endorsed right of strangers to hospitality, mentioned in chapter three, be translated into the complex world of deterritorialized politics and modern nation-states today? Surely the first step must be to decriminalize the worldwide movement of peoples and treat each person, whatever his or her political or economic status, with the respect he or she deserves as a human being. At present, citizens of relatively poor nations standing before an immigration official at a rich nation's embassy, let alone its ports of entry, find themselves in a situation totally uncharacteristic of normal legal procedures. Instead of being regarded as innocent until proven guilty, they are assumed to be fraudulent unless they can prove their stories are true. While for a rich person from a rich country borders are a mere formality, for a poor person from a poor country, the border is an obstacle to be confronted. If the poor person is also an asylum seeker, then the border becomes his or her permanent residence. As long as we have a world defined as a system of nation-states with tightly controlled borders and citizens legally distinguished in terms of their civic rights from alien residents, then an international human rights regime is needed that protects those who travel as migrants, asylum seekers or as refugees to enter another people's territory and become members of that society by a peaceful and open process.[44]

The current international legal documents that cover cross-border movements are fraught with unresolved tensions. Article 13 of the United Nations Declaration of Human Rights recognizes a right to leave a country but not a corresponding right to enter a country, while the second half of article 15 stipulates that "no one shall be arbitrarily deprived of his nationality nor denied the right to change his nationality." It is silent on the obligations of states to uphold the right of asylum, to grant entry to immigrants and to permit citizenship to alien residents. The Geneva Convention of 1951 relating to the status of refugees and its 1967 Protocol are binding on signatory states alone and are brazenly ignored even by the latter.

It is easily forgotten that, from the Atlantic slave trade to California's Silicon Valley, much of the prosperity of the rich world is owed to migration, forced or voluntary. In the United States today, where, unlike in Europe, being of immigrant origin carries more respectability, between a quarter and a third of living Nobel Prize winners and one-fifth of the membership of the National Academy of Sciences is foreign-born. Some of them came as refugees from totalitarian states, others were wooed and recruited by universities and corporations. Writing in 2002, the economist Nigel Harris notes that in the six leading states in the United States to which poorer immigrants head, three quarters of waiters and tailors, 78 percent of cooks and over half of taxi drivers and textile and garment workers are immigrants. Immigrants make up 18 percent of the Los Angeles construction workforce. In Washington State, 70 percent of the employed in the peak harvest time are said to be undocumented immigrants.[45]

It is a widespread fallacy that poor immigrants sponge off social security and don't pay taxes for the benefits they receive. In fact, whenever even undocumented workers buy things they pay the same taxes as citizens, and when they rent apartments the local rates are included in the rents they are charged. Ironically, many end up subsidizing resident citizens while not receiving social security at all. In the United States, Mexicans account for the greatest number of undocumented workers. Many of them are subsistence corn-growing farmers unable to survive on the land. They are victims of the North Atlantic Free Trade Agreement that pits them in unfair competition with state-subsidized agribusiness giants from the United States and Canada. Western nations never admit that enforced migrations may be the result of their own short-sighted and often selfish policies.

I noted earlier Kant's influential attempt, in his "Perpetual Peace" essay, to distinguish a universal moral duty to offer temporary sojourn to all, and the legal prerogative of the republican sovereign not to extend such temporary sojourn to full membership in the political community. Contra Kant, but embracing his cosmopolitan moral outlook, Seyla Benhabib argues that the right to membership must be viewed as a human right. She writes, "While the

prerogative of states to stipulate some criteria of incorporation cannot be rejected, we have to ask: which are those incorporation practices that would be
impermissible from a moral standpoint and which are those practices that are
morally indifferent—that is to say, neutral from the moral point of view?"[46]

Benhabib is advocating a system of porous rather than completely open
national borders. Moreover, she rightly observes that "defining the identity of
the democratic people is an ongoing process of constitutional self-creation."[47]
She does recognize that states have greater discretion to stipulate conditions
of entry in the case of immigration than they do when facing refugees and
asylum seekers. The latter peoples carry weightier moral claims. Although
democratic governments have the right to regulate the transition from first
admission to full membership, once first admission is granted, the laws governing naturalization must be subjected to human rights norms and also be
transparently formulated. They must not be left to the mercy of bureaucratic
capriciousness. What would be morally unacceptable is the absence of any
procedure for foreigners and resident aliens to become citizens at all or if naturalization were restricted on the basis of religious, ethnic, racial, or sexual
orientation.

Interestingly, Jacques Derrida's (1930-2004) later writings were often provoked by Kant's reflections on hospitality and Emmanuel Levinas's ethic of
responsibility to the "other." One recent commentator on Derrida argues that
for him "the question of hospitality or welcome is not only the ethical question, it is also in a certain way, the political question, the question of politics today."[48] Derrida traces Kant's cosmopolitanism to Pauline Christianity,
which "revived, radicalized and literally 'politicized' the primary injunctions
of all the Abrahamic religions. . . . Saint Paul gives to these appeals or to
these dictates their modern names."[49] In a speech to UNESCO in November 1999, titled "Globalization, Peace, and Cosmopolitanism," Derrida stated
that thinking of the world as a historical process and reality, which is not the
same as what is called globalization today, depends in important respects on
the Abrahamic traditions and especially the Pauline focus:

> It is because the concept of world gestures toward a history, it has a
> memory that distinguishes it from that of the globe, of the universe,

of earth, of the cosmos even (at least the cosmos in its pre-Christian meaning, which Saint Paul then christianized precisely to make it say world as fraternal community of human beings, of fellow creatures, brothers, sons of God and neighbours to one another). For the world begins by designating, and tends to remain, in an Abrahamic tradition (Judaeo-Christian-Islamic, but predominantly Christian) a particular space-time, a certain oriented history of human brotherhood, of what in a Pauline language—the language that continues to structure and condition the modern concepts of the rights of man or the crime against humanity . . .—of what in this Pauline language one calls citizens of the world (*sympolitai*, of the saints of the household of God), brothers, fellow men, neighbours, insofar as they are creatures and sons of God.[50]

ETHICS OF FREEDOM

Tzu-kung asked [Confucius] about government. The Master said, "Sufficient food, sufficient weapons, and the confidence of the common people." Tzu-kung said, "Suppose you had no choice but to dispense with one of these three, which would you forego?" The Master said, "Weapons." Tzu-kung said, "Suppose you were forced to dispense with one of the two that were left, which would you forego?" The Master said, "Food. For from of old death has been the lot of all men; but a people that no longer trusts its rulers is lost indeed."[51]

The question of trust also lies at the heart of modern states that style themselves as representative governments. Political leaders constantly call on us to trust their competence and good intentions. That many of us have become understandably cynical about our leaders is shown by the steadily falling percentages of citizens, especially in the older democracies, who bother to exercise their vote. Much of the political process is dominated by the lobbying power of business interests, and as long as popular newspapers and TV "news" care more for the salacious and scandalous than the truthful, and the general cultural environment stimulates the pursuit of private goods rather than deliberation about the common good, the prognosis for healthy democracies is fairly bleak.

Representative democracy, as the political philosopher John Dunn reminds us, was the model which the Western nations imposed on their defeated enemies at the end of the Second World War. It was also the model which, "after much preliminary foot-dragging," they bequeathed to most of their former colonies.[52] It has, however, proved remarkably resilient and been adopted "with some success in every continent, in societies with long and cruel experiences of arbitrary rule, cultures of great historical depth, and religious traditions which insist on the profound inequality of human beings . . . in East and South and South East Asia, in Latin America, and more sporadically and precariously, in Sub-Saharan Africa and even the Middle East."[53]

I have noted how, in recent years, in societies as wide apart as the United Kingdom, Canada, Sri Lanka and India, legal and political philosophers have devoted considerable attention to exploring how best to embody the ideal of democratic choice—its capacity to enhance and bring into play the full range of knowledge and experience of the entire citizen body—while also submitting such choices to universal moral norms. Every such deliberative democracy faces common challenges despite varying contexts: how to build a united and inclusive political community, how to protect vulnerable and insecure cultural-ethnic groups, how to promote human rights and dignity in the face of economic inequalities, how to ensure that the self-governing community is genuinely participatory. All these are hard issues. Not surprisingly, no single political ideology, whether libertarian, liberal nationalist, conservative, communitarian, socialist, revolutionary Islamist or Marxist, has proved adequate.

The church contributes best to these discussions by articulating theological insights drawn from both biblical revelation and its rich historical experience in East and West. All human conceptions of justice take different forms in different cultural and religious milieu. This is partly because our understanding of the demands of justice forms part of a wider worldview, something that is expressed implicitly in the societal culture to which we belong. Deliberating across cultures in mutually challenging dialogues, and the experiences of participating in overlapping communities (from transnational, environmental action groups to multicultural schools) can help bring about shared conceptions of social justice. Christians of all denominations and cultures have been in the forefront of such dialogues and justice initiatives around the world.

Despite great cultural and religious differences, the governments of most countries in the world have signed both the UN Declaration of Human Rights as well as the UN Millennium Development Goals, which seeks to halve poverty by the year 2015 by setting achievable practical goals in a number of fields such as maternity health, environmental protection and basic education. Such basic needs and primary goods to which all human beings should have equal access have already been identified as worthwhile universal goals, whatever else we may disagree on with respect to more comprehensive social and political goals. I see no reason why, in every democratic polity, rough-and-ready principles of social justice cannot emerge out of democratic debate and dialogue. But all this implies trust, not only of political leaders but of one another.

The doctrinaire advocates of a "value neutral" market order, which is central to most liberal democracies, have classically argued that the market is simply a mechanism to enable as many people as possible to get as much as possible of whatever it is that they want. It embodies no specific moral purpose other than encouraging individual choice. The consumer is sovereign. The aggregate outcomes of markets, being unintended and unforeseeable, are not susceptible to moral criticism and collective moral constraint. Here it will suffice to note that, far from operating in a sanitized social space, markets and business corporations inhabit a world (largely of their own making) of ruthless marketing techniques, hostile takeovers, chronic unemployment, subsistence wages, industrial espionage and environmental degradation. These are all profoundly moral issues.

Moreover, in everyday life we are held responsible for the unintended but reasonably foreseeable consequences of our actions, as, for example, in the case of manslaughter. Further, as the political philosopher Raymond Plant points out, there is something extremely odd in the claim that the consequences of markets are unforeseeable, when "for the past few years we have been treated to endless papers from politicians and think-tanks which argue for the extension of markets to more and more areas of our lives on the grounds of the beneficial consequences which might be thought to follow from this." Plant advances a counterclaim to the effect that "there is an aggregate judgment that one can make about free markets, namely, that those who enter the market with least are likely to leave it with least, and that for those at the margins of society the trickle-down effect without social intervention will not alter this. If this conjecture is right, then it follows that we can bear collective responsibility for those outcomes and that their consequences for those who are worse off can be compensated for."[54]

It has also been pointed out by critics that when the mentality of instrumental reasoning and individual consumer choice encroaches on every sphere of social life, it erodes the moral basis of society that markets presuppose for their proper functioning. The more a predatory, transnational capitalism absorbs cultures everywhere into the general process of commodity production, so that cultures are reduced to lifestyle choices and all human relationships become commercial and contractual, the legitimacy of capitalism itself is destroyed. As long as economic growth continues to benefit us and impending environmental catastrophe can be ignored, we don't need to raise moral and political questions to do with the legitimacy of the market order.

Interestingly, Francis Fukuyama, who considers liberal democracy and secularism inseparable, is obliged to recognize that liberalism itself requires public virtues which are sustained by religious communities if it is to survive:

> If the institutions of democracy and capitalism are to work properly, they must coexist with certain pre-modern cultural habits that ensure their proper functioning. Law, contract, and economic rationality provide a necessary but not sufficient basis for both the stability and prosperity of post-industrial societies; they must as well be leavened with reciprocity, moral obligation, duty toward community, and trust, which are based on habit rather than rational calculation. The latter are not anachronisms in a modern society but rather the sine qua non of the latter's success.[55]

If liberal democracy is parasitic upon and, in turn, has a corrosive impact on pre-liberal traditions, if it needs for its own survival values that it cannot itself produce (and even tends to undermine), then the liberal project has to look elsewhere for its coherence and plausibility. Rabbi Jonathan Sacks observes that what differentiates the seventeenth-century approach to liberty from twentieth-century advocates such as Friedrich Hayek, Karl Popper and Isaiah Berlin is that "these latter-day thinkers predicated their ideas of a free society on scepticism and uncertainty, and in so doing weakened the defence of liberty, making it vulnerable to those who fight in the name of certainty."[56] In the hands of Milton, Locke and others, religious liberty, for instance, meant "Faith is supremely important, and therefore everyone must be allowed to live by the faith which seems true to him." This is not relativism, but a deeply religious understanding that coercion does not lead to genuine faith. The philosopher John Plamenatz wrote, "Liberty of conscience was born, not of indifference, not of scepticism, not of mere open-mindedness, but of faith."[57]

A number of eminent thinkers in recent years, including Charles Taylor, Amartya Sen and Raymond Plant, have argued that human liberty makes sense only against the backdrop of a substantive account of what is valuable in human life.[58] There is no nonmoral conception of liberty. Negative freedom (freedom from coercion) is only intelligible in the context of the prior question, What we do want freedom for? If liberty merely means freedom from intentional coercion, then a primitive society with very few laws and meager economic resources would be more free than a modern society. This would be absurd. Laws and other social institutions serve some conception held within a particular society about what are the important human purposes that need to be protected and realized, and these involve deep moral judgments. Every defense of freedom thus implies an account of human capacities.

Plant gives the following example by way of illustration:

Before the invention of aeroplanes, and thus the generalised ability to fly, I do not think that it would make sense to ask the question, were people free or unfree to fly? The question would be unanswerable and absurd, because there was no general ability to fly. I think, therefore, it can be argued that a general ability to do X is a necessary condition for asking whether a particular individual is free or unfree to do X. If this is so, then there cannot be a categorical distinction between freedom and ability, and the neo-liberal's attempt to draw such a sharp distinction, to block the claim that freedom involves the resources necessary to realize abilities, has no force. In order to determine the most important types of freedom, we need an account of what are the most important general abilities that human beings have and value.[59]

Moreover, the "free" choices that we make are skewed by the way that power is distributed and exercised in a given society. Social pressure, the massive amounts of money that corporations spend on advertising, educational specialization from an early age and the ubiquitous presence of brand insignia and logos, all serve to narrow the range of choices actually open to people. The scandalous abortion of female fetuses in many Asian societies, with the number of "missing girls" in India alone amounting to some forty million or more, reveals the one-sidedness of "pro-choice" rhetoric.

If freedom presupposes moral purposes and responsibilities, then a community and a tradition of moral reasoning is inevitable. The two fundamental human needs for freedom and belonging are not in contradiction but rather inseparable. There is no true freedom without belonging, and there is no true belonging without freedom. In Dietrich Bonhoeffer's succinct words, "Being free means 'being-free-for-the-other', because I am bound to the other. Only by being in relationship with the other am I free."[60] When a guest of ours asks, "can I use your phone?" we sometimes answer "feel free," or, interchangeably, "feel at home." This domestic observation captures the fact that it is "being at home," or the sense of belonging, that enables us simply "to be" and nurtures the freedom to explore.[61]

The language of self-creation and self-determination, whether in its modernist or postmodernist forms, is dangerously misleading. It is true that we are not static beings, that we are the selves we are always becoming. But our creaturely freedom (as opposed to the mythical freedom of the gods) is a freedom to make something of what we are given already. It is a freedom wholly dependent on gift.

The theologian Richard Bauckham gives the following example:

If I make myself, for example, into a brilliant musician, then certainly
I am exercising a real freedom to make all the choices, some no doubt

very hard, that lead to this. But this freedom is entirely dependent, not only immediately and obviously, on being born with musical talent and having the opportunities to develop it (which have to be available even if one has to struggle to avail oneself of them). It is also dependent on a whole range of other facts about my circumstances that one would normally take for granted (but precisely for granted, that is, given!). For example, that there is music and that my culture has a musical tradition in which I can learn to love and to play music. Becoming a brilliant musician is therefore much more fundamentally gift than achievement. The same would be true of becoming a good parent, or a good friend, or just a good person. This is not to denigrate the achievement. But it is to recognize the priority of grace (to use the theological word for gift) to all human achievement. Pride and joy in the achievement are not in the least diminished by recognizing, with thankfulness and joy, that grace that made it possible.[62]

Contra liberal individualism, Bauckham also points out that the freely chosen commitments of friendships and common-interest groups are not the only models we have for human relationships. Most of our relationships are not chosen by us but given to us—in families and in cultural and national communities. It is in these that we discover the meaning of our created human freedom. In the parent-child relationship (including the responsibility of adult children to care for their elderly parents), in befriending a person for whom one accepts responsibility simply because circumstances places one in the position to do so or in putting up with difficult relatives, we are faced with situations "in which givenness rather than chosenness is constitutive of the relationship without detriment to freedom properly understood." Bauckham asks, "Is it really slavery to recognize obligations to people to whom we have not freely made even implicit promises of commitment? To insist that a person is only truly free when every aspect of life becomes a matter of choice between available alternatives is really to understand freedom as a rejection of finiteness."[63]

Consequently, perhaps the most fundamental human choice of all, on which all individual and political choices ultimately depend, is this: Do we accept the world as an unmerited gift from a gracious Giver with thanksgiving, respect and responsible service to others (human and nonhuman creatures like ourselves) who share this world, or do we regard it as a meaningless "resource" to be possessed and disposed of according to our desires? Human freedom, as supremely demonstrated by Jesus, consists in the full and glad alignment of our wills with God's character and purposes. To be enabled by grace to love God and to love neighbor—that is true freedom.

5

MYTHS OF SCIENCE

If, as I have been arguing, human beings are social, culture forming animals who are oriented in the depths of their nature toward a transcendental realm of value, meaning and purpose, then human freedom involves much more than liberation from political tyranny, exploitation, economic scarcity or cultural conformity. It will also be freedom from those definitions of the "human" which take the form of oppressive world pictures, acts of collective imagination that conceive of human beings and their world in such a way that important aspects of the human are either explicitly denied or subtly excluded from public acknowledgement. At the root of such collective worldviews lie originating images or metaphors that soon come to tyrannize over others. For instance, viewing the world as a machine profoundly changed the direction of much European thought from the seventeenth century until well into the twentieth. The invention of clocks and other complex pieces of machinery transformed the human imagination. Machines are easy to understand and are under human control; they can be taken to pieces and put back together in new ways. Viewing the world of humans and their societies, animals and plants, as essentially machines meant that they could be taken apart and reassembled in more satisfactory ways.

Thus no discussion of human dignity and freedom can bypass the role that science and technology have come to assume in contemporary societies. It has often been observed how we draw our collective self-images from the dominant technologies and science pictures of our time. Freudian psychology was

replete with thermodynamic and hydraulic imagery. Social Darwinists justified laissez-faire economics and decried welfare measures in the name of "the
survival of the fittest" (a term which Darwin himself had carefully avoided).
Both Nietzsche and Marx invoked "evolutionary struggle." In a computer age,
all human thinking is reduced to information-processing, and the human brain
itself is regularly likened to a supercomputer. The "selfish gene" has replaced
the social contract in some defenses of neoliberal individualism. The image of
the liberal individual—isolated, ahistorical, autonomous, self-sufficient—has
its counterpart in the image of science advanced by a host of popularizers of science from Bertrand Russell to Richard Dawkins—science as omnicompetent,
self-assured, self-generating and the sole standard of rationality in the world.

Primo Levi, describing his early education in fascist Italy, explains how he
and his friends took to chemistry largely out of disgust at the ideas presented
to them by other studies, simply to get away from "the stench of Fascist truths
which tainted the sky. . . . [T]he chemistry and physics on which we fed,
besides being nourishments vital in themselves, were the antidote to Fascism.
. . . [T]hey were clear and distinct and verifiable at every step, and not a
tissue of lies and emptiness like the radio and the newspapers."[1] However,
what Levi and his friends underestimated was the power of fascism and other
political ideologies to co-opt the "clear, distinct and verifiable" methods of
chemistry and physics. Scientists played a leading part in the initiation, administration and execution of Nazi racial policy. The Wannsee Conference,
which decided on the final solution of the Jewish problem, was attended by
many scientists, and the extermination of Jews in the death camps was largely
carried out by medically trained personnel.

Consequently, perceptive writers such as George Orwell sharply criticized
the fashionable postwar denigration of the arts and humanities in favor of a
"scientific education," and the appeal in some circles in Britain for scientists
to be "brought out of their isolation" and given a greater role in politics and
public administration. Orwell saw that the demand for more scientific education implied an implicit claim that if one has been scientifically trained one's
approach to all subjects will be automatically more intelligent than if one had
no such training. A scientist's political opinions, his or her opinions on sociological questions, on morals, on philosophy, perhaps even on the arts, will be

more valuable than those of a layperson. The world, in other words, would be a better place if scientists were in control of it. "But," Orwell asks,

> is it really true that a "scientist," in this narrower sense, is any likelier than other people to approach non-scientific problems in an objective way? There is not much reason for thinking so. . . . The German scientific community as a whole made no resistance to Hitler. Hitler may have ruined the long-term prospects of German science, but there were still plenty of gifted men to do the necessary research on such things as synthetic oil, jet planes, rocket projectiles and the atom bomb. Without them the German war machine would never have been built up.[2]

SCIENCE AS IDEOLOGY

It is significant that in the English language *science* has acquired a much narrower meaning than the Latin *scientia* or even the contemporary German *Wissenschaft*. The English word *scientific* is also the source of much confusion. There is a laudatory sense of the word, as when an inquiry that is rigorous, methodical and open to argument is described as "scientific." In this sense, history, political theory and theology can be as scientific as astronomy. But there is the other, more popular sense of the word, which refers to "what is done in the natural sciences" as opposed to other studies. When the two meanings are mixed up, it is inevitable that the methods peculiar to the natural sciences (observation, theory formation, laboratory experimentation and so on) are praised as being scientific and the only intellectually respectable methods to deal with any subject matter. Indeed the expressions *rational* and *scientific* come to be identified in the popular mind. All other knowledge depends, more or less, on prejudice, emotion, superstition, myth or whatever, and as such is inferior in trustworthiness to scientific knowledge. Because the scientist is engaged in a superior activity, he or she should receive special admiration and respect in society. Rudolf Carnap, a leading figure in the Vienna Circle that developed after the First World War, provides us with a typical statement of this position: "When we say that scientific knowledge is unlimited, we mean that *there is no question whose answer is in principle unattainable by science*."[3]

This way of thinking seems to have first emerged with the "positivism" of August Comte in the early nineteenth century and later in the circle of naturalists who gathered around T. H. Huxley, a great defender of Darwin and one who applied Darwin's ideas of natural selection to human society. Comte sought to establish a "scientific-humanist" church and, ironically, it was not Paris but Calcutta that witnessed the first community of his religion of humanity "with its full paraphernalia of man-oriented rituals."[4] The group around Huxley in Britain, which included Herbert Spencer and Francis Galton, also organized themselves into a "Church Scientific," with the avowed intent of attacking and undermining the credibility of the Church of England. The Church Scientific organized "lay sermons" on scientific subjects, dressed in gowns imitative of the clergy, set up Sunday Lecture Societies to compete with the Church of England Sunday schools, sang hymns to "Nature" at mass meetings and distributed pamphlets and tracts which proclaimed scientific naturalism and denounced Christianity as the chief obstacle to scientific progress. Even buildings set up as monuments to science, such as the Natural History Museum in London, were designed as secular cathedrals. A whole new "history" of science was written, now regarded as utterly worthless (save for the light it sheds on the motives of the writers and their social setting), to show that science and religion had always been bitter enemies, with Mother Nature replacing God, and Copernicus, Galileo and Darwin assuming a heroic status as the knight-saints of the modern world. Thus a new mythology was created. The idolization of science, with its new priestly class of professional scientists, was now complete.[5]

Comte's positivist legacy seems to have survived in the thought of Jawaharlal Nehru, India's first prime minister. Born into an eminent Brahmin family and educated in the elite British institutions of Harrow and Cambridge, Nehru's vision for India was shaped by the Fabian socialism and progressive Enlightenment idealism that he absorbed in his youth. Addressing the Indian Institute of Science in 1960, Nehru asserted that "it is science *alone* that can solve the problems of hunger and poverty, of insanitation and literacy, of superstition and tradition, of vast resources running to waste, of a rich country inhabited by starving people. . . . The future belongs to science and to those who make friends with science." The contrast Nehru draws between "science," on the one hand, and "superstition and tradition" (note the assumed link), on the other, was basic to his secularist program for India. Like so many nonscientists of his time (and ours), the incompatibility between science and religion was simply taken for granted. Science was a new moral force, the bearer of secular humanist values for a secular age. Observe how Nehru called on all Indians not just to use science but to "make friends with science."

Nehru and his technocratic advisers' faith in science issued in centralized economic planning, heavy investment in large industrial enterprises (including civil nuclear reactors) and the development of nuclear-weapons capability as a means to enhancing India's status and power in the West-dominated world of realpolitik. From its inception under the leadership of Nehru's friend, the brilliant and ambitious physicist, Homi Bhabha, the Indian nuclear program was military as well as civilian. The founders of India's Atomic Energy Authority welcomed the options its military dimension gave to India. They did this in 1948—before the communist victory in China and long before any military threat from China or any other nation was publicly recognized.[7]

The philosopher Mary Midgley ponders:

Supposing we were to ask Nehru: can you really rely on science alone? Aren't you also going to need good laws, effective administrators, honest and intelligent politicians, good new customs to replace the old ones, perhaps even a sensitive understanding of the traditions that you mean to sweep away? Might you not even need to know a good deal of history and anthropology before you start on your destructive cleansing of tradition? Now Nehru knows of course, that he is going to need all these things. But he is assuming that all are included in what he means by science. He includes in "science" the whole world-view which he takes to lie behind it, namely, the decent, humane, liberal attitude out of which it has actually grown. . . . He expects that the scientific spirit will include within it wise and benevolent use of those discoveries. He is certainly not thinking of science as something likely to produce industrial pollution, or refined methods of torture, or opportunities for profiteering, or a concentration on weaponry, or overuse of chemicals on farms, or computer-viruses, or irresponsible currency speculation made possible by the latest computers, or the wholesale waste of resources on gadgetry.[8]

For much of the twentieth century, in the "developing" world no less than the "developed," the word *scientific* was constantly invoked in this value-laden sense. It represented not so much a particular body of knowledge as a political ideology. Policymakers, industrialists and academics who claimed that we "live in a scientific age" did not just mean an age that used science. They meant, as Midgley puts it, "an age that is guided by science, an age that, in some way, chooses its ideals as well as its medicines and its breakfast foods on grounds provided by scientific research. This new system was certainly not seen as value-free but as a moral signpost that could take the place of religion."[9]

Sometimes this program is stated explicitly and in lofty language, as when the sociobiologist Edward Wilson wrote some thirty years ago:

> I consider the scientific ethos superior to religion. . . . The core of scientific materialism is the evolutionary epic. . . . The evolutionary epic is probably the best myth we will ever have. It can be adjusted until it is as close to truth as the human mind is constructed to judge the truth. And if that is the case, the mythopoeic requirements of the mind must somehow be met by scientific materialism. . . . Scientific materialism is the only mythology that can manufacture great goals from the sustained pursuit of pure knowledge.[10]

Wilson is perceptive in recognizing that it takes new myths (large-scale, imaginative stories) to sustain or rejuvenate a political culture. But this conversion of a biological theory (evolution by natural selection) into an all-encompassing worldview (scientific materialism) is what, understandably, provokes a hostile rejection of the theory by religious fundamentalists in the United States and elsewhere. Creationism and evolutionism are simply mirror images of each other.[11] The former reduces the Christian doctrine of creation to the level of a scientific account of chronological origins, and the latter elevates the biological theory of evolution into a total worldview. Paradoxically, creationists and evolutionists have more in common than they each realize:

both work within a "universe-as-machine" picture of the world, so that God's relationship with the world can only be conceived in the form of engineer-type interventions which have to be scientifically inexplicable.*

Darwin himself stressed that the concept of natural selection was strictly a biological one, and even in biology he steadily rejected the claim that it was an all-embracing explanation. He reemphasized this point strongly in the sixth edition of *The Origin of Species:*

> As my conclusions have lately been much misrepresented, and it has been stated that I attribute the modification of species exclusively to natural selection, I may be permitted to remark that in the first edition of this work, and subsequently, I placed in a most conspicuous position—namely at the close of the Introduction—the following words: "I am convinced that natural selection has been the main, but not the exclusive, means of modification." This has been of no avail. Great is the power of steady misrepresentation.[12]

[Evolution is an indisputable fact of life. Darwin's formulation of the mechanisms of evolutionary change, combined with twentieth-century discoveries in genetics and molecular biology, accounts for both the astonishing diversity and interconnectedness of all living beings on the earth. However, when it comes to interpreting and narrating the details of evolution, there is much less agreement and often acrimonious debate.[13] An ultra-Darwinist orthodoxy identifies evolutionary change almost exclusively with random genetic mutations and contingency. Biological forms and behavior are what they are purely by happenstance. Any notion of *telos* or progress in the unfolding story is mere illusion. In recent years, several biologists, as well as physicists and mathematicians, have challenged this received wisdom.] They have pointed

---

*This is what has often been called "the god-of-the-gaps": "God" is invoked to explain the gaps in our contemporary knowledge of the world. So as the gaps are reduced, this "God" shrinks. I must humbly confess that, while I welcome the way the so-called intelligent design (ID) movement in the United States exposes the hollow pretensions of Wilson-type scientific materialism, I cannot see how it is much more than a return to the old god-of-the-gaps approach to understanding creation. To anticipate what follows in the main body of the text, there is no "natural world" and "designed world," but one world, a creation, that has to be understood at different levels of meaning. What a scientist may call "natural processes" or "natural laws" are the expression of God's normal way of working. Medieval theologians adopted a sophisticated understanding of multiple causality (efficient, formal, final) that both atheistic scientists and ID advocates seem to have lost.

out that most mutations are harmful and maladaptive, and that holistic, directional principles of biological organization (hitherto little understood) must also be at work. Simon Conway Morris, for example, who is professor of evolutionary paleobiology at Cambridge University, draws our attention to the well-known phenomenon of evolutionary "convergence," namely, the recurring tendency for biological organization to "navigate" toward the same solutions for particular "needs."[14] "Not all is possible," observes Morris, "options are limited, and different starting points converge repeatedly on the same destinations. . . . The 'landscape' of biological form, be it at the level of proteins, organisms, or social systems, may in principle be almost infinitely rich, but in reality the number of 'roads' through it may be much, much more restricted."[15]

Moreover, the origin of life itself remains a scientific mystery. There is no reason to doubt that life emerged by natural means, but the details of that process (how inanimate organic molecules bring about animate matter) remain stubbornly elusive.[16] We know that all life is underpinned by a simple array of building blocks: principally, the five nucleotides that comprise DNA (and RNA), and twenty-odd amino acids that when strung in chains form the proteins. The entire story of evolution is seemingly encapsulated within this molecular substratum. However, we know very little about the links between the latter and a particular living organism. Again, contrary to received wisdom, recent genomic mapping studies have revealed that the overall quantity of DNA an organism possesses bears little relationship to its complexity. Single-celled organisms may contain more DNA than humans. A simple worm, with a simple body plan and a fixed number of cells, has more genes than the fruit fly (Drosophila) with its compound eyes, gyroscopic stabilizers and complex brain with the ability for memory and courtship.[17] Claims in popular science books for the primacy of the gene have distorted biology.

Sociobiologists, whose studies of animal behavior are intended to breakdown the narrow, exclusivist humanism that denies our oneness with the rest of nature, often end up attributing human characteristics to the insects or rodents that they study. Words like *blind*, *altruism* and *selfishness* are initially used in a strictly technical way—the latter, for example, when referring to genes means something like "able to be selected alone." The authors, however, move back and forth between this technical meaning in biology and the everyday usage of the word. So Richard Dawkins begins his most famous book, *The Selfish Gene*, with the assertion that "we are survival machines—robot vehicles blindly programmed to preserve the selfish molecules known as genes. . . . We and all other animals are machines created by our genes." But very soon this "selfishness" of the genes takes on a moral quality. Dawkins writes as if the genes were personally motivated by selfishness, even qualifying it with words like *ruthless*, and warns his reader that this motive— "selfishness" in the ordinary moral sense—is part of our human nature that needs to be resisted: "If you wish, as I do, to build a society in which individuals co-operate generously and unselfishly towards a common good, you can expect little help from biological nature. Let us try to teach generosity and altruism, because we are *born selfish*."[18] This advice is repeated solemnly in the last paragraph of his book.

These anthropomorphic sleights of hand are not simply bad arguments. They have an obvious dishonesty about them, preying upon wider social and moral understandings in which the science is embedded, while claiming superiority for science as a worldview. Dawkins, having spent page after page trying to persuade us that we are nothing but gene machines, whose sole purpose for existence is to replicate our DNA and pass it on to our offspring, ends with a passionate appeal to ignore the Darwinist picture when it comes to the ordering of human affairs. He summons us to defy the tyranny of our genes and to cultivate "pure and disinterested altruism." But why should we rebel? And from where do we derive countervalues? And, if we are able to rebel, does not that prove that there are other purposes for our existence than the transmission of DNA? No answers are ever given.

It is a striking and curious fact that as twentieth-century physics, the archetypal exact science, decisively turned away from the crude materialism and reductionistic views of reality advocated on its behalf in the late nineteenth century, biologists such as Dawkins, Wilson and Francis Crick seem to be stuck in an outdated metaphysics. Human beings and all other living organisms seem to have been reduced to their genes, and genetic determinism is the new myth in town. Yet any decent biologist without an ideological ax to grind knows full well that genes can do nothing on their own. DNA is an inert molecule that only works when part of living cells. As the biologist Steven Rose explains:

> Far from being isolated in the cell nucleus, magisterially issuing orders by which the rest of the cell is commanded, genes . . . are in constant dynamic exchange with their cellular environment. What brings DNA to life, what gives it meaning is the cellular environment in which it is embedded. . . . Genetic theorists with little biochemical understanding have been profoundly misled by the metaphors that Crick provided in describing DNA (and RNA) as "self-replicating" molecules or replicators, as if they could do it all by themselves. But they aren't and they can't. . . . You may leave RNA and DNA for as long as you like in a test-tube and they will remain inert: they certainly won't make copies of themselves. . . . The functioning cell, as a unit, constrains the properties of its individual components. The whole has primacy over its parts.[19]

Overlapping with sociobiology, an entire new branch of psychology has emerged, evolutionary psychology, which atomizes the human mind itself into a string of separate molecules and seeks to correlate particular genes with particular kinds of human behavior. Genetic mutations plus adaptive success in our primate past are weaved together into a just-so story of how every human activity from adultery to warfare has arisen (but, not so far, to my knowledge, evolutionary psychology). The cultural determinism of anthropologists and the economic determinism of crude Marxists have now been replaced by the genetic determinism of some evolutionary psychologists. To believe that our genetic heritage is not simply a prerequisite for our reasoning but actually determines the content of that reasoning is to be plunged back into the prescientific fatalism from which Nehru wanted to liberate us.[20] It is hard to exaggerate the implausibility of such reductive approaches to understanding human reality. All that is most profound and intriguing is trivialized or ignored. This approach to complex problems is typified by the story of the man who lost his keys and was seen searching for them under a streetlight. When asked whether this was where he had dropped them he answered, "No, but this is where the light is."

Why can we not accept that evolution accounts for some features of human life but cannot explain others—and that this need not surprise us, given that human beings are underdetermined by their biological heritage? Indeed, what are most intriguing and fascinating about human behavior are precisely those aspects that distinguish us from the ant colonies, vampire bats and chimpanzees regularly studied by sociobiologists and ethologists. We seem to be the only animals around who inspect our anatomical parts and physiological functions—and laugh. ⌣ lol

The assault on human freedom and responsibility also stems from some sections of the glamorous discipline of brain science. But here it is our neurones and their linkages that have replaced humans as the principal actors in the story. Colin Blakemore, in a book revealingly titled *The Mind Machine*, states with astonishing boldness:

> The human brain is a machine which alone accounts for all our actions, our most private thoughts, our beliefs. It creates the states of consciousness and the sense of self. It makes the mind. . . . To choose a spouse, a job, a religious creed—or even to choose to rob a bank—is the peak of a causal chain that runs back to the origin of life and down to the nature of atoms and molecules. . . . [W]e feel ourselves, usually, to be in control of our actions, but that feeling is itself a product of our brain, whose machinery has been designed, on the basis of its functional utility, by means of natural selection. . . . It seems to me to make no sense (in scientific terms) to try to distinguish sharply between acts that result from conscious intention and those that are pure reflexes or that are caused by disease or damage to the brain.[21]

Nowhere does Blakemore attempt to explain how natural selection could "design, on the basis of its functional utility" a capacity which has absolutely no effect on our behavior, nor how it could then delude us into supposing that it did have such an effect. It is mere "handwaving," a habit developed into a fine art form, especially among those in the fields of evolutionary psychology and cognitive science. It is extremely revealing to observe how, in much of the literature, "natural selection" is personified, taking on the role of the seventeenth-century Cosmic Designer. Perhaps the implications of an impersonal, atheistic universe are existentially unbearable.

The human brain is often referred to as the most complex item in the universe. It is common sense, though, that brains only exist by themselves in laboratory jars on the shelf of autopsy rooms. There they are simply inert slabs of pinkish-gray meat. An active, functioning brain is part of a living body, and a living body is part of a society, and a society is a part of a wider, living world. It is such living persons who act, and every parent, schoolteacher, lawmaker, jury and judge knows that there are important distinctions to be drawn between actions for which persons are to be held responsible and those for which they are not. Of course it is true that this border line is not sharp, but it exists. We do not hold seriously brain-damaged people responsible for their actions, because, in their case, the agent's thoughts do not provide an adequate explanation for his actions. The latter can only be explained causally, by invoking neural processes in the way that Blakemore does.

So we must not confuse claims about brains with claims about persons. It is not brains but people—conscious cognitive agents—who think and make decisions, freely or otherwise, while their brains go through the corresponding changes. The analytical philosopher Jerry Fodor is even more blunt in challenging the handwaving of cognitive scientists and evolutionary psychologists:

> There isn't one, *not one*, instance where it's known what pattern of neural connectivity realizes a certain cognitive content, innate or learned, in either the infant's nervous system or the adult's. To be sure, our brains must somehow register the contents of our mental states. The trouble is: Nobody knows how—by what neurological means—they do so. Nobody can look at the patterns of connectivity (or of anything else) in a brain and figure out whether it belongs to somebody who knows algebra, or who speaks English, or who believes that Washington was the Father of his country. By the same token, nobody can look at an infant's brain and tell from the neurological evidence whether it holds any or all of these beliefs innately. The sum and substance is that we would all like our cognitive models to be brainlike because we all believe, more or less, that one thinks with one's brain. But wishing won't make them so, and you can't make them so by proclamation either. Nobody knows how to make a brainlike cognitive model, classical or connectivist, because *nobody knows how the cognitive brain works.*[22]

If our everyday belief that our conscious, deliberative efforts do make a difference to ourselves and to the world is really an illusion, like our belief in the solidity of tables or the rising of the sun, we have no basis for confidence in our powers of reasoning. We may as well give up scientific research altogether. Academics whose work is denounced for plagiarism or superficiality do not usually answer their critics by blaming their neurons. If we really believed Blakemore's picture of human agency, we have no grounds on which to either praise or criticize scientists for their efforts. We should not be rewarding them with doctorates, professorships and Nobel Prizes, since the conscious effort they put into their work is not their own. Instead of paying Blakemore his book royalties, perhaps his publishers should have injected his brain with euphoric, hallucinogenic drugs. Whenever scientists exempt their own work from the world picture they advance, we can be pretty sure they don't believe it themselves. So why should we?

TWO WIDESPREAD MYTHS

From science as ideology or dominant social myth, let us turn to two more erroneous views about the practice of science that are still widespread.

Science as encouraging an atheistic worldview. There is a persistent belief, often advocated by popular science writers such as the ones I have cited, that developments in modern science not only challenge notions of human freedom and uniqueness but are also hostile to the entire theistic—especially Christian worldview, which has historically undergirded that conviction of human significance. This belief is deeply ironic. For the practice of science itself is primarily a great act of faith. To devote one's life to scientific research requires some basic assumptions, namely, (1) that there is a real world outside our minds, and that world is structured in an orderly and intelligible way; (2) that this rational order is contingent, it cannot be deduced in advance by logical reasoning but has to be discovered, thus calling for a basic posture of humility before the world whose rationality we seek to articulate through our theories and experiments; and (3) that the intelligibility of the universe is accessible to the human mind: our epistemic abilities, though not unlimited, are adequate to this task.

The very success of science has hidden from view the radical nature of this last assumption. For, materially speaking, humans are microscopic specks of dust on a very ordinary planet revolving around an average-sized star in a remote corner of a galaxy that comprises a hundred billion stars and is itself only one among a similar number of galaxies. And if the geological and neo-Darwinian theories concerning the formation of the earth and the emergence of life on earth give us a reliable picture of what has happened on our planet, then human life is indeed a very recent event on a universal time scale. Some astronomers and biologists proclaim that these discoveries have "put man in his place," and they pour scorn on the traditional Christian emphasis on a human being's intrinsic value and distinctiveness. For instance, the astrophysicist Chandra Wickramasinghe, in an attempt to show that modern cosmology is a vindication of Buddhist philosophy, once wrote: "The sobering lesson of astronomy, a lesson that still continues to unfold, is that our planet and humans upon it are truly insignificant on a cosmic scale. Our egocentric, ethnocentric and anthropocentric interests must surely pale into total insignificance in a cosmic context."[23]

Supposing we were to come across a magnificent diamond ring on an immense beach, buried among tons of sand. Is it reasonable to conclude that that solitary ring has no value because of its rarity? Those who seem to delight in belittling human significance commit the childish error of confusing size and age with value or importance; but they also fail to see that astronomy and evolutionary theory themselves are products of that same insignificant human mind! To use human theories to attack human significance is to destroy the plausibility of those same theories. Why believe in the products of the human mind, such as cosmology and neo-Darwinian evolution, if the mind itself is a chimera or mere quirk of chance? A hundred years ago G. K. Chesterton pointed out, with characteristic pungency, "Evolution is either an innocent scientific description of how certain earthly things came about; or, if it is anything more than this, it is an attack upon thought itself. If evolution destroys anything, it does not destroy religion but rationalism."[24]

Darwin himself confessed that "with me the horrid doubt always arises whether the convictions of man's mind, which has been developed from the mind of the lower animals, are of any value or at all trustworthy. Would any one trust in the convictions of a monkey's mind, if there are any convictions in such a mind?"[25] Surely the very success of science itself bears eloquent testimony to the significance of human thought. As the mathematician Blaise Pascal reminded his seventeenth-century colleagues: "Through space the universe grasps me and swallows me up like a speck. But through thought I grasp it."[26] Paul Davies, an Australian theoretical physicist and prolific writer for lay audiences, observes that "The very fact that the universe is creative, and that the laws have permitted complex structures to emerge and develop to the point of consciousness—in other words, that the universe has organized its own self-awareness is for me powerful evidence that there is 'something going on' behind it all. The impression of design is overwhelming."[27]

A common objection to this is that, even if there were an intelligent and purposeful divine Creator, he is wasteful and indifferent to human life, since he has brought into existence a universe that is so vast and so old. But what cosmologists have discovered in recent years is that the universe needs to be this vast and this old for elements such as carbon and oxygen to be synthesized, and so for carbon-based life forms (the only life we know) to be able to emerge. Size and age are related in an expanding universe. The biochemist Denis Alexander points out,

> If the universe were the size of our solar system, then it would last for only one hour. Even if the universe contained as much as a single galaxy, such as our own Milky Way, containing "only" 100 billion stars, instead of the 1000 billion galaxies that it in fact contains, it would have expanded only for about a month. Our universe needs its 10^{22} stars in order for us to exist. As we look up into the night sky, the vastness of its myriad stars and galaxies should remind us of how small we are, but the fact remains that without those stars we would not exist.[28]

really?
if true
COOL!

The stars were the furnaces in which the elements that make up our human bodies were cooked. Chemically speaking, we are animated stardust.

Recently cosmologists have marveled at the delicate fine-tuning of a set of physical constants and their interdependence in the early phase of the cosmic big bang, a fine-tuning that eventually made possible the emergence of carbon-based life on the planet earth. A universe that, when it was only a million millionth of a second old, was just a hot soup of elementary particles,

has now given birth to artists, political revolutionaries and scientists. This
hardly suggests purposelessness, that we are accidental byproducts of the
cosmic process. The late Stephen Jay Gould was fond of pointing to the contingency of evolutionary history—if you replayed the tape of life again, said
Gould, then you would end up with a very different scenario. Not so, argues
Simon Conway Morris. The ubiquity of evolutionary convergence means that
if you replay the tape of life again, things are going to look pretty similar. The
emergence of human intelligence "is a near-inevitability."[29] Morris notes:

> What we do see through geological time is the emergence of more com-
> plex worlds. . . . [W]hen within the animals we see the emergence of
> larger and more complex brains, sophisticated vocalizations, echoloca-
> tion, electrical perception, advanced social systems including eusocial-
> ity, viviparity, warm-bloodedness, and agriculture—all of which are
> convergent—then to me that sounds like progress.[30]

This calls into question the assumption that the human is merely an accidental and insignificant twig that sprang out of the tree of life.

Mind and personhood are not merely froth on the surface of matter, rather
they are central to the unfolding story of the universe.[31] The multilayered
texture of reality is wholly intelligible within a theological account of creation. God is not a god of the gaps and the edges of explanation, nor did
God's creative activity cease fourteen billion years ago. If God is truly God
then he is the God of the whole show. An evolutionary world understood
theologically is a world enabled by the Creator to "make itself," to explore
its creaturely potentialities. The astonishing fruitfulness and novelty in the
world is the gradual unfolding of a complex interplay between chance and
necessity, both built into the fabric of reality by the Creator.

The fact that science is possible is itself a fact that points us beyond science. Even when we use mathematics to unlock the secrets of the physical
universe, something very strange is happening. For these mathematical patterns are abstract human creations conjured up by human thought. Time and
time again the breakthroughs in fundamental science have occurred because
someone has chosen to trust a theory simply because of its elegance and simplicity from a mathematical point of view, and then discovered that it does

indeed generate empirically successful results in the physical world around us. This "unreasonable effectiveness of mathematics" (a famous phrase of the Nobel laureate Eugene Wigner) is a source of wonder to many philosophically inclined mathematicians and physicists.

The science journalist Timothy Ferris poses the question:

> Why then does science work? The answer is that nobody knows. It is a complete mystery—perhaps the complete mystery—why the human mind should be able to understand anything at all about the wider universe. . . . Perhaps it is because our brains evolved through the working of natural law that they somehow resonate with natural law. . . . But the mystery, really, is not that we are at one with the universe, but that we are so to some degree at odds with it, different from it, and yet can understand something about it. Why is this so?[32]

As Ferris observes, evolutionary psychology will not help. It may well be true that if there was no congruence between the workings of our minds and the way things really are we would have perished long ago in the evolutionary struggle. But what counts for adaptive cognitive strategies of survival relate to the world of our everyday experience (that is, the world of gravity and pain, rocks and trees). Euclidean geometry, arithmetic and simple mechanics can help in coping with that world. But we are not talking at this mundane level. We are dealing here with counterintuitive theories about the behavior of the subatomic world and of vast galaxies at distances we cannot even imagine, with strange entities such as black holes, gluons and quarks all predicted by abstract and sophisticated mathematical ideas. How can Lie algebras, Hilbert spaces, gauge fields and string theories be mere spinoffs from our evolutionary adaptation? Even the dream of people like Stephen Hawking to have a mathematical "theory of everything" simply begs the question. A theory of everything, if it is to be truly a theory of everything, must include within it the most intriguing question of all: from where does the desire of Hawking-like creatures, accidentally thrown up like flotsam in an obscure part of the universe, for an explanation of everything—and their confidence of success—originate?

Why does the universe harbor a being with an insatiable desire to know?

"There is a surplus in both subjectivity and intelligence," writes John Haught, "that escapes even the Darwinian understanding that has lately become the court of final appeal in the life sciences."[33] Haught goes on to argue (contra the naturalist who believes that nature is all there is):

> While Darwinian science can go a long way toward laying out a natu-ral history that led up to the existence of our minds, it is too undersized to function as a worldview that accounts fully for why we are purpose-driven, meaning-seeking and truth-oriented beings. Darwinian ex-planations by themselves, after all, do not rule out the possibility that nature can create a kind of conscious organism that finds illusions more adaptive, than truth. In fact, since truth can often be unsettling, and obedience to it demanding, the flight into fiction could conceiv-ably be much more adaptive than facing up to facts. Some Darwinian naturalists understand religion in precisely this way. Religion is adap-tive, they claim, because it allows people to avoid facing reality even while it is giving purpose to their lives. Such a view, however, makes it all the more difficult to state in purely Darwinian terms how the naturalist's own mind came to be guided by an exceptionally pure passion for truth.[34]

The existence of such truth-seeking human minds cannot be simply a mere quirk of fate, an incidental blip in the great cosmic drama. We can choose to believe the latter, but it is hardly something that the scientific ac-count requires; rather, it is a view that derives from the wider culture that the naturalist/atheist scientist inhabits. Taken as an ultimate explanation of the world and ourselves, materialistic accounts are self-contradictory. Truth, in order to function as a value that gives meaning to the scientific enterprise and all our other pursuits of knowledge, must derive from a realm of being that transcends both nature and culture. Truth is not something we possess or construct, but that which invites our unconditional surrender.

Of course human creativity enters into all our construals of truth. But all such construals, if they are to count as truthful, transcend our minds. We are addressed by truth, invited to participate in it and to represent it in our finite ways. Truth persuades, compels, excites and gives purpose to our lives. To explain this attraction and power will require us to move beyond a naturalist worldview. The philosopher-theologian Thomas Torrance reminds us,

> Behind and permeating all our scientific activity, whether in critical analysis or in discovery, there is an elementary and overwhelming faith in the possibility of grasping the real world with our concepts, and, above all, faith in the truth over which we have no control but in the service of which our rationality stands or falls. Faith and intrinsic rationality are interlocked with one another.[35]

Now, if we are creatures made in the image of the Creator, sharing the earth with other creatures, animate and inanimate, yet called to wise dominion over it, it is not presumptuous of men and women to seek to understand their Creator's world. Both the rationality of the universe and the rationality of the scientific explorer are grounded in the ultimate rationality and faithfulness of the Creator. Therefore, given other grounds for faith in a God who is the Creator of the world, and whose character and relationship with humankind is disclosed most fully in the biblical revelation, the entire scientific enterprise becomes perfectly reasonable.

Science as inherently reductionistic. We have already encountered examples of this in the writings of Dawkins and Blakemore. It is easy to shock people who know little about science but are impressed by the prestige science and scientists enjoy with words like the following: "Morality, or more strictly, our belief in morality, is merely an adaptation put in place to further our reproductive ends."[36] Or the Nobel laureate Francis Crick's equally audacious claim, "[Science has shown that] 'you,' your joys and your sorrows, your memories and your ambitions, your sense of identity and free will, are in fact no more than the behaviour of a vast assembly of nerve cells and their associated molecules."[37] Similarly, Dawkins's well-known polemic: "We are machines built by DNA whose purpose is to make more copies of the same DNA. . . . That is exactly what we are for. We are machines for propagating DNA, and the propagation of DNA is a self-sustaining process. It is every living object's sole reason for living."[38]

Notice the language of "merely," "nothing but" or "no more" that is smuggled into what appears to be a scientific discussion. No biologist would deny that a property of all biological organisms is the passing on of DNA to their progeny. But if everything human beings do, including the quest for scientific understanding and writing books about it, is reduced to a story of DNA and nerve cells, then we are in serious trouble. As I mentioned earlier, the authors of such sensationalist remarks exempt themselves from the deterministic and reductionist view of human persons that they want their book-buying public to accept.

How much more rational and humble is the position of other scientists like Steve Jones, himself a well-known geneticist: "Science cannot answer the question that philosophers—or children—ask: why are we here, what is the point of being alive, how ought we to behave? Genetics has almost nothing to say about what makes us more than just machines driven by biology, about what makes us human. These questions may be interesting, but scientists are no more qualified to comment on them than is anyone else."[39] The illusion of omniscience is encouraged by our academic specializations. The university is a place of tribal warfare, and every academic tribe feels that the only way it can gain social recognition is by exalting itself over others. A moment's reflection will reveal the absurdity of such moves. If we liken the acquisition of knowledge to mapmaking, why regard a map that shows world climatology, for instance, as more "fundamental" than another which shows world energy distribution or world political groupings or world food production? They are all about one world, and we need all these maps and many more to understand it. What we regard as "fundamental" will depend on what particular questions we are asking.

In some branches of physical science, it makes sense to analyze separately each component or aspect of a complex phenomenon. This *methodological* reductionism can be a useful and often necessary approach to understanding. But if such a scientist were to go on to claim that the adequacy of his or her story at its own reductive level rules out other accounts that deal with the phenomenon as a whole, that would be a false move. For that would be to fall into the trap of *metaphysical* reductionism, namely, the failure to perceive the hierarchical character of reality which requires description and understanding at other levels of meaning. Even within physics, it is only the simplest phenomena (called linear systems) that can be analyzed or reduced to their individual parts. In nonlinear systems, which comprise the bulk of everyday reality, the whole is much more than the sum of its parts, and the properties of the whole are usually unpredictable and mathematically complicated. As we move to higher levels of complexity, as in self-organizing systems and living organisms, new properties emerge that require new explanatory concepts and theories which cannot be reduced to lower-level accounts. Thus it is absurd to talk of reducing human sociology to individual psychology, or psychology to biology, or biology to quantum physics.

A physicist may legitimately describe a Beethoven symphony as "a pattern of longitudinal vibrations of nitrogen, oxygen and other gas molecules that make up air," but this is of no interest to any nonphysicist and especially to a musician or musicologist. Indeed the latter will remind the physicist that he or she has quite simply missed the point of the work as a whole. This is not, however, a fault of the physicist, for the appreciation of music is outside the scope of physics. The concept of a symphony is not found in any physics textbook. But, granted that the physics-level description is true, there is a higher-level description which requires new concepts to do justice to all that is happening in the room. If, however, the physicist were to deny the musicologist's account simply on the grounds that musical concepts cannot be expressed in terms of physics, he or she would be committing the reductionist fallacy.

Similarly, an electrical engineer may explain the behavior of a computer in terms of integrated circuits and other components of its hardware. The mathematician may say that the computer is behaving in a certain way because it is being controlled by a program (software) which, let us assume, is working out the income tax returns of a company's employees. The income tax laws that determine the output of the computer cannot be reduced to the laws of electro-magnetism that determine the computer's circuitry. The two descriptions complement rather than contradict one another. Both are required, but for different purposes.

When it comes to human agency, a host of causes and conditions are necessary to bring about an action—social causes, educational causes, economic causes, political, climatic, nutritional, genetic, besides the subjective and neural angles that I have mentioned. Each of these sets of causes may partly explain the action. But none of them invalidates the others, and to ask which of them counts as the explanation in a given case depends entirely on our interests, on what we want to find out. If you asked me why the kettle on my kitchen stove is boiling, I can either answer "Because the vapor pressure has equalized with the atmospheric pressure" or "I am making a pot of tea." The second presumes the first is true (otherwise boiling does not occur) but sets the physical event within a wider matrix of human relationships and intentions.

From a theological viewpoint, our biological inheritance and embodiment is the God-given matrix within which our created freedom shall operate. It is this kind of creature that God has actually created as a human being through the evolutionary process. The mental and the physical are not two kinds of stuff but two aspects of life, two points of view—inside and outside, subjective and objective, the agent's view of why he or she performs an action and that of the psychologist who studies it. These two angles often need to be distinguished for thought. But both of them are essential and inseparable aspects of our normal experience, and we move back and forth between them. How they relate is still shrouded in deep mystery. Most scientists now acknowledge that some form of top-down causation—that is, from mind to brain, the whole affecting the individual parts—is what makes the study of the brain so complex and fascinating. The linkages between brain cells (synapses) are not genetically determined but depend profoundly on the inputs from learned experiences in the cultural environment. These create new connections or change the density of present connections. How we nurture and educate our children affects their brain circuitry.[40]

The medieval scholar Etienne Gilson reminds us that Aristotle, the philosophical father of teleological thinking, "never denied that the mechanism of Empedocles was true, but [rather] reproached him with presenting it as a total explanation of reality in the order of living beings." Gilson also points out that while it is a rare mechanist who grants that there may be final causes in nature, even rarer, "exceedingly rare—if they have ever existed—are those finalists who deny mechanism and its natural function in natural beings."[41]

The theological concept of creation is a higher-order account of reality than the cosmological and evolutionary explanations of the natural scientist. The reason we say it is a higher-order account is simply because, even as the musicologist's analysis of music assumes that the physics-level analysis is true (there would be no music if there were no molecular vibrations in the air), so to say that we are persons created in the image of God assumes that the biological-level description is valid. Our personhood is embodied in physical and biological structures, just as, to use a rough analogy, Beethoven's symphony is embodied in the complex patterns of sound waves in the air. What would happen if the air sucked out of the room? The symphony can still be performed in another place. Likewise, even when our bodies are destroyed in death, our Creator can reembody our personhood in new structures of his choosing. That is his freedom, and it is the basis of a Christian hope that is grounded in the bodily resurrection of Christ.

Finally, we have seen that students don't acquire knowledge for the first time when they start to study science. There is a whole background of knowledge, implicitly accepted, which acts like a foundation for their study. Many of the presuppositions of physical science—including the reality of the external world and of other minds, the value of intellectual inquiry, the trustworthiness of their memories and the reports of other colleagues both past and present, and much else besides—all count as knowledge, and it is only by treating this as knowledge that it becomes possible to do any science at all. The scientific community is also undergirded by shared moral values: for example, truth-telling (in work and reporting of results), the right of free expression and access to information, team work, patience, honest debate and mutual criticism, and so on. Whenever these values have been flouted (and they have, as anyone familiar with the history of science knows) the scientific world is deeply shocked. So, neither is the scientific enterprise value neutral (as some claim), nor are its values derived from science itself (as others do). It is a practice that tacitly assumes the reality of a whole range of other social practices, moral values and human ends. There is something perverse about a worldview that casts doubt on the reality of the physicist's mind or the social institutions in which he works while embracing the ideas produced by that mind.

John Haught charges such reductionist naturalists with inconsistency.

Typically they deny in their philosophy of nature what they implicitly affirm in their actual ethical and intellectual performance. For example, evolutionary naturalists clearly treat truth as a value that judges their own work, and therefore as something they did not invent. Some of them even devote their whole lives to its pursuit. It is what gets them up every morning. In effect they are serving a cause that they tacitly know will outlast them. Their implicit sense of the lastingness of truth gives continuity to their efforts and satisfaction to their careers. Like the rest of us they are grasped by truth and have submitted their minds to it. At the same time, however, some of their own writings portray truth and other values as pure creations of human minds and, ultimately, of genes. They generally fail to see the logical contradiction between their almost religious obedience to truth-telling on the one hand and their evolutionary debunking of it on the other.[42]

For John Polkinghorne, mathematical physicist and Anglican theologian, science and Christian faith are "intellectual cousins under the skin." "Both are searching for motivated belief," he writes, "Neither can claim absolutely certain knowledge, for each must base its conclusions on an interplay between interpretation and experience. In consequence, both must be open to the possibility of correction. Neither deals simply with pure fact, or with mere opinion. They are both part of the great human endeavour to understand."[43] However, when it comes to the more profound questions of life, detached scientific "objectivity" is useless. For here it is the inclination of our hearts, the openness of our wills, that shapes our beliefs and our responses. God does not merely satisfy our curiosity. The encounter with God, unlike our engagement with physical reality, not only illuminates the mind but calls for a radical commitment that reorients our lives on a different axis. "I believe in quarks," says Polkinghorne, "but the acknowledgment of their existence does not touch or threaten me in my own being. It is very different with belief in God, which has consequences for all that I do and hope for."[44]

SCIENTIFIC RESEARCH AND MORAL RESPONSIBILITY

Looking back on the heady days of the Manhattan Project (the secret U.S. project during the latter part of World War II to develop an atomic bomb), Robert Oppenheimer, its director, remarked a decade later: "When you see something that is technically sweet, you go ahead and do it and you argue about what to do about it only after you have had your technical success. That is the way it was with the atomic bomb."[45] Similarly, another physicist, Freeman Dyson comments, "Nuclear explosives have a glitter more seductive than gold to those who play with them. To command nature to release in a pint pot the energy that fuels the stars, to lift by pure thought a million tons of rock into the sky, these are exercises of the human will that produce an illusion of illimitable power."[46] It is far easier to delight in the technical aspects of our craft than to face up to tough, moral issues which call for an emotional and spiritual maturity which as scientists we may lack.

Dyson worked as a mathematician in Royal Air Force Bomber Command during World War II. "Technology has made evil anonymous," he wrote later.

> Through science and technology, evil is organized bureaucratically so that no individual is responsible for what happens. Neither the boy in the Lancaster aiming his bombs at an ill-defined splodge on the radar screen, nor the operations officer shifting papers at squadron headquarters, nor I sitting in my little office in the Operational Research Section and calculating probabilities, had any feeling of personal responsibility. None of us ever saw the people we killed. None of us particularly cared.[47]

The combination of profound creativity with moral naiveté, intellectual passion with personal and national ambition, has made science an instrument of great violence today. Ironically, side by side with its massive benefits, in the name of science more violence has been inflicted on human beings and other living creatures in the past century than in the entire history of humanity. Science is less and less a quest for understanding, a humble delight in truth. It is tied to military power and huge commercial interests. It is estimated that almost half of all scientists and engineers in the world today are involved in research connected to military interests. This represents a terrible waste of human talent, let alone of the earth's natural resources. We now possess the satellite technology to survey every square yard of our planet, but we are still unable to provide the cities of the world with safe and reliable electric power or a pollution-free public transport system. Moreover, according to a United

Nations Report from not too long ago ("Making New Technologies Work for Human Development"), "Public research, still the main source of innovation for much of what could be called poor peoples' technology, is shrinking relative to private research. Gaining access to key patented inputs—often owned by private firms and universities in industrial countries—has become an obstacle to innovation, sometimes with prohibitive costs."[48]

Since scientific research today is big business, prestigious universities around the world are reinventing themselves as corporations, and many research scientists enjoy a new status as entrepreneurs. More funds are necessary to secure top faculty, build new facilities and finance scholarships. University administrators feel they have no choice: they have to move away from the education of students to be well-informed and critical citizens; instead, they have to concentrate more on producing people who can contribute to the world of commerce. Commercial undertakings are, in the nature of the case, in it for the money. If they fail to make money, they go out of business. Their idea of truth is purely instrumental. Knowledge is now one more commodity to be traded.

Derek Bok, a former president of Harvard University, has described the damaging effects of this pervasive commercialization of science in a report on academia, *Universities in the Marketplace*.[49] The concerns of research, he argued, have become skewed toward answering questions that are concerns of industry, not of the public. Researchers working for corporate sponsors find themselves signing confidentiality agreements that limit what they can publish and when. Bok cites a couple of high profile cases where researchers were harassed by drug companies who wanted them not to publish their findings—they had their competence challenged and their research methods impugned. It was worsened by the connivance of academics and administrators who were themselves in the pay of the pharmaceutical companies. Secrecy has undermined a productive collegiality among scientists, leading to waste and inefficiency as investigators are forced to duplicate the secretive work of others. Even scientific journals are owned by publishers and scientific societies that receive huge earnings from advertising by drug companies. There are both overt and covert pressures on editors to adopt positions that favor these industries. Thus, through patents and confidentiality agreements, often publicly supported research is being turned into private wealth.

Richard Horton, the editor of the prestigious British medical journal *The Lancet*, notes that about a quarter of scientists working in medical research have some sort of financial relationship with industry. Not surprisingly, the conclusions such scientists draw from their research is closely tied to their commercial sponsorship. "Scientists who argue in favour of a particular product are more likely than their neutral or critical colleagues to possess a financial stake in the company that is funding their research or the product they are studying. And, for the most part, these conflicts of interest are not reported when research is either presented at scientific meetings or published in medical journals." Horton further observes:

> The problem is not only institutional. An extraordinary culture of gift giving now exists within scientific research, a culture that has altered the way in which new discoveries are shared and debated. Take virtually any major medical conference . . . these meetings are usually billed as scientific conferences. It is true that keynote lectures, together with symposiums at plenary sessions and parallel meetings, make up a substantial proportion of the program. But the visitor cannot help being struck by the scandalous bargain that has been made between professional societies and industry—namely, that in order for science to be reported and discussed among a professional society's membership, sponsors will be given free rein to market their products to attending physicians. The venality of those taking part in this corrupt covenant is difficult to square with a profession that is quick to squeal at the mere suggestion of government intrusion into the delivery of health care. Any claim that the science and practice of medicine are disinterested is utterly groundless.[50]

World sales of the larger pharmaceutical companies exceeds the GNP of many Third World nations. Countries in which clinical trials are now conducted are often too poor to pay for the medicines that are successfully tested and patented. And the people recruited for those trials very seldom get the kind of medical care that the participants in trials in prosperous countries can expect. The major international codes on human experimentation, including the principles proclaimed at Nuremberg in 1947 and the World Medical Association's Declaration of Helsinki in 1964, all say that the well-being of the subject should take precedence always over the needs of science or the interests of society, and that doctors must obtain "the subject's freely informed consent." But whether these codes covering the treatment of people who are the subjects of research can and should be applied in Africa and Asia has become a bitterly debated question.[51] As compensation to their subjects for enrolling in the research, should investigators be required to leave their subjects medically better off? Should the latter receive the benefits of treatment now, not in some distant future when pharmaceutical companies may, or may not, reduce the price of their drugs or vaccines so that citizens in poor countries can afford them?

Such is the intense pressure that results from the combination of massive financial investment, national prestige, media "hype" and personal vainglory that researchers are tempted to unethical practices and fraudulent claims. In March 2004, a South Korean group led by Hwang Woo-Suk reported in the prestigious journal *Science* that they had generated a human stem cell line from a cloned human embryo. In June 2005, this same group reported that they had generated eleven patient-specific stem cell lines from cloned human embryos and had dramatically improved their success rate to better than one in twenty attempts, bringing cloning into the realm of the possible for routine treatment of human medical conditions. In Korea, Hwang was hailed as a national hero and recommended for the nation's highest honors. However, the purported miracle proved to be a sham. Colleagues of Hwang raised serious concerns about his published studies. Following an investigation, it was conclusively shown in December 2005 that all of Hwang's alleged cloned stem cell lines were fakes.

The scandal surrounding Hwang raised numerous concerns about the ethics of embryonic stem cell research. Hwang had used thousands of human oocytes for his unsuccessful attempts. Since the medical risks associated with egg donation include both sterility and death, it raises serious questions about the morality of conducting basic research on human cloning. The neurobiologist Maureen Condic asks:

Given that Hwang pressured junior female colleagues into donating eggs for his research, how can the interests of female scientists be protected from such professional exploitation? Given that thousands of human eggs from more than a hundred women were used by Hwang and not even a single viable cloned human embryo resulted from this research, how can the medical risks to women entailed by this research possibly be justified?[52]

GENETIC ENGINEERING

Molecular biology and genetics have taken over from nuclear physics as the media's new "glamour science," and thousands of biotechnology firms have mushroomed almost overnight. It is widely believed that the Henry Fords and Bill Gateses of the twenty-first century will emerge from this new industry. Recombinant DNA technology offers us the prospect of changing the genetic map of living organisms to suit our own cultural, political and economic aspirations. The genetic modification of organisms, whether bacteria, plants or animals, is the fruit of the immense advances in molecular biology that have occurred over the past few decades. The technology has generated huge scientific, political and economic expectations all over the world, and the economies of countries such as Singapore and South Korea are increasingly being reorganized around the burgeoning biotech industry as the successor to information technology. Transnational pharmaceutical and agribusiness companies are staking out exclusive rights to patent genetic material taken from the Third World's forests. They are heavily lobbying governments to allow the patenting of all human, animal and plant tissue. This raises profound ethical questions which reach beyond the scientific community.[53]

Is genetic modification a continuation of the long history of human transformation of nature, or are we moving into a qualitatively different stage in our relationship with the natural world? Is the unease about genetically modified organisms expressed in many parts of the world, but especially in Europe, simply a familiar and irrational failure of nerve when faced by a new technology? Not all genetic engineering entails moving genes from one species to another. Often genetic engineering simply speeds up a process that could equally be carried out by conventional inbreeding, the essence of a biological species being that within it individuals are able to breed among themselves. The modification of yeasts to improve bread and beers has involved using the tools of genetic engineering to move genes between strains or varieties of yeast but still within the same species. Another example would be introducing an artificial gene into tomatoes to inhibit the normal gene that hastens the softening of the fruit from working, thus enabling them to stay fresh longer after being picked.

Most examples of genetic engineering, and those of most concern to the general public and professional ethicists, involve cross-species transfer of genes by scientists. Although such horizontal gene transfer does occur naturally, genetic engineering breaches species boundaries in a way that is not found in nature. Some applications have brought medical benefits. The gene in humans responsible for producing the hormone insulin has been moved into bacteria and used to produce drugs for the treatment of diabetes that arises in young people. Is there any ethical significance in the fact that bacteria confined to fermenters in pharmaceutical factories contain human genes if the final outcome is to produce life-saving drugs?[†] Why bother that pigs are being engineered genetically with human genes so that their internal organs may provide alternatives to human organs in transplant surgery? An increasing number of farm animals such as sheep and pigs are being genetically engineered for research into the production of human proteins in milk and for xenotransplantation. While genetic modification is not as advanced as the claims of its most enthusiastic advocates, there is a genuine public concern that creatures will be produced with overtly human features or human beings will give birth to creatures with nonhuman properties. Most people, not unsurprisingly, suspect that, given the enormous commercial investments at stake, what can be done technically will be done. If governments in Western countries introduce tighter regulations on such research, companies and their laboratories can always move to parts of the globe where there are less ethical scruples on the part of lawmakers, or where an educated, democratic voice is muted.

[†]Talk of "human genes" can be misleading here, as there are no strands of DNA found exclusively in the human genome, and the excision or insertion of DNA so as to replicate a human gene may not involve any actual transfer of human material.

If we argue that no sentient animal should ever be used merely as a means to the profit of another allegedly superior animal, then we would have to argue that all dairy and livestock farming should be banned. That extreme position clearly belongs to a small minority of opinion. So the realistic question concerns the nature of the harms that are inflicted on any animals and the possible justification for such harms. Harm cannot be limited to the infliction of pain or lethal disease, as in a primitively utilitarian pain-pleasure calculus of moral reasoning. The violation of species integrity or a species-specific life means that an animal is unable to live a decent life after its kind because it has been deprived of that ability, either genetically, chemically or mechanically. Whatever difficulties attach to such notions, it is an important aspect of mature moral reasoning to pay attention not only to immediate or foreseeable outcomes, but also to the agent's motivations and goals. Experiments on animals or human embryos with the motive of gaining academic kudos or making money will be clearly morally unacceptable. But more subtle are the changes in public attitudes that may be induced over a time if animals were increasingly regarded as merely tools or organ factories for human use.

In an essay titled "Biotechnology and the Yuk Factor," Mary Midgley rightly reminds us that feelings of disgust and outrage are not in themselves irrational. "Someone who does not have such feelings—someone who has merely a theoretical interest in morals, who doesn't feel any indignation or disgust and outrage about things like slavery and torture—has missed the point of morality altogether."[54] Midgley recollects how a deepening of moral sensitivity in relation to cruelty occurred in sixteenth-century Europe when "a few bold people, such as Montaigne, began to express disgust and outrage about judicial torture and the use of cruel punishments, and also about the abuse of animals. They said that these customs, which had largely been taken for granted as perfectly normal and justified before, were monstrous, unnatural, and inhuman. Because of the strength of their indignant feeling, other people listened and gradually began to agree with them. The notion of what is human took a surprising turn to include this kind of response to suffering."[55]

Feelings are an essential part of our moral life, though, of course, not an infallible guide. We need to reflect on our emotions, sorting out what springs from unfamiliarity or mere physical revulsion, such as a horror of snakes. The feeling of Yuk that carries moral weight is the sense that something is being violated, and must be distinguished from mere squeamishness. It is tied up with our intuitive sense (blunted by urban, technocratic environments) of the sacredness toward which all reality is oriented. This is difficult to discuss in scientific circles because of the widespread positivist ideology discussed earlier—namely, that scientific inquiry, proceeding by way of quantifiable observation and dealing only with efficient causal mechanisms, is the sole bearer of valid knowledge.

The main incentive for the genetic engineering of crops is the improvement to farming productivity. Scientists and agronomists claim that genetic modification of staple crops such as wheat, maize and rice (leading to high-yielding varieties such as Golden Rice) are the only way we can deal with global hunger, feeding the growing populations of the poor nations and reducing the cost of food in the rich nations. However, all these claims are made without any reference to the large body of social scientific literature on the causes of famines.[56] We know from the literature that, while raising food production is important, the principal causes of global hunger are not low farm productivity but growing landlessness, rural unemployment and the poor distribution systems for available food. India's grain silos have been bursting for the past few years and a record surplus is being built up, yet tens of millions of Indian children are undernourished and hundreds of farmers commit suicide every year. Is it possible to discuss the role of genetically modified crops in tackling global poverty without simultaneously addressing the horrendous inequities and double-standards associated with state-subsidized agribusinesses in Europe, the United States and other rich nations; or the global shift from subsistence agriculture to cash-crop farming for export markets, enforced on many poor countries by organizations such as the World Bank and the International Monetary Fund?[57]

It may be salutary to remember the famous Green Revolution of the 1960s. Certain high-yielding miracle seeds were developed by agrarian research institutes in Mexico and the Philippines, and introduced to other agricultural societies such as India. Here was a technology designed to increase local food production and so alleviate malnutrition and rural poverty. However, these seeds, being artificially nurtured, required high doses of pesticides for protection against pathogens; they also needed good irrigation and high inputs of fertilizer. Most agricultural countries are economically poor and have to import fertilizers and pesticides. They also had to rely on foreign experts for advice and on seed banks owned by multinational institutes. So the import bills increased more rapidly than did agricultural exports. Moreover, the vast majority of subsistence farmers could not afford fertilizers and pesticides, nor did they have adequate irrigation facilities for their small holdings; so they sold their land to the wealthier farmers. This resulted in more landlessness and worsening rural poverty.

To whom did the Green Revolution bring a lucrative harvest? The Indian writer Claude Alvares is blunt in his answer: "To those who designed the project, including American private foundations like Ford and Rockefeller; multinational corporations, who manufactured the seeds, equipment and nutrients; the banks who provided the credit and certain categories of very large farmers."[58] It is with hindsight that we realize that the alleviation of famine and rural poverty has much more to do with land reform, cooperative ownership of technology and the purchasing power of the poor than with the raising of national food productivity.

A handful of powerful corporations such as Cargill, Ciba Geigy, Dow, Monsanto and Zeneca dominate agricultural research today, and they also control the global seed and agricultural chemical markets. Industrial patents originally designed to protect inventions are now being used to grant ownership of genetic material and seeds to private corporations. Patents on germplasm can be imposed on every farmer in every country in the world, from the Chinese peasant small farmer to the large mechanized farmers of the American prairies. Many of the seeds developed or modified by American corporations were collected in the southern hemisphere, but no royalties are ever paid to local farmers in that hemisphere nor claimed by their governments. But when those farmers use germplasm over which American seed companies have patents, or even seek to reuse the seeds in new plantings, they are immediately accused by the U.S. government of piracy and of violating intellectual property rights.

From a business point of view, the practice by farmers of saving and exchanging seeds is a threat to sustaining profitability. So a number of technologies have been developed to make farmers continually dependent on the seed-manufacturing companies. These all make use of a recombinant gene that has a "promoter" region (the region of the gene that determines where, when, for how long and how fast a gene expresses itself) that is sensitive to an externally applied chemical. This gene is used as a chemical switch or trigger. The activation or dormancy of the gene can be used to bring about sterility, so forcing farmers to buy either a fresh crop of seeds or the chemicals that switch off the genes that inhibit germination. Other techniques are available to produce seedless fruits, induce a plant to kill itself, control the genes that confer resistance to pests and disease, or trigger toxic substances in plant cells that makes the harvest inedible. The technologies are collectively referred to as Genetic Use Restriction Technologies (GURTS) or Technology Protection Systems (TPS). The development of these technologies came to public attention since their patent applications were registered at the World Intellectual Property Office with a list of designated states in which the inventor intends to get patents.

The environmental theologian Michael Northcott envisions a different world where "Genetic engineering would be used to enhance the sustainability and lower intensity of agriculture, to reduce soil erosion, enhance biodiversity, increase tree cover in arable farm regions, reduce water usage and eliminate chemical dependence."[59] Such a vision would require that those involved in biotechnology research would be helped (perhaps by public funding) to service this form of agriculture by developing seeds which were less dependent on chemical inputs, which could be intercropped to take advantage of natural cycles for replenishing the soil between plantings, and which had a hardy resistance to the vagaries of climates and pests. Similarly it would be possible to breed animals that had low requirements for drugs and special mechanical care systems, which could live in the open air for most of the year while still producing high-quality meat.

The American conservationist and poet Wendell Berry castigates our destruction of nature as not just "bad stewardship, or stupid economics, or a betrayal of family responsibility" but as the "most horrid blasphemy." "It is flinging God's gifts into His face, as if they were of no worth beyond that assigned to them by our destruction of them."[60] Berry sees the deleterious effects of mechanized, chemical agriculture on rural communities, wild species and the soil as the product of bad work, work which dishonors God, work which lacks awareness of the divine origin and destiny of the world and of the extent to which all the creatures of God participate by their very being and continued existence in the life of God.

According to the Christian biblical tradition, the earth and all its creatures belong to the Lord (Psalm 24:1). The ancient covenant people of God were taught repeatedly that they were guests in the land on which they dwelled, and only when they saw the land not as a commodity for commercial exchange but a community to which they belonged would they use the land rightly. Respect for the natural order, an order not alien to human beings but a shared realm of creaturely dependence, flows out of this recognition that we receive the world as a gift, not as a possession. Human worship and prayer is part of a cosmic act of praise that the whole creation, consciously or unconsciously, offers to its Creator. "All things affirm Thee in living; the bird in the air, both the hawk and the finch; the beast on the earth, both the wolf and the lamb; the worm in the soil and the worm in the belly."[61]

Traditionally, Christian theology has described human responsibility toward the nonhuman creation in terms of stewardship. The weakness of this language is that it suggests, in many contexts, an image of humanity as separate from nature and all embodiment. It can perpetuate the corresponding image of an active humanity and an inert nonhuman property (natural resources) awaiting *management*, even *reconstruction* through continual human intervention. It can downplay the wildness of nature and the many biblical passages that speak of God's independent relation with nonhuman nature. We care about wild nature because it is an integral and constitutive part of who we are as human beings. It is our metaphorical mother. Our fundamental attitude toward nature is one of gratitude, recognizing that our dominion (as the unique bearer of the *imago Dei*) is exercised as part of a "fellowship of creation," hierarchically ordered toward the fulfilment of God's purposes.[62] Thus our use of nonhuman nature is subordinated to the deep telos of creation and the telos of our own true being which centers on loving mutuality. We can use animals for medical experimentation that has a therapeutic purpose, for us or for them, provided we treat them decently, respectfully and not inflict on them gratuitous pain. Humanity is part and parcel of nature while exercising dominion over it, and nonhuman nature finds its eschatological fulfillment in the redemption of humanity.

From this perspective, genetic engineering at its most rampant and manipulative expresses an instrumental approach that sacralizes itself. It treats animals, plants and natural processes purely as commodities that serve human interests, narrowly defined. Therefore, as long as we remain strictly within the stewardship paradigm of understanding our relation to the material order, whether human or nonhuman, we may fail to perceive how the techniques of genetic modification, taken as a whole and promoted in a global consumerist culture by powerful commercial interests, radically alter our view of nature and therefore of human nature itself. The colossal scale on which this whole enterprise is proceeding, the way it distracts public policy from other fruitful avenues of exploration, the rate at which money flows into it rather than in other directions, all seem to imply a religious belief that all social problems are amenable to this kind of biochemical solution.

THE RETURN OF EUGENICS

The origin of modern eugenics can be traced to Francis Galton, a cousin of Charles Darwin, who coined the word in 1883. For Galton, eugenics had to do with "using our understanding of the laws of heredity to improve the stock of humankind." He held that, while we may disagree about morality, "all creatures would agree that it was better to be healthy than sick, vigorous than weak, well fitted than ill-fitted for their part in life." Eugenics seeks "to give the more suitable races or strains of blood a better chance of prevailing over the less suitable than they otherwise would have had."[63]

By the beginning of the twentieth century we find eugenic views widely defended by the ablest advocates of the so-called humanist movement.[64] Sidney Webb, H. G. Wells, Bertrand Russell, John Maynard Keynes and George Bernard Shaw all supported eugenic policies, Shaw even calling for a "eugenics religion." Leonard Darwin, Darwin's son, who was chair of the London eugenics society from 1911 to 1928, spoke of eugenics as giving "life new meaning and purpose." Darwin himself, who was a gentle, rather squeamish man, deeply sensitive to suffering in the world, would have been shocked by the uses to which the evolutionary metaphors would be put, but Social Darwinists could legitimately claim that Darwin himself was their forebear. His book *The Origin of Species* carried as its full title *On the Origin of Species by Natural Selection, or The Preservation of Favoured Races in the Struggle for Life*. From its publication in 1859 the alternative title was used to give scientific support to the views prevalent among mid-nineteenth-century British colonial administrators, businessmen and settlers that it was natural for "favoured races" to displace "savage" or "lower" ones. Darwin himself believed that aboriginal people would become naturally extinct and was skeptical of Christian missionary attempts to improve their living conditions.

By the late 1920s twenty-four states in the United States had passed enforced sterilization laws (affecting poor black people or those with learning difficulties). The 1924 Johnson Act, which selectively restricted immigration, was used in the 1930s to turn back boats of refugees from Nazi Germany. Such eugenic policies were regarded as liberal, progressive and the embodiment of scientific planning. The most comprehensive sterilization law ever framed, in Nazi Germany on July 14, 1933, was based on the American model. Disabled people were the first victims of Hitler's extermination policies. A decree of August 18, 1939, instructed that all children under the age of three with disabilities be killed by lethal injection or excessive doses of medication. What began with babies ended up with murder of teenagers and adults for "defects" as varied as schizophrenia, depression, mental retardation, dwarfism, paralysis, epilepsy, sometimes even delinquency, perversion, alcoholism and antisocial behavior. The move from here to the extermination of an entire "antisocial" race, as the Nazis viewed the Jews, wasn't such a dramatic leap.

Eugenics has become respectable again. Early eugenicists appealed to the then socially prevalent ideas of duty and self-sacrifice to encourage healthy individuals to marry and propagate abundantly. The new eugenics claims the virtue of relieving suffering, of respecting private choice and expressing compassion. In a liberal, capitalist context, where market choice and self-determination are the only acceptable public values, the new eugenics is presented as a benevolent extension of the sovereignty of the consumer. "A world in which prenatal screening followed by abortion of children diagnosed with defects has become a routine part of medical care for pregnant women," writes the ethicist Gilbert Meilaender, "that is to say, our world is one into which eugenics enters not through government programs but precisely as government removes itself from what is seen as entirely a private choice."[65]

Gene therapy can be employed according to traditional medical practice, correcting defective genes in the embryo. While pre-implantation genetic diagnostic (PGD) techniques were first developed to detect embryos with rare and severe genetic disorders, such as Huntington's chorea, as the technology becomes cheaper and more powerful its range of application will widen. The sheer availability of the technology can put enormous social pressure on couples and doctors to weed out embryos and fetuses considered abnormal by the standards of their society. Whereas the old eugenics selected the "right" parents, the new genetics aims to select the "right" offspring. However, as Kendall Soulen points out, the contrast between the old and the new eugenics must not be overdrawn:

> Galton himself hoped that eugenic goals would be achieved through parental choice. The essence of Galton's eugenic principle is not coercion (nor, for that matter classism or racism) but *selection*, preferring the existence of some individuals over others on the basis of desired or undesired traits. Seen from this perspective, *the new eugenics embodies the core principle of eugenics much more successfully than did the old*. It replaces clumsy and indirect modes of selection with vastly more powerful and direct ones. In this respect, the new eugenics is eugenics *par excellence*.[66]

The new technology can transform profoundly the role of the medical profession in a way very similar to what legalized euthanasia threatens to do. Whereas traditional medicine was about healing the patient or alleviating his or her suffering, the new medicine is about killing off the patient altogether, and in the case of eugenic diagnosis and selection it is about replacing one "patient" with another. It is important for us to note that, behind all the window-dressing of "compassion," "improvement," "maximizing advantage for future couples" and so on, eugenics is actually about selecting certain people for existence and rejecting the life of others. This surely is the "playing God" aspect of the new medical regime that rightly troubles many people. It prefers healthy individuals to unhealthy ones, smart ones over dumb ones, and (this will rarely be openly stated in Western liberal democracies) fair-skinned people over darker-skinned. It reinforces our fallen, sinful human tendency to regard our fellow human beings as a burden to us, and so to avoid painful sacrifices for the sake of others and the bearing of one another's infirmities.

Therefore, not only does genetic selection undermine human solidarity, but it also blatantly violates the moral principle that affirms the equal worth and dignity of each human being. It says to those born with defects or deformities: You are of inferior value and therefore do not have the right to exist. Action taken against such embryos or fetuses is intrinsically unjust, whatever may be our view of the moral status of the embryo or fetus. For, as Kendall Soulen rightly observes, "people who make eugenic judgments do so with respect to the relative fitness or desirability of the kind of human being a given embryo or foetus is likely to become."[67] Living children and adults with mental or physical disabilities are being sent powerful social signals that their lives are not worth living. Once again the incoherence and hypocrisy of secular liberal rhetoric about human dignity and of human rights stands exposed.

We have seen in chapter three that the defense of equal worth and dignity requires a theological framework. The entire biblical narrative attests to God's solidarity with and selection of the weak and "insignificant" that they may be the vehicles of his redemptive love to the rest of his creation. The Suffering Servant of Yahweh had "no form or majesty that we should look at him, nothing in his appearance that we should desire him," he was "acquainted with infirmity; and as one from whom others hide their faces he was despised, and we held him of no account" (Isaiah 53:2-3). The new creation announces not that the last will be eliminated but that the last will be first. In God's household, the strong are dependent on the weak. The apostle Paul reminds his readers in Corinth: "God chose what is foolish in the world to shame the wise; God chose what is weak in the world to shame the strong; God chose what is low and despised in the world, things that are not, to reduce to nothing things that are, so that no one might boast in the presence of God" (1 Corinthians 1:26-29).

Around the turn of the new millennium there were numerous scientific and medical pronouncements in the media concerning the promise that stem cells, derived from human embryos, were said to hold for millions of people suffering from fatal or medically debilitating conditions. Despite the profound ethical concerns regarding the use of human embryos for medical and scientific research, many scientists, university administrators, venture capitalists and politicians embraced this promise and the seemingly miraculous hope it offered. However, there is a huge discrepancy between the promise and the reality. Repeating something with a loud voice does not make it true. There is no scientific evidence to date to support the popular claim that that embryonic stem cells in the laboratory can readily be induced to form all the cells comprising the mature human body. When cells derived from embryonic stem cells are transplanted into adult animals, their most common fate is to die. The rapid death of transplanted embryonic stem cell-derived cells stands in striking contrast to the robust survival of bona fide adult cells when transplanted to adult tissue. To date, all the successful medical treatments using stem-cell lines have used adult rather than embryonic stem cells.

In a review article on stem-cell research, published in January 2007, Maureen Condic concludes:

> Over the past thirty years, hundreds of billions of dollars and countless hours of research by dedicated professionals worldwide have been devoted to solving the problems of immune rejection and tumour formation, yet these issues remain serious scientific and medical challenges. The mysteries of embryonic development have been plumbed for more than a hundred years by some of the most brilliant biologists of history, and yet, despite the clear progress we have made, we are nowhere near the point of having a "recipe book" for cooking up cellular repair kits to treat human disease and injury. Immune rejection, tumour formation, and embryonic development have proved themselves to be profoundly serious scientific challenges, and they are likely to remain so for decades into the future.[68]

Condic also reveals that Ron McKay at the National Institutes of Health acknowledged in a *Washington Post* interview in June 2004 that scientists have not been quick to correct exaggerated claims of the medical potential of embryonic stem cells, yet McKay justified this dishonesty by stating, "To start with, people need a fairy tale. Maybe that's unfair, but they need a story line that's relatively simple to understand. Isn't it time Americans recognize the promise of obtaining medical miracles from embryonic stem cells for the fairy tale it really is?"[69] We have returned full circle to E. O. Wilson's attempt, a quarter of a century ago, to create a pseudo-religious myth out of the biological sciences.

POST/TRANSHUMANISM

Given the overriding mindset of consumer choice, free-floating selves and technological hubris, it is but a short step to fantasies of not only weeding out human beings considered defective and inferior in other ways, but of proactively redesigning human nature itself. In a book significantly titled *Remaking Eden* and written at the dawn of the new millennium, Lee Silver, an American molecular biologist, anticipates what the combination of genetic and reproductive technology will lead to over the next fifty years. If we are prepared to produce genetically engineered plants and animals, to enhance some valued property in them, why not extend the techniques to enhance the capabilities of human beings?[70] Hence the vision of a society where prospective parents can survey a portfolio of desirable genes and cherry pick which traits they want in their offspring. This is the ultimate shopping experience—designing our progeny in advance, subjecting them to quality control, purchasing them in the biological marketplace and continually upgrading individual parts.

This fantasy of "designer" or "virtual" children is based on the scientifically unsubstantiated idea that by adding a gene we can enhance a normal function, or that even if we could, it would not also involve unpredictable changes in other brain functions as well. Moreover, as the British neurochemist Susan Greenfield argues, do we really want a world of two species of humans, one "enhanced" and the other "naturals"? The current global discrepancies in health, education and income are serious enough to threaten global stability. But "Closer to home," Greenfield writes, if enhancement were a commodity just for the rich, for the stratum in society, say, that can currently channel income into private education, then might such segregation even occur within a single society, a return to the rigid class divide of old, only even more definitive? The non-negotiable hierarchy of *Brave New World* might become a reality.[71]

Gregory Stock, a former adviser in biotechnology to President Bill Clinton, remarks in the opening chapter (called "The Last Human") of his book *Redesigning Humans: Changing Our Children's Genes* that we "are on the cusp of profound biological change, poised to transcend our current form and character on a journey to destinations of new imagination." This journey has become possible because "the technological powers we have hitherto used so effectively to remake our world are now potent and precise enough for us to turn them on ourselves. . . . With our biological research we are taking control of evolution and beginning to direct it."[72]

Homo sapiens have been directing their evolution from the time they first appeared on the earth. Technology, in the sense of tools and the making of artifacts with our tools, lies at the root of all human cultures. Once the latter develop in sophistication, humans build for themselves "other worlds"—through language, religious rituals, music, the visual arts, economic production and exchange, political institutions, and so on—and technology is often the medium through which such cultural achievements are expressed. Technologies are more than human appendages, and they do more than sustain long-term habitation in hostile natural environments. They transform our experiences and understanding of what it means to be human. Human beings have "co-evolved" with their environments, tools and technologies.

However, what writers such as Silver, Stock and a host of others are claiming is that developments in genetic, reproductive, cybernetic and computer technologies in recent decades have brought about a world (at least the First World) where the boundaries between human and machine, nature and technology, are being erased. Thus "nature" and the "human" are being redefined by technological progress. The bionic human is the human being of the future. We already have people walking around with cochlear implants, heart pacemakers and silicone breasts continually linked via mobile phones and the

Internet to a global community of disembodied, "virtual" beings. Does the emergence of what are called cyborgs or cybernetic organisms, as hybrids of biological and technological components, signal the dawn of a postbiological existence?

The posthuman has become a shorthand metaphor for talk of a new phase of human evolution, albeit one technologically driven rather than by natural selection. It goes beyond the scientific and medical prospects of enhancing human physical and intellectual powers by means of cybernetic implants or genetic modification. For some commentators, the new technologies promise to liberate us from the limitations of fleshly existence entirely. As Elaine Graham notes, "Technology has moved from being an instrument or tool in the hands of human agents, or even a means to transform the natural environment, and become a series of processes or interventions capable of reshaping human ontology."[73] The vision of a transformation of human ontology can be exhilarating for those who dream of attaining a godlike state in overcoming all limitations to knowledge and power. Conquering death, the final frontier, by means of cryogenic regeneration and cellular repair techniques is included in such intoxicating dreams.

The acme of such intoxicating plans for the future is to be found in the ideology of transhumanism, which as Graham notes is the "hi-tech heir to Enlightenment humanism" with its vigorous assertion of free inquiry, self-mastery and self-determination. Transhumanism is an interdisciplinary movement that seeks to harness advanced technologies in the pursuit of human perfection: the construction of artificial intelligence to augment intellectual functions and the use of biomedical transplants, prostheses, genetic modification, and cryonic preservation to stave off disease and aging. One of its high priests, Nick Bostrom of the Oxford-based Future of Humanity Institute, calls for "a more proactive approach to technology policy" and writes, "Transhumanists view human nature as a work-in-progress, a half-baked beginning that we can learn to remold in desirable ways." One of the desirable ways that he envisions is as follows:

> It may be possible to upload a human mind to a computer, by replicating in silico the detailed computational processes that would normally

take place in a particular human brain. Being an upload would have many potential advantages, such as the ability to make back-up copies of oneself (favorably impacting on one's life-expectancy) and the ability to transmit oneself as information at the speed of light.[74]

Gregory Stock urges his readers to embrace the challenges and goals of these transformative technologies as "an act of extraordinary faith." We cannot know in advance where self-directed evolution will take us, but "In offering ourselves as vessels for potential transformation into we know not what, we are submitting to the shaping hand of a process that dwarfs us individually."[75] This mystical act of worship would be laudable if it were indeed Stock and his fellow scientist elites who were offering themselves up as passive vessels to this mysterious process rather than our unfortunate descendants.

It is important to grasp these strong religious resonances in much of the post/transhuman literature. The invocation of faith is no mere hyperbole. One writer has described virtual communities as "techno-pagans" who equate the sacred not with the natural order but with the technological, where digital networks perform the power of earlier magi who promised to transport their acolytes into new realms of disembodied experience.[76] Mortality remains the final challenge to the euphoric technocracy in the United States that believes it can vanquish every obstacle.

Christians cannot help but see a reincarnation of the ancient heresy of Gnosticism which dogged the Western Christian church from the middle period of the second century A.D. The Gnostics rejected orthodox Jewish and Christian belief in the goodness of creation, replacing the Creator with a Demiurge who was responsible for the prosaic, material world of nature and human bodies. Salvation was understood as a flight from human finitude, embodiment and dependence into a "spiritual" realm of godlike existence. Such visions of transcendence and human perfection were profoundly challenged by the Christian proclamation of a God who had not only created and sustained the material world but who had himself embraced finitude, vulnerability, dependence and even evil and death through the incarnation, crucifixion and resurrection of Jesus. This is what love entails—the capacity to be hurt by the other and to transform that hurt into creative action. The resurrection represented not the overcoming of the human but its fulfillment. A perfected humanity is a Jesus-like humanity.

Thus, what both the ancient and today's posthuman gnostics see as salvation is, from the perspective of Christian hope, simply a deepening of the problem. When we empathize with another human being, it's because we feel their vulnerability, their frailties and suffering. But in a world that comes to expect a gnostic perfection in its offspring, can empathy really survive? The human attempt to become an invulnerable God, rather than live as the image of a vulnerable God, is the very essence of sin—and sin, as Jesus emphasized, enslaves. In thinking that we are the architects of our humanity we end up losing our humanity. In our striving for total mastery over creation we reduce ourselves to objects to be manipulated—exemplifying Marx's classic account of the alienation of labor under the conditions of modern capitalism: technology, a product of human labor, becomes reified and acquires a "life of its own" independent of the human laborer who now experiences himself as an object of technology.

Not surprisingly, scientific research into a posited "transhuman future," involving genetic, biochemical, computer and nanotechnology, finds its biggest sponsor in the U.S. military. Turning fallible human foot soldiers into transhuman machines who need neither sleep nor food, and are incapable of resistance and independent thought, is a Napoleonic dream. And the wannabe Napoleons in the Pentagon are willing to invest massive public funds into translating fantasy into reality.

GODS OR NOTHINGS: THE FALSE CHOICE

In surveying the state of the natural sciences today, we seem to have moved in a closed circle. Two contradictory views of the human both claim the authority of science. The first imprisons human beings in a story told by their genes or neurons, thereby ridiculing the notion of human freedom. The other proclaims an unlimited capacity for self-design on the part of technocratic magi of the future, thereby trivializing the exercise of human freedom. When human freedom is not received as divine gift, only meaningful within a web of relationships and responsibilities, it will always oscillate between godlike pretension and nihilistic denial.

The biotechnician is like the alchemist of an earlier age, a quasi-religious power fantasist, intoxicated with the idea of being in touch with the invisible force at the heart of the universe. The alchemist had to indulge in aggressive hype in order to persuade his rich patrons to invest some of their gold in his project so that they could make some more. The new algenist, eager for grant money from powerful multinational corporations that are investing heavily in the technology, has to promote a similar vision. The vision, as we have seen, is based on a simplistic understanding of biology. There is a strange contradiction at the heart of this high-priestly vision: on the one hand, we are told that human beings are at the mercy of their genes, being simply vessels for their transmission. Hence the idioms of fate and of passive surrender to an unknown future. On the other hand, the biotechnician can cut and splice our genes in such a way that new humans can emerge free of their limitations and inherent weaknesses. All our moral and social problems have biochemical solutions. Hence the idioms of "control" and "self-directed" evolution.

For those of us who love science, the challenge is twofold: on the one hand, to rescue science from its cultural detractors—from those who want to reduce science to simply one culturally constructed language game among many, with no pretensions to universal validity, let alone to something called "truth." On the other hand, we have to rescue science from those who want to reduce all human knowledge, goals and experience to talk of physics and biology, and to impose a scientific imperialism on other branches of learning as well as on public policy. The landscape of reality is so rich that no single perspective can do justice to it. We need all the available resources at hand: professional theologians need to attend to the natural sciences for the broadening of their horizons as much as scientists need to pay attention to the wider social, political and moral dimensions that shape their work. Both the fear of science and the idolatry of science that are now commonplace in the late modern world have the same roots, namely, the lack of a coherent, satisfying worldview within which science can be cherished and also put in its proper place.

A Christian theological anthropology recognizes the multidimensional nature of human experience. Academic specializations such as sociobiology, cognitive science, evolutionary psychology, rational-choice economic theory and so on have (no doubt with a view of boosting their public status) over-reached themselves in elevating their narrow perspectives on the human into new social myths. In doing so they have stifled human creativity, which is always framed between divine reflection and creaturely dependence. Theologically understood, human beings and the universe belong together. They form what we mean by world in its relation to God. And God has made the universe to express itself, to bring forth its own order in ever richer forms, and in that way to find its fulfillment as the creation of God. This is what takes place through us human beings, for we are "that unique element in the creation through which the universe knows itself and unfolds its inner rationality."[77]

6

MYTHS OF POSTCOLONIALISM

DECENTERING WORLD HISTORY

We belong to one world. The German sociologist Ulrich Beck writes of a new "globality" that means "that from now on nothing which happens on our planet is only a limited local event; all inventions, victories and catastrophes affect the whole world, and we must reorient and reorganize our lives and actions, our organizations and institutions, along a local-global axis."[1] However, the novelty of this phenomenon should not be exaggerated. One of the persistent myths about globalization is that it is a late-twentieth-century phenomenon and initiated largely by Western capitalism. Undoubtedly the scope and intensity of globalizing practices has increased in recent decades, but we have seen in earlier chapters how cultures have always interacted and influenced each other through the movement of commodities, peoples and ideas. Cultures did not—and do not—merely stand by as passive recipients or bemused observers. A. G. Hopkins reminds us that globalization has taken different historical forms, from seaborne and land-based globalizing expeditions of the Byzantine and Tang Dynasty periods to the Islamic and European Christian expansionisms of the 1500s, to the spice trade of the East India Companies and imperialistic colonization, to the opening of the Suez Canal, to the dispersion of the Jewish, Chinese and other diasporas. Lipton Tea was the first global drink, predating Coca-Cola and Starbucks.

A number of recent historical studies have challenged typical Eurocentric readings of globalization, arguing that modernity should be seen as a multicentered enterprise, involving the active participation of many societies around the globe.[2] The late eighteenth and early nineteenth centuries saw a profound unsettling of the old agrarian regimes around the world, with pressures for change being strongly evident in China, India, Persia and Arabia. But they erupted explosively in the American and French revolutions, unleashing a truly global struggle for power. Viewed in this wider context, the future of nineteenth-century Europe was decided as much by events in Egypt, India and the West Indies as by the Peninsular Wars or the French Revolution. Napoleon himself indirectly acknowledged this when he remarked that the Battle of Waterloo had been lost in India.[3] Events ricocheted around the world. The Taiping Rebellion in China, the so-called Indian Mutiny and the American Civil War were all global events (though triggered by local causes) that reflected and further propelled the forces of ideological, economic and political change. Christopher Bayly has shown how "the creation of yet stronger, more intrusive states, European, colonial, and extra-European, was the most potent legacy of the age of revolutions," and that the events of the years from 1780 to 1820 greatly sped up the emergence of "the resolute, aggressive modern nation-state" and the rise of "polite, industrious, and commercial societies" around the world.[4]

What Bayly writes concerning the nineteenth-century world bears a remarkable semblance to our own:

> As world events became more interconnected and interdependent, so forms of human action adjusted to each other and came to resemble each other across the world. . . . This growth of uniformity was visible not only in great institutions such as churches, royal courts, or systems of justice. It was also apparent in what this book calls 'bodily practices': the ways in which people dressed, spoke, ate, and managed relations within families. . . . Yet, at the same time, these connections could also heighten the sense of difference, and even antagonism, between people in different societies, and especially between their elites.[5]

Bayly continues:

> In fact, a kind of international class structure was emerging. This greater specialization gave rise, paradoxically, to an impression of uniformity. The ruling groups, professions, and even working classes of different

societies looked more and more similar, were subject to similar types of pressure, and began to harbour similar aspirations. Convergence, uniformity, and similarity did not mean, again, that all these people were likely to think or act in the same way. At the very least, though, they could perceive and articulate common interests which breached the boundaries of the nation-state, even if they were profoundly influenced by it.[6]

Thus the conventional geographical compartmentalizing of history, embodied in the writing of "national histories," is as distorting of reality as is the geographical compartmentalizing of theology. The globalization that has occurred in the period from 1800 to the present day is in some crucial respects very different from its predecessors. Nevertheless, prior to that period significant flows of goods, resources, currencies, capital, institutions, ideas, technologies and peoples flowed across regions to such an extent that they transformed societies in different parts of the world. Knowledge systems had always been interactive, as, for instance, when Chinese literati came into contact with the ideas of Aristotle through the good offices of the Jesuits. The complexity of non-European thought in the nineteenth century was never simply derivative of Western norms, but European ideas were taken up and used by indigenous rulers and intellectuals who were already attempting to forge intellectual tools with which to grapple with their own "early modernities." Robert Holton maintains,

> A global history need not take the form of a single uniting process [or metanarrative] such as the triumph of reason or western civilisation. Nor should it be taken to imply an inexorable process of homogenization to a single pattern. . . . [T]he minimum that is required for us to be able to speak of a single global connecting thread is that tangible interconnections exist between distinct regions, leading to interchange and interdependency.[7]

Recent historians of the British empire such as Linda Colley and Peter van der Veer have pointed out that it is impossible to understand nineteenth- and early twentieth-century British society apart from the wider context of its global empire.[8] It was not simply a matter of recognizing how British national identity came to be defined over and against the threatening "other" (increasingly "Hindu India" rather than "Catholic France"), but how profound transformations in the concepts of religion, race and secularism all occurred in the interaction between the periphery and the margins. If India today cannot be understood apart from British history, no less can Britain be understood apart from Indian history.

John Hobson has taken the story further back in presenting the case for an "Oriental globalization" that was "the midwife, if not the mother, of the medieval and modern West."[9] He seeks to replace the notion of an autonomous or pristine West with that of the "oriental West." The East (which was more advanced, technologically and economically, than the West between 500 and 1800) played a crucial role in enabling the rise of modern Western civilization. Hobson argues that the East enabled the rise of the West through two main processes, diffusion and appropriation:

> First, the Easterners created a global economy and global communications network after 500 along which the more advanced Eastern "resource portfolios" (e.g. Eastern ideas, institutions and technologies) diffused across to the West, where they were subsequently assimilated, through what I call oriental globalization. And second, Western imperialism after 1492 led the Europeans to appropriate all manner of Eastern economic resources to enable the rise of the West.[10]

Before 1800, few of the major players in the world economy at any particular time were European. Many of the technologies that proved crucial to the agricultural, military and political revolutions in Europe from medieval times to 1800 diffused from the East—for example, the stirrup, the horse-collar harness, the watermill and windmill, the iron ploughs and horseshoes, guns and gunpowder, cannon, compasses, square ship hulls and multiple mast systems, papermaking and movable metal-type printing presses. It was only as late as the mid-nineteenth century that Europe caught up with Asia and the Ottoman empire.

A hundred years before the first European conquistadors set sail for the Americas and the East Indies, China controlled half the world's oceans. With its formidable navy it could easily have grasped the other half. But it did not. The great treasure fleets of the Chinese (Muslim) admiral Zheng He (Cheng Ho) had, after traversing the Indian Ocean, rounded the Cape in the autumn of 1421 and sailed up the west coast of Africa as far as the Cape Verde islands.[11] Some of his ships went on to explore Antarctica and the Arctic, North and South America, and had crossed the Pacific to Australia. "They had solved the problems of calculating latitude and longitude and had mapped the earth and the heavens with equal accuracy."[12] On Zheng He's return to Beijing in 1423, he found that China had undergone not only a regime change but an abrupt reversal of its foreign policy. China suddenly turned inward, renouncing overseas trade and forbidding its people to travel. All charts and documents commemorating its momentous maritime discoveries and scientific exploits were destroyed by the Chinese court. The traditional rural gentry were back in power, and China entered a long period of isolation and xenophobia.

Europe has never been a self-enclosed geographical reality. Invoking ancient Greece as the fount of European civilization is problematic, not least because the Greeks borrowed so much from others. Europa itself was the daughter, in Greek mythology, of the daughter of the king of Tyre, a kingdom on the coast of modern Lebanon. Most European dishes are imported from elsewhere. The pizza was first made in ancient Egypt. It was later embellished in the United States and returned as Italy's "national dish." The Arabs introduced the cultivation of rice and saffron into Sicily and Spain (which enabled the making of paella). Chocolate came from South America, spices from Southeast Asia, and coffee from Ethiopia (derived from the Arabic term *kahwa*). Europe's importing of software engineers from India today was foreshadowed centuries ago by European dependence on Chinese technical expertise. As Michael Edwardes has noted:

> Those responsible for the first segmental arch bridges in Europe—such as the Ponte Vecchio, spanning the Arno at Florence (1345)—must have been influenced by pioneering Chinese expertise. Indeed, the fame of China's technicians persisted [over the centuries] and Peter the Great of Russia, in process of modernizing the country, called in Chinese engineers in 1675 for his bridge-building projects.[13]

It was the Jesuits who first challenged the Eurocentric version of world history. From the days of the first Jesuit mission to China under Matteo Ricci in 1610, a steady stream of letters, reports and books on China emerged in Europe which showed Europeans that gunpowder, the mariner's compass, paper and printing had been Chinese inventions. Louis XIV of France sent six Jesuits to China in 1685 with a long list of topics (drawn up by the French Academy of Science) to gather knowledge in a number of areas ranging from science, flora and fauna to agricultural production. The German philosopher and mathematician Gottfried Leibniz (1646-1716) urged the Jesuit mission in China to send information pertaining to the manufacture of metals, tea, paper, silk, porcelain, dyes and glass as well as advanced military and naval technologies. He also requested the Jesuits to transport back to Europe machines and models of agricultural and manufacturing technologies. The numerous Jesuit letterbooks, travel accounts and translations of Chinese texts stirred up the imagination of European intellectuals and monarch alike.[14] The Jesuit missionaries were followed by other adventurers and sailors who not only sent back descriptions of all aspects of Chinese life but brought back with them a number of models and machines which were later copied and adapted to spearhead the agricultural and industrial revolutions.[15]

According to the standard economic history taught in undergraduate textbooks, Britain became the first industrial nation in the world in the latter half of the eighteenth century, and this industrial revolution was the crucial material pivot in the birth of modernity and the triumph of Western civilization. This unique breakthrough is, moreover, attributed to what is often called the "British genius": native ingenuity, amateur innovators, self-help individualism. Walter Rostow, the grandfather of "development economics" believed that "the British case of transition was unique in the sense that it appeared to have been brought about by internal dynamics of a single society, without external intervention." Similarly, the British Marxist scholar Perry Anderson asserts that the British "industrial revolution . . . was a spontaneous, gigantic combustion of the forces of production, unexampled in its power and universal in its reach."[16]

This Anglocentric view has been challenged in recent years by a number of historians, many of them British.[17] A wider, world-historical reading locates the British "Great Transformation" as part of a cumulative story of global economic development that links thirteenth-century Sung China's industrial revolution with the global agrarian revolutions of the mid-eighteenth century and the rise of British imperialism. The renowned economic historian Paul Bairoch estimated that in 1750 the East (Asia and Africa) contributed 77 percent to world manufacturing output, while the West's contribution was about 23 percent.[18] China's per capita income was equal to that of Britain's in 1750, and it was responsible for a remarkable one-third of total world manufacturing output. This was sixteen times that of Britain. The ratio between Chinese and British contributions to world manufactures dropped to 6.7 in 1800 and 2.15 in 1830. Britain's gunboat diplomacy and the shameful Opium Wars of 1839–1842 deepened the slide, but it was only as late as 1860 that the British share finally equalled that of the Chinese.

The British genius was for copying, appropriating and adapting the technological breakthroughs of others, notably the Chinese. What Europeans accused Japan of doing after the Meiji reforms and again after 1945—copying and improving on the technology of the West—was exactly what the British were adept at doing, but without acknowledging their indebtedness to other peoples. Hobson argues that Britain was like any "late developer" or newly industrializing country in that it enjoyed the "advantages of backwardness" and was able to assimilate and refine the advanced technologies that had previously been pioneered by early developers.[19] Bayly notes that "Europe connected, subjugated, and made tributary other peoples' industrious revolutions."[20]

Perhaps the clearest sign of Europe's economic backwardness was its perennial trade deficit with Asia until about 1800. There was little that was produced in Europe that Asian consumers wanted. By the end of the fifteenth century, China probably published more books than the rest of the world combined. Even as late as 1840 all that the British could sell to the Chinese was opium grown in India. European powers paid for the trade deficit with bullion (normally silver) that was plundered from Africa and the Americas, and used American natives and African slaves to extract the bullion. Desperate to bridge the huge trade deficit with China and to stop the draining of bullion from Britain, which that gap ensured, the British turned to the cultivation of opium and tea in its Asian colonies. Tea production in

India and Ceylon reduced the dependence on Chinese tea. By 1828 Indian opium comprised 55 percent of all British exports to China (despite a ban on its consumption by the Chinese authorities). When the Chinese government sought to curtail the drug trade in 1839, Lord Palmerston seized on the action as a pretext for war in the defense of "free trade." The British government employed the same methods as Afghan warlords and Colombian drug cartels today, namely, drug-pushing backed up by military power. As long as the Chinese were hooked on opium and the British on drinking tea grown in India (and later Ceylon), the trade deficit could be reversed.

What this historical discussion has shown is that the binary polarizations of Eastern and Western, national and foreign are as problematic as the popular distinction between the secular and religious. The origins of modernity lie not exclusively in Western Enlightenment, superficially understood as an atheistic project, but in the complex, historical interplay of European and non-European civilizations beginning from the eighteenth century onward. The origins of change in world history have always been multicentered. World history thus needs to be decentralized. As Peter van der Veer maintains:

> Modernity has a global history. This does not imply a single origin of concepts and blueprints that are developed in the Enlightenment (both American and French) and exported, resisted, and adopted, elsewhere. Nor does it imply the dialectic between an already finished idiom of modernity that confronts an already existing idiom of tradition, out of which a synthesis emerges. Rather, it manifests a history of interactions out of which modernity, with its new historical problematic, arose, offering creative tensions, not solutions.[21]

THE COLONIAL LEGACY

The great Dutch historian Johan Huizinga concludes his masterly biography of Erasmus of Rotterdam with the comment, "The history of Holland is far less bloody and cruel than that of any of the surrounding countries. Not for naught did Erasmus praise as truly Dutch those qualities which we might also call truly Erasmian: gentleness, kindliness, moderation, a generally diffused moderate erudition."[22]

I remember my immediate reaction to this passage in Huizinga: What about the brutality of the Dutch East India Company, including the displacement and enslavement of whole populations and the burning of the entire town of Jakarta in order to create a new colonial center?[23] Or what about the forcible rebaptism of Roman Catholics in Ceylon and Malacca into the Dutch Calvinist church? As for the Dutch legacy in South Africa, perhaps the less said the better. But the point is that not only is national stereotyping dangerous but failing to read one's national history against a broader world canvas is to seriously distort it and to arouse ire in others.

It is a remarkable fact that as recently as the 1930s 84 percent of the earth's surface area was under European colonial rule. Formal decolonization was a central event of the second half of the twentieth century, and one that has had profound repercussions for societies all over the world, the colonizers as much as the colonized. European colonialism not only plundered wealth from the colonies but violently reshaped physical territories, social terrains, knowledge systems and human identities. The economies of colonized peoples were restructured and locked into those of Europe so that there was a flow of human and natural resources between colonized and colonial countries. Just as opium was transported to China from India by the British East India Company in exchange for tea that was then shipped to England, slaves were moved from Africa to the Americas, and the Caribbean plantations produced sugar for consumption in Europe. When slavery was abolished in the British Empire, it was replaced by a system of indentured labor: low caste "coolies" from southern India were shipped to east and south Africa and the Caribbean to work on colonial plantations under conditions not much different from slavery.

The two major industries of the British industrial revolution were iron/steel and cotton. As late as 1788, however, British iron production levels were still lower than those achieved in China in 1078! What is particularly striking here is that in both these industries, India led the way up to around 1800. Indian Wootz steel was exported to Persia, where it provided the foundation for the famous Damask steel. Moreover, Indian steel was both superior to and cheaper than steel produced in Sheffield. As late as 1842 the number of blast furnaces in India was about fifty times the number found in Britain and was still ten times the number in the peak year of 1873.[24] When the British finally became interested in steel production, it was, naturally, to India and China that they looked. They started manufacturing it in large quantities only from 1852 when steel became cheaper to make after the discovery of the Bessemer conversion process (which itself was influenced by earlier Chinese methods).

A similar story unfolded with respect to cotton. India was also the foremost cotton-textile producer in the world and also made silk textiles on an impressive scale. Words such as *khaki, dungarees, pajamas, calico, chintz* and *shawl* are all of Indian origin and have passed into everyday English usage as proof of the dominant Indian influence in the textile industry. While in the seventeenth century the British economy was a net importer of Indian textiles, by the mid-nineteenth century India had been transformed into a raw cotton supplier for the Lancashire industry, which in turn exported the finished product back to India. The British began by imposing high tariffs on Indian cotton manufactures and then, in the name of "free trade," pushed their own, more expensively produced, textiles into India unimpeded. Having noted the superiority of Indian industrial development over British in the period prior to the establishment of British rule, Felipe Fernández-Armesto wryly observes, "with an exactness rare in history, India's industrial debacle coincided with the establishment of British rule or hegemony. . . . The potential competition of its economy could be stifled. No single episode was more decisive in shifting the balance of the world's resources than this shift in the sources of control."[25]

In his savage indictment of colonialism, the Algerian psychiatrist and political activist Frantz Fanon (1925-1961) claimed that Europe was "literally the creation of the Third World" in the sense that "the wealth which smothers her is that which was stolen from the under-developed peoples." Europe's opulence had been "founded on slavery" and nourished by "the sweat and the dead bodies of Negroes, Arabs, Indians and the yellow races."[26] Not too dissimilar views were held by a man of a more irenic temperament than Fanon— Sir Mohammed Iqbal (1877- 1938), the poet-philosopher behind the concept of Pakistan, and a man who, like Fanon, owed much intellectually to the West and even received a knighthood from the British. In his *Persian Psalms*, published in 1927, he declared:

Against Europe I protest,
And the attraction of the West.
Woe for Europe and her charm,
Swift to capture and disarm!
Europe's hordes with flame and fire
Desolate the world entire.[27]

While profits flowed from the colonies to the "mother" country, there was also a flow of people from the latter to the former. They went as administrators, soldiers, merchants, adventurers, missionaries, scholars, chaplains and settlers. In some societies European colonialism penetrated more deeply than in others. The forms of colonial domination varied widely, from rule (with varying degrees of harshness) through native elites in the Indian subcontinent to the gun-boat diplomacy and opium wars of the 1840s in East Asia and the wholesale massacre of tribes by white settlers in southern and western Africa.

However, even the most repressive alien rule required not only concessions but also the partial incorporation of the ideas and practices of the dominated. The Italian Marxist Antonio Gramsci's (1891-1937) work on hegemony has inspired many postcolonial analyses of colonial societies and has fueled resistance movements and postcolonial discourse.[28] Hegemony is power achieved through a combination of coercion and consent. Gramsci noted that subjectivity and ideology are central to the processes of domination. He argued that the ruling classes achieve domination not by coercion alone but by inducing subjects to be willing collaborators in their subjugation. Ideology is the medium through which the ideas of the ruling class are transmitted and accepted by the ruled, and is crucial in manufacturing consent.

Modern-day Britons, like their predecessors in the time of the Raj, have an inveterate tendency to think of their empire as essentially benign. Yes, there were unfair trading practices, the occasional military atrocity and the corrupt administrator or vicious police officer, but these were blemishes on an otherwise disciplined and high-minded enterprise. Historians have noted that the British, convincing themselves of their moral superiority, invented their oldest traditions in the second half of the nineteenth century. Once they had abolished the trade in slaves, which had been the mainstay of their colonial economy until it became economically unviable, the British made the abolition of slavery a moral crusade, part of their "civilizing mission" in Africa and elsewhere. Lord Curzon, a viceroy of India in the heyday of the British Raj, claimed that "In empire, we have found not merely the key to glory and wealth, but the call to duty, and the means of service to mankind."[29]

Liberalism and representative democracy became part of British political tradition despite their effective suppression at home and abroad. Indeed, the experience of the French Revolution, eloquently denounced by Edmund Burke, turned liberal as well as conservative opinion in Britain against a rapid extension of the franchise. Holding a stake in property or commerce was an essential qualification for exercising political judgment. On this view, people had to be economically independent in order to exercise independent judgment. The specter of Louis Napoleon's dictatorship in France, which had conceded universal male suffrage in 1830, haunted proposals to create universal male suffrage. Even where relatively full franchises had been created by the 1890s, powerful checking and balancing mechanisms were put into place. The House of Lords, which represented mainly the landed interest, retained a veto over legislation until 1911.

In the French colonies of Africa and Indo-China, similarly, the idea that people had to achieve a level of "civilization" (in this case "French civilization") was used to scotch any idea of the universal right to political representation until well into the twentieth century. French colonial settlers saw to it that the barriers to French citizenship for nonwhite people were very high indeed. In many Western states, universal suffrage came into being only after the Second World War—in the United States only in 1965 (with the passing of the Voting Rights Act) and in Switzerland as late as 1971. So much for the argument that democracy is an "ancient European tradition" that the rest of the world needs to learn from the West.

POSTCOLONIALISM

Postcolonial studies take their cue from such internal contradictions of colonial discourse, whether that discourse be found in the form of official governmental papers, Victorian novels, travelers' journals, missionary newsletters, scientific catalogs, historical reports or biographical narrative. However, the term *postcolonial* has become fraught with controversy in academic circles. If it is used in a purely temporal sense—meaning the historical process of political decolonization—then debates rage as to whether decolonized societies are truly independent or still locked into forms of economic and political dependence that were established in the heyday of colonialism. If *postcolonial* is used in a critical sense—meaning the continuing process of resistance to hegemonic discourse—then debates rage as to whether it is adequate to understanding both the past and the present oppressions of postcolonial societies.

Many contemporary writers generalize about colonialism from their knowledge of it in a specific place or time. Thus, in the work of Gayatri Spivak, a prominent postcolonial literary critic based at Columbia University, it is nineteenth-century India, and particularly nineteenth-century Bengal, that becomes the model for theorizing about the colonized world. Often, *postcoloniality* becomes a general term for dissecting any discourse that marginalizes or excludes any group of people, from tribal women in India to Hispanic immigrants in New York, and the specificities of locale and history rarely matter.

Although postcolonial studies is such a wide-ranging discipline, encompassing everything from literary analyses to contemporary critiques of global capitalism, some themes prominent in most postcolonial writings are:

The understanding of colonialism as an ongoing subjective phenomenon. As the Caribbean novelist George Lamming put it, "the colonial experience is a live experience in the consciousness of these people. . . . The experience is a continuing psychic experience that has to be dealt with and will have to be dealt with long after the actual colonial situation formally 'ends.' "[30] In this context, some writers have suggested that we interpret the "post" in *postcolonialism* as the contestation of all forms of domination, thus integrating the history of anticolonial resistance with contemporary resistances to Western imperialism and to dominant Western (especially American) culture. This would allow us to include people geographically displaced by colonialism such as African Americans or people of Asian or Caribbean origin in Britain as "postcolonial" subjects although they live within metropolitan cultures.

Jorge de Alva suggests that postcoloniality should "signify not so much subjec-

tivity 'after' the colonial experience as a subjectivity of oppositionality to imperi-
alizing/colonizing (read: subordinating/subjectivizing) discourses and practices."
He justifies this by arguing that new approaches to history have discredited the
idea of a single linear progression, focusing instead on a "multiplicity of often
conflicting and frequently parallel narratives." Therefore, he suggests that we
should "remove postcoloniality from a dependence on an antecedent colonial
condition" and "tether" it to poststructuralist theories of history.[31]

So, a strong strand in postcolonial theory shifts the focus from social locations and institutions to individuals and their subjectivities. In part the
dependence of postcolonial theory on literary and cultural criticism is responsible for this shift. Influenced by Gramsci's insights into hegemonic discourse, literary critics have pointed out that the teaching of English literature
in British India was a way the ruling colonial power convinced the Indian
middle classes of their cultural inferiority. In her justly celebrated book *Masks
of Conquest*, Gauri Viswanathan argues that "no serious account" of the development of English teaching in nineteenth-century India can ignore "the
imperial mission of educating and civilizing colonial subjects in the literature
and thought of England."[32]

The reading of colonialism itself as a literary text. This follows from the
fact that what is circulated as "postcolonial theory" has largely emerged from
within English literary studies departments in American and European
academies, and from the "poststructuralist turn" in many of these departments. Colonialism is analyzed as if it were a text, a method of representation
of colonial subjects. These representations are available to us through a range
of writings, as mentioned earlier. Even when writings on colonial or postcolonial discourse do not explicitly privilege the textual, they do so implicitly by
interpreting colonial relations through literary texts alone.

> The meaning of "discourse" shrinks to "text" and from there to "literary
> text," and from there to texts written in English because that is the cor-
> pus most familiar to the critics. . . . [C]olonialism-as-text can be shrunk
> to a sphere away from the economic and the historical, thus repeating
> the conservative and humanist isolation of the literary text from the
> contexts in which it was produced and circulated.[33]

The recovery of the "other" that was suppressed by colonialist discourse. No
area of human knowledge was left untouched by colonialism. Much of what
was considered scientific, objective knowledge—especially knowledge about
other peoples and their societies—was embedded in colonial practices that
accompanied, justified and used that knowledge in the service of colonial
domination.

Ania Loomba explains:

> In any colonial context, economic plunder, the production of knowl-
> edge and strategies of representation depended heavily upon one an-
> other. Specific ways of seeing and representing racial, cultural and so-
> cial difference were essential to the setting up of colonial institutions
> of control, and they also transformed every aspect of European civil
> society. Guns and disease, as a matter of fact, cannot be isolated from
> ideological processes of "othering" colonial peoples. The gathering of
> "information" about non-European lands and peoples and "classifying"
> them in various ways determined strategies for their control. The dif-
> ferent stereotypes of the "mild Hindoo," the "warlike Zulu," the "bar-
> barous Turk," the "New World cannibal," or the "black rapist" were all
> generated through particular colonial situations and were tailored to
> different colonial policies. In Africa and India, by attributing particu-
> lar characteristics to specific tribes and groups, colonial authorities not
> only entrenched divisions between the native population, but also used
> particular "races" to fill specific occupations such as agricultural work-
> ers, soldiers, miners, or domestic servants.[34]

The Palestinian-American Edward Said's hugely influential book *Orientalism: Western Conceptions of the Orient* inaugurated a new study of colonialism.[35] Said looked at how representations of the Orient in European
literary texts, travelogues and other writings contributed to the creation of a
dichotomy between Europe and its "others," a dichotomy that was central to
the maintenance and extension of European hegemony over other lands.

Said's principal focus was on Napoleon's expedition to Egypt in 1814
and the subsequent transformation of studies on "Middle Eastern" societies.
When Napoleon arrived in Egypt in 1798—on board a ship called L'Orient—

he brought with him an entire scientific academy, the Institut d'Egypt. By occupying Egypt he planned to damage British trade in the eastern Mediterranean and threaten British India. But he also presented himself to the Egyptian people as their liberator, restoring a state of true civility to the Orient. In the words of the massive *Description de l'Egypte*, which appeared in twenty-three volumes between 1809 and 1828, Egypt, which had transformed its knowledge to so many nations, was now, under its Mamluk and Ottoman rulers, plunged into barbarism. From this unhappy condition Napoleon, the "Muhammad of the West," as Victor Hugo later called him, had come to release it and, while he was there, "to make the lives of the inhabitants more pleasant and to procure for them all the advantages of a perfect civilization."[36] This civilization was to be predominantly French, yet it was also to be a civilization that would preserve what the French regarded as the true spirit of the Orient—the wisdom of the pharaohs in happy alliance with the pieties of Islam. In Napoleon's view it was the French, despite being Christians, and not the Mamluk rulers, who by restoring to the Egyptians their cultural inheritance were "the true Muslims."

Using Michel Foucault's method of discourse analysis (which traces the way that power works through language, literature, culture and the institutions that regulate our daily lives), Said moved away from a narrow understanding of colonial authority. He showed how it functioned by generating a discourse about the Orient—structures of thinking which were manifest in literary and scientific writings and more specifically, in the creation of Oriental studies. Said's basic thesis is that Orientalism, or the study of the Orient, was an instrument of Western imperialism, in the form of "an accepted grid for filtering through the Orient into Western consciousness" whereby, in setting out to "discover" the cultures of Asia, Orientalists reshaped an Orient to suit their own Occidental prejudices. Thus knowledge about non-Europeans was part of the process of maintaining power over them. It was

> a political vision of reality whose structure promoted the difference between the familiar (Europe, the West, "us") and the strange (the Orient, the East, "them"). . . . When one uses categories like Oriental and Western as both the starting and the end points of analysis, research,

public policy . . . the result is usually to polarize the distinction—the Oriental becomes more Oriental, the Westerner more Western—and limit the human encounter between different cultures, traditions, and societies.[37]

Said's assault led to a spectacular volte-face in departments of Oriental studies in the 1980s as Western academics desperately sought to correct their political positions. The term *Orientalism* today carries heavy pejorative overtones while, in the words of Charles Allen, the "Orientalist is judged in much the same terms as those Orientals whom he himself, according to Said, once sought to judge, study, depict, discipline, illustrate, contain and represent."[38]

TOWARD A MORE NUANCED UNDERSTANDING

Said's work, and the numerous extensions of his work to other fields, is of permanent merit insofar as it highlights the way that representations of the East as the essentialized and stereotypical "other" of the West serve to suppress the rich complexity and diversity of both the East and the West. Any writer who claims to have uncovered the essence of, say, "the Chinese mind" or "American culture" needs to be treated with a heavy dose of skepticism, even ridicule. Similarly, all binary oppositions (e.g., Europe and Asia, us and them, tradition and modernity) can no longer be regarded as fixed and stable.

However, there are also several ambiguities, tensions and omissions in Said's work. These have been submitted to many rigorous critiques, and I do not intend to rehearse those criticisms here.[39] What I shall do in the remainder of this chapter is to make some observations on the ironies and paradoxes involved in both Orientalist and anti-Orientalist discourses, especially in relation to South Asian religion and politics, and then to interrogate briefly contemporary academic discussion about "postcoloniality" as it engages with Christian theology.

1. Stress is often laid on how aggressive European powers were in the past in relation to other continents. However, what made possible the growth of British colonialism in the age between the end of the Napoleonic Wars (1815) and the beginning of World War I (1914) was the relative absence of conflict between the European powers. Linda Colley notes that "in every

century during the first and second millennium—with only one conspicuous exception—Europeans have devoted more energy to hating, fighting and invading each other, than to hating, fighting and invading peoples outside Europe."[40] Colley also notes that the lower ranks of British soldiers, mostly Irish working-class men, experienced the brutality of the British Raj (for example, routine corporal punishment) far more than most Indians: "British soldiers stationed here often perceived themselves as the lowest of the low. They were captives of an alien environment, captives of their own state, and captives of a situation where their sepoy counterparts were in some respects better treated because they were deemed more important."[41]

Moreover, European colonial paternalism was directed not only toward "Oriental" peoples. According to Bayly:

> Recent studies of Napoleonic armies and government in Italy have shown how strongly held was the notion that the Italians were degenerate, unable to move beyond primitive, family-based values and corruption. According to condescending French administrators, they lacked a civil society and a sense of "mine" and "yours." Their civic institutions would need to be purged of old privilege, their landed society freed of feudal accretions, and power within it invested in powerful landowners protected by strong and transparent property rights.[42]

2. Postcolonial writings routinely ignore the indigenous colonial narratives and practices that British colonialism simultaneously displaced *and* reawakened. The Orientalist discourse, as depicted by Said and his followers, tends to be a purely Western construction imposed on an Oriental tabula rasa. But Orientalist productions were shaped by native elites (religious pundits and rulers) on whom scholars had to depend. The native ideologies which influenced, informed and resisted Orientalist positions (often in order to protect their own hegemonies) are often absent in postcolonialist narratives. The goal of the traditional Hindu king was universal empire, and long before the Anglicists appeared in India with their notorious project of "forming a class of persons, Indian in blood and colour, but English in taste, in opinions, in morals, and in intellect,"[43] the priestly Brahmanical ideologues were subverting vernacular cultures through the imposition of Sanskrit (the so-called lan-

guage of the gods). As one scholar of Indian religions observes, "Sanskrit was the principal discursive instrument of domination in pre-modern India and . . . it has been continuously reappropriated in modern India by many of the most reactionary and communalist sectors of the population."[44]

Ironically, "to ignore the role played by Asians themselves in the construction of Orientalist discourses results not only in the myth of the passive Oriental but also perpetuates precisely the East-West dichotomy that is such a feature of Orientalist discourses."[45] The construction and the appropriation of Orientalist discourses by different, competing groups (both for colonial and anticolonial ends) followed convoluted and multiple trajectories. A simplistic association of Orientalist discourses with Western colonial aspirations masks both the massive debt that present academic scholarship and Asian religious communities owe the early Orientalists, but it also fails to appreciate the way that discourses develop and are transformed over time.

In his fascinating story of the discovery of Buddhism in India and Ceylon by Western scholars, both humanists and Christian missionaries, Charles Allen poses the question:

What Professor Said and his many supporters have consistently failed to ask is where we would be without the Orientalists . . . [for it was they who] initiated the recovery of South Asia's lost past. The European discovery of Buddhism and the subsequent resurgence of Buddhism in South Asia arose directly out of their activities. They also established the methodology upon which the subcontinent's own historians, archaeologists, philologists and students continue to base their studies.[46]

Allen also notes,

Thanks to the efforts of men like Jones, Buchanan, Prinsep, Cunningham and Marshall, as well as of those who have followed them, the great Buddhist monuments of Ajanta, Sanchi and Sarnath are now visited and admired by hundreds of thousands of visitors each year. Many Indian nationals seem unimpressed—perhaps India has so much antiquity that they have become blasé, or perhaps they have yet to understand the richness of their heritage. But the pilgrimage trails that Fa Hian and Huan Tsang trod so long ago are now followed by thousands of new pilgrims, some of them tourists but many more of them Buddhists, drawn from all over the world.[47]

3. Orientalist scholarship led to the creation of Hinduism as a world religion and its identification with a corpus of Sanskrit texts (Vedas, Upanishads, etc.) painstakingly edited and translated into Western and modern Indian languages. These texts were then bestowed with canonical authority over Hindu practices in a manner similar to the Semitic faiths. It led to the periodization of Indian history into Hindu, Muslim and British stages, with "Indian civilization" identified with the earliest stage and the Muslim and Christian presence effectively occluded. In the hands of men like Swami Vivekananda (1863-1902), founder of the Ramakrishna Mission, and Mohandas Gandhi (1869-1948), Orientalist notions of India as otherworldly and spiritual, in contrast to the nihilism and materialism of modern Western society, were embraced and presented as India's gift to humankind. Thus colonial stereotypes were perpetuated and reemployed in the anticolonial nationalist struggle.

Moreover, it was an Orientalist history that attributed the modern concept of *tolerance* to Hinduism even though as a doctrinal notion it had no specific place in Hindu discursive traditions. Modern Hindu thinkers have come to interpret hierarchical relativism in Hindu discourse in Orientalist terms, as tolerance. Wilhelm Halbfass argues convincingly that the step to reconcile all religious and philosophical traditions was not taken prior to the colonial period.[48] And the characteristic manner in which it was done was by relativizing truth claims and including all religious traditions within the Vedanta, the spiritual essence of pure philosophical Hinduism, as in Radhakrishnan's famous saying, "The Vedanta is not a religion, but religion itself in its most universal and deepest significance."[49]

A comparable role was played by Zen Buddhism in the period of Meiji nationalism in Japan. Aspects of Buddhism attractive to Western audiences—mystical experience and the absence of institutional religious forms—have been marketed in Europe and the United States by prolific authors such as D. T. Suzuki. Vivekananda's neo-Vedanta and Suzuki's version of Zen became the stereotypical "religions of Asia" for spiritually jaded Westerners seeking an exotic alternative to institutional Christianity. "Suzuki's abstract, universalized and non-institutionalised 'Zen,' like the neo-Vedanta of Vivekananda and Radhakrishnan, provided a classic example of the universality of 'mysticism,' increasingly conceived as the experiential 'common core' of the various 'world religions.' "[50]

4. Orientalist writing on Indian texts was largely done in Germany, where university chairs in philology and Sanskrit mushroomed almost overnight. Germany had no imperialist agenda in Asia, while Japan, which was subjected to Orientalist discourses, was never colonized by a Western power. Moreover, German Orientalist studies on Indian Vedic texts profoundly affected Germany by providing an Indo-European myth of a pure Aryan race, which eventually became the ideology of the National Socialists in their colonization and domination of Europe itself.

Max Müller (1823-1900), a German scholar who devoted his entire life to the study of ancient Indian texts from his library in Oxford, was critical of pretensions of racial superiority in the British nationalism of his time. His work was enthusiastically embraced in India to support a Hindu nationalism built on the racial superiority of the Hindu Aryans. "They used philology in the way the Germans used it in their own country. Sanskrit philology provided them with the tools to dig up the origin and essence of the nation, that is, the Hindu nation. It also gave them a scientific language to exclude 'latecomers' such as Muslims, as outsiders to the story of the nation."[51] A significant number of modern-day Hindus, quite understandably, want to construct their religion as historically ancient, cohesive and centered, as a viable world religion able to compete with Islam and Christianity in global society.

Similarly, it is doubtful whether until the advent of Western scholars Tibetans, the Sinhalese or the Chinese saw themselves as Buddhists. "Pure" or "authentic" Buddhism was "discovered" by these scholars not in the actual lives or actions of living Buddhists in Asia but rather in the edited manuscripts of European university libraries and archives. Frits Staal points out that "The inapplicability of Western notions of religion to the traditions of Asia has not only led to piecemeal errors of labelling, identification and classification, to conceptual confusion and to some name-calling. It is also responsible for something more extraordinary: the creation of so-called religions."[52] Once again, the irony is that middle-class, Western-educated Buddhists in Sri Lanka and other parts of Southeast Asia continue to talk of a pure Buddhism, which they distill, in true Orientalist fashion, from the metaphysical commentaries on Pali texts. What has come to be called "Protestant Buddhism" in Sri Lanka, heavily shaped by the American theosophist Henry Olcott (1832-1907) and his native disciple Anagarika Dharmapala (1864-1933), was wedded to a Sinhalese nationalist discourse. It is propagated today to Western tourists and by Buddhist missionaries to Europe and the United States as the "ancient wisdom" of the land.

5. Anticolonial narratives, such as secular or religious nationalisms, are embedded in specific histories and cannot be collapsed into some pure oppositional essence. Nationalist struggles in Algeria against the French were very different from Indian resistance to the British, and neither can be equated to Korean and Chinese struggles against Japanese imperialism. Slavery in Africa was begun by Arabs and continued by Arabs after its abolition in the British empire, frequently with the connivance of local tribal leaders. The attempts by Christian missionaries, such as Thomas Fowell Buxton and David Livingstone, in the mid-nineteenth century to spread commerce along with Christianity as a means of breaking the economic stranglehold of slavery has usually been vilified by postcolonial writers who have not paid attention to the specific contexts in which these missions worked.

There is a new scramble for Africa raging today. The history of Western corporate involvement in Africa is one of forced labor, plunder, wars, the undercosting of resources, tax evasion and collusion with dictators and warlords. Today that role is being taken over by Chinese (and to a lesser extent, Indian) companies who are wooing the worst regimes in order to obtain oil and other mineral mining rights. Africans working in Chinese factories are paid subsistence wages and denied labor representation. Chinese investment in Africa in the twenty-first century seems likely to mirror the worst aspects of the European colonial heritage, but non-Western forms of imperialism are glaring in their omission from postcolonial studies.

6. Many postcolonialist writers display a marked indebtedness to the early work of Michel Foucault. The latter conceived of power as ubiquitous in modern societies, not emanating from a centralized state or at the peak of

a few institutional hierarchies but as dispersed by a kind of capillary action throughout the spheres in which it operates:

> Power comes from below; that is, there is no binary and all-encompass-
> ing opposition between rulers and ruled at the root of power relations,
> and serving as a general matrix—no such duality extending from the
> top down and reacting on more and more limited groups to the very
> depths of the social body. One must suppose rather that the manifold
> relationships of force that take shape and come into play in the machin-
> ery of production . . . are the basis for wide-ranging effects of cleavage
> that run through the social body as a whole.[53]

In the field of colonial discourse analysis, Homi Bhabha has developed Foucault's ideas to argue (against Said) that colonial power and discourse were not so all-encompassing that the colonized were left without any re-sources for resistance. Bhabha applies the Derridean notion of différance, denoting the endless differentiation and deferral of meaning within texts in order to highlight the inherent ambivalence of colonial discourse. Since dis-courses cannot be controlled once they have entered the public arena, they can be contested, appropriated and even inverted by others. There is always a gap in the blanket of power through which the repressed can return. Bhabha suggests that colonial authority is rendered "hybrid" and "ambivalent" by the process of replication of colonial identities, thus opening up spaces for the colonized to subvert the master discourse.[54]

Thus for Bhabha the key to anti-colonial resistance is the subversive mim-icry of the colonialist by the colonized native. Hybridity "reveals the ambiva-lence at the source of traditional discourses of authority and enables a form of subversion, founded on that uncertainty, that turns the discursive conditions of dominance into the grounds of intervention."[55] The ambivalent figure of the English-speaking Indian in British India represents the instability of the colonizer-colonized dichotomy, and it is not surprising that it is he or she (and not the vernacular-speaking lower classes) who are central to Bhabha's analysis of colonial discourse. Bhabha and other English-speaking writers of the In-dian diaspora can now invest themselves with new heroic identities as subversive voices for the voiceless, even in their own mimicry of an arcane literary style.

Since, in Bhabha's view, it is the failure of colonial authority to reproduce itself completely that allows for subversion, he has been criticized for
not considering alternative sources of anticolonial intellectual and political
activity. More seriously, his conception of the agency and resistance of the
colonized as primarily mimicry seems to require the continuing authority
of the colonial discourse, thereby (paradoxically) reinscribing colonialism as
a totalizing process. The totalizing discourse cannot be contested from any
other position. As Benita Perry puts it, the only option available to the colonized subject is "to place incendiary devices within the dominant structures
of representation and not to confront these with another knowledge."[56]

7. It is ironic that while many postcolonial writings, especially those influenced by poststructuralist readings of texts and histories, stress fragmentation, diversity and hybridity, they routinely posit a universal postcolonial
subject, a postcolonial condition, even a postcolonial woman. Writing about
the "universalizing tendency" in Bhabha's work (and other writings inspired
by it), Ania Loomba makes the pertinent observation that this

> derives partly from the fact in it colonial identities and colonial power
> relations are theorised entirely in semiotic or psychoanalytic terms.
> While theories of language and the psyche have given us sophisticated
> vocabularies of subjectivity, we also need to think about how subjectivi-
> ties are shaped by questions of class, gender and context. We need to
> peg the psychic splits engendered by colonial rule to specific histories
> and locations. In making the point that "there is no knowledge—po-
> litical or otherwise—outside representation" Bhabha reduces colonial
> relations to a linguistic interchange.[57]

Postcolonialism is a word that is useful only if we use it with qualifications.
If the word is uprooted from specific historic and cultural locations, the nature of postcolonial oppressions cannot be meaningfully investigated, and
the term may well obscure the very relations of domination that it seeks to
uncover. Postcoloniality, like patriarchy and racism, is articulated alongside
other economic, social, cultural and historical factors, and therefore, in practice, it works differently in different parts of the world.

Many doyens of postcolonial theory are well-heeled, self-exiled Asians ensconced in the Western academy. Indeed, a prominent critic Arif Dirlik asks, "When exactly does the 'postcolonial' begin? . . . I will supply here an answer that is only partially facetious: when Third World intellectuals have arrived in First World academe."[58] It is tempting to suggest that much of their popularity in Western academic circles (much more so than in the "Third World") is due not only to their playing on "postcolonial Western guilt" but also on the romantic image of the intellectual "exile," epitomizing the fissured identities and hybridities generated by colonial dislocations and celebrated in some postmodern works.

> But while of course there are themes in common across different kinds of diasporic experience and exiles, there are also enormous differences between them. The experiences and traumas generated by the single largest population shift in history—the division of India and Pakistan—are quite different from that of immigrants from once-colonised nations to Europe and America.[59]

Dirlik argues that the "language of postcolonialism is the language of First World post-structuralism." The "cult of the fragment" tends to confound ideological metanarratives with the actualities of power. The purely theoretical rejection of global narratives can end up silently supporting the latter. For *rejection* can mean two very different things—"opposition to" and "denying the existence of." Therefore, postcolonialism, which appears to critique the universal pretensions of Western knowledge systems and "starts off with a repudiation of the universalistic pretensions of Marxist language ends up not with its dispersal into local vernaculars but with a return to another First World language with universalist epistemological pretensions."[60]

In a similar vein, the Ghanaian-born social anthropologist Anthony Kwame Appiah has argued,

> Postcoloniality is the condition of what we might ungenerously call a comprador intelligentsia: a relatively small, Western-style, Western trained group of writers and thinkers, who mediate the trade in cultural commodities of world capitalism at the periphery. In the West they are known through the Africa they offer; their compatriots know them

both through the West they present to Africa and through an Africa they have invented for the world, for each other, and for Africa.[61]

POSTCOLONIALISM AND RESISTANCE FROM THE MARGINS

It has often been said that whatever is true of India, the opposite is equally true. Living day by day with the contradictions of ostentatious affluence and degrading poverty, luxury condominiums and appalling slums, internationally renowned management schools and rampant illiteracy is an overwhelmingly painful experience for many visitors as well as local Indians with a social conscience. The contrasts are as great, if not greater, than in precolonial and colonial times. Indian universities produce more engineering graduates each year than North America and Europe combined, but India's literacy level is only 65 percent. Despite the hype surrounding India's software industry and its "booming economy," the information-technology sector employs less than 1 percent of India's total pool of labor and is unlikely to be an answer to the hopes of the majority of its job-hungry masses.

One of the most polemical, anti-Christian Indian writers in recent years has been the journalist Arun Shourie. At the beginning of his book *Missionaries in India*, Shourie asserts:

> I believe that the interests of India as a whole must take precedence—overwhelming precedence—over the supposed interests of any part or group, religious, linguistic or secular. . . . [T]he movements which are currently afoot ostensibly to "liberate" and "empower" those groups may well break India. . . . [T]hose who foment them . . . ought to be dealt with using the full might of the State.[62]

Nowhere does Shourie explain who decides what are "the interests of India as a whole," nor how they are to be determined. The ominous, authoritarian tone of his pronouncement reflects the fear among wealthy, upper-caste Hindus that the voices from below and their clamor for justice will not only discredit their depiction of India as an emerging global superpower but erode their own privileged positions. It is tribal Christians and poor Muslims who have borne the brunt of violence at the hands of Shourie-inspired fanatics in recent times.

The postcolonial nation-state, like the nationalist movements that gave it birth, has often deepened the exclusions of European colonialism. Despite having an egalitarian constitution (largely the brainchild of the dalit leader Bhimrao Ramji Ambedkar), it could be argued that the continuing exclusions and oppressions of caste and patriarchy in India are far more degrading for ordinary folk than the oppressions of colonial rule. Women's movements, peasant struggles or caste and class-based dissent, both during and after colonial rule, expose the distance between the rhetoric and the reality of the nation-state. In recent years the effort to uncover the histories and standpoint of people excluded by nationalist projects has multiplied across the disciplines. Histories from below have attempted to tell other stories of rebellion and struggle as well as to relate them to the narratives of nationalism and decolonization.

The Subaltern Studies Collective, a group of (largely diaspora) Indian historians, is perhaps the best-known example of this approach. It shifts the crucial divide from that between colonial and anticolonial to that between "elite" and "subaltern."[63] The early work of this group focused on forgotten moments of insurgency (before, during and after British rule in India) when peasants and other subaltern groups rose up in often violent resistance to elite domination. However, this model of resistance conceives the everyday life of subaltern communities as comprising long periods of submissiveness punctuated by sudden, violent irruptions and contestations of elite power. More nuanced accounts, often inspired by feminist critiques, have emerged which draw attention to the various strategies and modes of resistance undertaken by disempowered people in the course of their daily lives. The conventional separation of the political from other spheres of human activity, such as the religious, the cultural and the domestic, is rightly challenged by this approach.

Not only does the Subaltern Studies project reject colonial and elite nationalist historiographies, but it has gradually distanced itself from the traditional Marxist approach of locking the subaltern into supposedly universal and fundamental categories such as worker and peasant. Marxist, universal teleologies ride roughshod over the specificities of subaltern struggles and interests, depriving such groups of their own autonomous agency. From the outset the project was faced with the formidable obstacle of a lack of any reliable historical material that describes the acts of resistance and social practices of subaltern groups in their own terms. The only way to recover the political voice and agency of the subaltern was through a critique of colonial and elite representation.

However, Subalternist historians have in turn been criticized on two principal fronts. Traditional Marxists argue that supposedly local narratives and struggles are penetrated and woven together by the forces of global capitalism. Others influenced by European poststructuralist thought find problematic the notions of autonomy, collective consciousness and subjective agency applied to the subaltern, notions that they believe belong within the realm of liberal humanism and the colonial historiographies criticized by the Subalternist project. These representations fail to register the complex power relations which efface the agency of the subaltern, especially women. In the oft-debated essay "Can the Subaltern Speak?" Gayatri Spivak argued that all attempts to retrieve subaltern voices perpetuated the same privileging of men as the actors in politics that characterized official historical discourse: "Both as object of colonialist historiography and as subject of insurgency, the ideological construction of gender keeps the male dominant. If, in the context of colonial production, the subaltern has no history and cannot speak, the subaltern as female is even more deeply in shadow."[64] She has turned to subaltern women's literature as an alternative space to discuss the involvement of women in insurgency and resistance in the social context of postcolonial India.

Several attempts to write histories from below have been charged with "essentializing" the identities of peasants or tribal communities. In trying to show how peasant struggles in India were distinct from the elite anticolonial movement, the Subalternist historians, Rosalind O'Hanlon suggests, construct an essential peasant identity in India, not fractured by differences of gender, class or location. But at the same time she is also deeply skeptical about accepting fully poststructuralist or postmodern views about identity:

> Some conception of experience and agency are absolutely required by
> the dispossessed's call for a politics of contest, for it is not clear how
> a dispersed effect of power relations can at the same time be an agent

whose experience and reflection form the basis of a striving for change. To argue that we need these categories in some form does not imply a return to undifferentiated and static conceptions of nineteenth-century liberal humanism. Our present challenge lies precisely in understanding how the underclasses we wish to study are at once constructed in conflictual ways as subjects yet also find the means through struggle to realize themselves in coherent and subjectively centered ways as agents.[65]

These are familiar issues to feminist scholars. Postmodernist and poststructuralist moves to dissolve all unities into more complex heterogeneities have been seen by some as undermining the legitimacy of the search for an identity by oppressed groups. The problem of aligning oneself with a radically antirepresentationalist stance is aptly summed up by Nancy Hartsock: "Why is it that just at the moment when so many of us who have been silenced begin to demand the right to name ourselves, to act as subjects rather than objects of history, that just then the concept of subjecthood becomes problematic?"[66]

Postcolonial theory thus seems to be torn by a clash of agendas: between, on the one hand, a romanticized search for a heroic underclass, and, on the other, a radically deconstructionist stance that remains skeptical of the existence of anything outside of discursive power relations. And here we come back full circle to Said himself. For Said vacillated between an acknowledgement that the Orient is more than a colonial cognitive construction (i.e., there are authentic features to be discovered) and a Foucauldian, antirepresentational position. But, as several critics have noted, his passionate moral outrage reveals a cosmopolitan humanist in the Enlightenment tradition. In an interview in 1986, he remarked, "Orientalism is theoretically inconsistent, and I designed it that way; I didn't want Foucault's method, or anybody's method, to override what I was trying to put forward. The notion of a noncoercive knowledge, which I come to at the end of the book, was deliberately anti-Foucault."[67]

SOME THEOLOGICAL REFLECTIONS

We have seen that postcolonial criticism has come to mean different things to different people, depending on the context of the writer. For some, it is fundamentally a challenge to Eurocentric ways of thinking, speaking and acting; to others, resistance to the totalizing discourses of the nationalist project or to the epistemic violence of Western imperialism; and to still others, a generalized commitment to an emancipatory, egalitarian political agenda.

1. Whatever its use or abuse, postcolonial criticism reminds us as Christian theologians that our social location shapes our speech. Hence it is important to pay attention not only to what is said in theological discourse but also who says it and how that discourse may be received and perceived by others. For example, who is the "we" in statements such as "We believe that . . ." or "We have moved beyond traditional ideas like . . ."? All theology has to be self-reflexive, in the Gadamarian sense of recognizing our prejudices rather than aspiring to a Godlike "objectivity."

In a work criticizing those historians who seemed to write unaware of the way in which their view of the past was influenced by their understanding of the present, the late British historian Herbert Butterfield (himself a Christian) makes the interesting observation that "it is not a sin in a historian to introduce a personal bias that can be recognised and discounted. The sin of historical composition is the organization of the story in such a way that bias cannot be recognised."[68]

2. The "we" in Christian speech always arises out of local contexts, but it is disciplined by our belonging to the global body of Christ. The church is the only truly global community, and it is largely a church of the poor. More spectacular than the resurgence of Islam—or the spread of New Age spiritualities in the Western world and Hindu or Buddhist nationalisms in the Indian subcontinent—has been the growth of indigenous Christian movements in the postcolonial South.

Recent mission historians have drawn attention to this southward shift of the center of gravity of the Christian church. It was in the decades following decolonization that Christianity outpaced Islam in Africa. As I. M. Lewis has noted, the "total effect of the pax colonica, as much involuntary as intended, was to promote an unprecedented expansion of Islam," and that "in half a century of European colonization Islam progressed more widely and more profoundly than in ten centuries of precolonial history."[69] The main bearers of African Christianity seem to have been the young, women, the oppressed and others lacking monetary and organizational power. This is in striking contrast with the spread of Islam in Africa or Hindutva among the Indian middle-class diaspora.

These facts seem to be hidden from postcolonial critics as well as the secular Western media. In typically Orientalist fashion, Christianity is usually naively identified with Europe and the United States in most postcolonialist writings, and all Christian missionaries of the colonial age are assumed to have been mere pawns in the hands of colonial administrators. No major work of Indian history, whether nationalist or subaltern, even mentions the contribution of, say, Bartholomew Ziegenbalg (1683-1719) and Henry Plütschau (1678-1747), William Carey (1761-1834) and the Serampore Mission, Christian Friedrich Schwartz (1726-1798), Constanzo Beschi (1680-1747), Robert Caldwell (1814-1891), George Pope (1820-1908), and a host of other foreign Christians who pioneered education for women and dalits, and opposed both the Orientalists and the Anglicists in rescuing vernacular tongues and cultures from relative oblivion. As for Africa, "it is remarkable," observes Andrew Walls, "that the immense Christian presence in Africa is so little a feature of modern African studies, and how much of the scholarly attention devoted to it is concentrated on manifestations that in Western terms seem most exotic."[70]

There are, of course, many shameful stories to be told of Western missionary complicity in colonial practices of domination. But the more typical stories of missionaries and local Christian leaders in India, Africa or the South Pacific who courageously defended native interests and combated racist theories and stereotypes propagated by their fellow countrymen are missing from the anti-Orientalist corpus.[71] From the initial commercial ventures of the East India Company to the heyday of the British Raj, colonial administrators were mostly hostile to Christian missionaries and made every effort not to interfere with local customs, religious beliefs and values. Ironically, and contrary to anti-Orientalist writers, it was only when the Serampore missionaries and Ram Mohan Roy (the Bengali reformer who was deeply influenced by Western education) convinced the governor, Lord Bentinck, that sati (the practice of widow self-immolation) had no authority in the sacred Hindu texts, did the British abolish the practice in 1829. Gayatri Spivak's influential reading of sati (in her essay "Can the Subaltern Speak?") is flawed by her lack of attention to such historical detail. Likewise, it is rarely mentioned that some British Christians in India such as C. F. Andrews were criticizing British racism and advocating full independence for India rather than dominion status within the empire long before Gandhi and the Congress Party took it up in 1924.[72] So impressed was Gandhi himself by Andrews's integrity that, in order to break the deadlock between Congress and the Muslim League, he made the remarkable proposal to the Viceroy Lord Mountbatten in 1947 that Andrews be appointed as the first president of independent India.[73]

3. We have seen, in chapter four, of how the equality of human beings that the gospel implies also extends to their languages and cultures. The West African scholars Lamin Sanneh and Kwame Bediako have shown how revolutionary is the Christian attitude to religious language. That ordinary people (including the "subalterns" of postcolonial discourse) should understand the Word of God in their own speech was a view with momentous consequences for social and cultural awakening. God's universal purposes did not supplant their own social enterprises but included them. Sanneh observes that the Christian view that all cultures may serve God's purpose "opened the way for the local idiom to gain the ascendancy over assertions of foreign superiority."[74] This had far-reaching social, cultural and political consequences. It is perhaps another of the many ironies of church history that such indigenous cultural renewal should have later turned into antimissionary sentiment (partly due to the identification of missions with European power) and into a chauvinistic nationalism.

David Smith, a former missionary in northern Nigeria, observes:

> Tribal peoples in Africa, South America and Asia facing various forms of oppression and experiencing the painful dislocations resulting from the impact of modernization have discovered a renewal of hope and a path leading toward cultural revitalization as the result of the work of such missionaries. Moreover, in contrast to social anthropologists, multinational business executives, TV crews and travel writers—all of whom return to the West after relatively brief cross-cultural sojourns

to continue well-paid academic, commercial or literary careers—many missionaries have been committed to an immersion in local cultures which required living for years in remote village locations, entering deeply into local life and, crucially, taking the time and effort needed to master indigenous languages.[75]

4. The Christian understanding of sin and evil enables us to have a more nuanced perspective on the politics of domination and exploitation. The subaltern-elite binary opposition is itself destabilized; not only is the subaltern situated along many conflicting axes of domination (gender, class, ethnic, etc.), but one can be a subaltern in one context and an elite in another. The subaltern is best regarded as a shifting signifier, not a homogeneous community devoid of its own hierarchies and hegemonies. "The very condition of being oppressed," writes the political scientist Fred Halliday in a critique of some types of anti-Orientalism:

> in a collectivity as much as in an individual, is likely to produce its own distorted forms of perception: mythical history, hatred and chauvinism towards others, conspiracy theories of all stripes, unreal phantasms of emancipation. . . . Those forces that are often deployed against the oppressive and global—the local, the indigenous, the communal—may therefore conceal as much confusion, and as much instrumentalism and coercion, as the structures they claim to challenge.[76]

This is why political ideologies that take either a Manichaean approach to the oppressed and the oppressor or emphasize the structural aspects of evil at the expense of the personal are not radical enough. Yesterday's poor migrant in Europe, for instance, is often today's most rabid opponent of new asylum-seekers. To use the old Exodus paradigm, it is easier to get the people out of Egypt than Egypt out of the people. Of course one must be committed to both, and the precise strategies adopted will vary from context to context. If conservative Christians need to be challenged to see how the individual cannot be conceptualized without the structural, those influenced by a secular liberal agenda that can only see people as victims of evil systems (or as "sinned against" and never as "sinners," except in the sense of passivity in the face of structural evil) need to be challenged to recover a biblical realism about our own responsible agency as well as our endless capacities for self-deception and self-destruction. This is not, of course, to say that our sins are equal or that we all sin in the same way. Rather it is to point to the complex ambivalences of human beings. It is interesting that Nancy Hartsock argues that Foucault's rather pessimistic world is one "in which things move, rather than people, a world in which subjects become obliterated or, rather, recreated as passive objects, a world in which passivity or refusal represent the only possible choices."[77]

Some postcolonial historians want to have their cake as well as eat it. It is commonly argued that the peasant, the tribesman, the woman or the working-class man is an autonomous agent of resistance. Yet, when it comes to sentiments like patriotism, nationalism or pan-national religious identities, of which they disapprove, that agency is denied to ordinary people who are treated as docile victims of state or elitist manipulation. In fact, while wars started by states have certainly reinforced such sentiments, "patriotism, jingoism, and inter-communal hatreds have also proceeded from the people and influenced otherwise cautious statesmen, rather than vice versa. . . . Nationalism was not simply a sentiment forced on hapless and naive peoples by wicked power-brokers and greedy capitalists."[78]

In his introduction to the revised edition of his classic *A Theology of Liberation*, Gustavo Gutiérrez observes,

> It is not enough that we be liberated from oppressive socio-economic structures: also needed is a personal transformation by which we live with profound inner freedom in the face of every kind of servitude. . . . Finally, there is liberation from sin, which attacks the deepest root of all servitude; for sin is the breaking of friendship with God and with other human beings, and therefore cannot be eradicated except by the unmerited redemptive love of the Lord whom we receive by faith and in communion with one another.[79]

It was the recognition of the universality of sin, variously expressed in different cultures, that prevented more biblically minded Christian leaders from joining the racist chorus of British imperialism in the nineteenth century. David Smith writes:

It is worth recalling that when the founder of the Salvation Army, William Booth, published his controversial study of social conditions in British cities and gave it the title *In Darkest England and the Way Out*, he was deliberately challenging racist models of humankind and subverting Stanley's depiction of the African continent. The darkness, Booth suggested, is not limited to distant lands which we classify as "uncivilized"; it is found in the back alleys of the slums of London and, indeed, when the causes of the degradation of the poor are investigated, we shall have to conclude that it is also to be found in Whitehall and the City of London.[80]

5. We have seen that postcolonial criticism is often impaled on the horns of the following dilemma: whether to align itself with humanist notions of an autonomous, sovereign subject and so run the risk of subsuming heterogeneous identities and histories into an abstract essentialism, or of embracing a poststructuralist antihumanism and so denying any universal moral platform from which to contest the material and epistemic violence of the colonial encounter. Gayatri Spivak has suggested a "strategic essentialism" as a way of resolving this dilemma: that while theory recognizes only the dispersal of "subject-effects," emancipatory practice requires us to adopt an essentialist stance toward the colonized self.[81] We saw that Said distanced himself from Foucault precisely because of his commitment to a universal human solidarity.

Russell Jacoby, who belongs to the more traditional school of Marxist critics, warns that "Once writers and scholars isolate local conditions from universal categories, they lose the ability to evaluate them. They become cheerleaders, nationalists and chauvinists." He goes on to argue,

> The universal also has its claims. Even, or exactly, the protest of the individual against a political system taps into universal rights and equalities. Without these universals, which weaken in the face of appeals to localism and authenticity, the opposition crumbles. In the name of universals, the protest not only protests, but affirms a world beyond degradation and unhappiness; it hints of utopia.[82]

It is important to note that this clash between humanist and antihumanist discourse, which has been imported from post-Nietzschean European

philosophy and which generates a corresponding split between theory and
practice for some postcolonial critics, is itself a result of marginalizing other
discourses in the secular academy. Christian theology, for instance, transcends this dichotomy. What it means to be human can only be grasped in
its full scope on the basis of God's saving self-communication with us. For
the triune God, plurality and the "play of difference" are not alien territory.
Identity and difference are held together within a defining narrative. When
the patristic theologians used the word *person* (*hypostasis* in Greek)—whether
in connection with God or human beings—they meant a distinct identity, an
otherness, which only made sense in relationship. But *person* soon became a
word for a different kind of otherness: an aloneness, a naked individuality of
the mind closed in on itself. Trinitarian theology insists that persons are not
autonomous centers of consciousness; rather they participate in one another's
lives, whether or not they recognize it. In the eternal life of self-giving and
self-responsive love that we call God, the persons so indwell one another that
we cannot speak of any one person without implying something about the
other two as well.

Thus, although human persons are not to be confused with the divine
persons, there is a distinctively Christian ontology of humanness that points
beyond both Enlightenment humanism and postmodern antihumanism.
There is no sovereign, autonomous human subject at the center of history;
nor are there only subterranean force fields throwing up the multiplicity of
human "subject effects." All human history is framed by the unfolding divine
economy, which is definitive of what it is to be human and to act humanly.
God gives to his creatures the capacity to choose their own futures, to form
and act for reasons and ends of their own. But this creative freedom is for
the sake of a love, a mutuality: "we have distance for the sake of nearness,
autonomy for the sake of exchange and love, irreducible otherness for the sake
of genuine union."[83]

So identity is neither a self-sufficient fortress that has to be always defended; nor is it simply a wound in the flux of difference, an infinitely pli-
ant self, like the ever-changing screensavers on our computer monitors. To
switch the metaphors, we do not have to peel away layer after layer to uncover
the authentic self of modernity, nor do we have to reject interiority utterly

in order to settle for the surface fluctuations of the postmodern self. We are both "a coming from" and "a going toward"; and the divine conversation which enfolds us human beings and into which we are invited gives a new direction to otherwise false or fractured life stories.

How does one build genuine community with the hopeless and excluded, those whose identities have been fractured and decentered by oppressive discourses, whether colonial or postcolonial? Not by celebrating further fragmentation. There is all the difference in the world between dispensing with foundations and essences because you have a secure sense of your own worth, and dispensing with them when you are not sure who you are and need a secure identity to become all that you want to be. Liberal irony and postmodern jouissance are options only available to those whose lives are not constantly threatened with erasure. If you are a woman selling trinkets in a Delhi street and about to have your makeshift shelter torn down by municipal bulldozers, it helps to have a secure sense of self arising from another narrative (than what the powers-that-be dictate) if you are to resist and demand compensation.

Lacking a coherent narrative that can mediate between identity and difference, rationality and spontaneity, freedom and belonging, the ideological pluralism on which some forms of postcoloniality depend dissolves, paradoxically, into a predictable uniformity. Without an overarching normative structure that can articulate difference, it is impossible to recognize genuine difference, let alone be challenged by it. Unless human experiences are commensurable and we can communicate intelligibly across our differences, we remain isolated within our own ways of seeing and doing things. We are thus immune to criticism and change. We are left with empty rhetoric about our "responsibility" to "the other," but the basic questions *why* and *how* are sidestepped. The "other" is left nameless, and concrete particularities are dissolved into abstractions. How can one love and care for that whose nature is unknown to us? It is so much easier to ignore this insubstantial other or to reduce the other to the satisfaction of my desire, the answer to my lack. Also, as Jacoby's previous comment indicates, fashionable though it may be in some academic circles to proclaim the mantras of antihumanism, all who are driven by a passion for a universal justice (as Derrida himself was in his later years) are actually parasitic on more substantial (usually religious) understandings of the human—as much as Marx's own passion for justice was parasitic on his Judeo-Christian upbringing.

6. Who speaks for the voiceless? That too is a topic that has provoked heated argument among postcolonialist theorists and subaltern historians. We have pointed out the anomalous position of Ivy League professors dwelling in an arcane world of literary texts claiming to speak for those who have been robbed of speech and will by the forces of neo-colonial global capitalism. This invites charges of paternalism and a self-serving academic industry. Indeed, some critics have suggested that the new discipline of "postcolonial literature" is less a subversive field than a career move for largely upperclass Asians in American universities. Commenting on the way Derridean and Foucauldian texts are appropriated, Russell Jacoby observes, somewhat cynically:

> In a world composed of texts, no texts are central. Conversely, if there is no center, anything is marginal to something. This is music to the ears of many academics, who, no matter how esteemed and established, often claim to be marginalized, victims lacking proper recognition and respect. They see themselves as outsiders, blasting the establishment. Like uptown executives cruising around in pricey jeeps and corporate lawyers in luxurious utility trucks, they pose as rugged souls from the back country; they threaten the seats of power as they glide into their own reserved parking spots.[84]

No less important is the question, Who are the voiceless? In the Indian subcontinent, the term *subaltern* has been so expanded to cover such a disparate range of people (including upperclass women, simply because they are women) that it has become quite vacuous.[85] At the same time, the selectivity of the deconstructionist reading practices promoted by critics such as Spivak reveal a clear left-wing Western academic bias in the causes they espouse. For instance, abortions in postcolonial India have been legal and widespread for decades. Yet, it was only when the gravity of the male-female birth ratio in Indian society was recently highlighted by social scientists that feminist groups and other social activists began to campaign against the practice of fetal screening for gender. "Female feticide" has become the new battle cry, and the voice of the male fetus has been effectively silenced. The male-female polarity becomes rigid and the "ideological construction of gender" returns with a vengeance.

Furthermore, in the postcolonial lexicon, diasporic hermeneutics and the experience of hybridity and hyphenated identities by Third World academics and artists living in the West seem to have a privileged place. However, it is salutary to remember that it is Africa, not Europe or North America, that is host to the largest number of refugees in the world (with millions of Christians among them), followed by South Asia. These are people whose experiences are remote from those of cosmopolitan postcolonial theorists; the majority of the latter have fled not persecution or war but less lucrative academic jobs in their native countries. The relative absence of these people from postcolonial discourse betrays the parochialism, indeed Eurocentrism, of much postcolonial writing.

Unlike postcolonial theory, liberation theology (in its scriptural witness to God's "preferential option for the poor") stresses not representation but solidarity, concrete friendship with the poor. The subaltern is not simply a represented victim of history but one who is dignified and empowered by the incarnation to become an agent of a transformative historical project known as the kingdom of God.

7. Similarly, who speaks for Third World theology? A number of dictionaries and anthologies that have appeared in recent years on Third World theology, Asian hermeneutics and the like are usually written by Western Christians or by non-Western Christians domiciled in Western academics. There is also a curious selectivity shown in the way these anthologies are usually compiled. Asian theologies are taken to be theologies addressing what is called, in typical Orientalist fashion, the Asian context; and the latter is reduced to poverty, women's empowerment and the presence of ancient world religions (Hinduism, Buddhism and Islam to some extent; rarely primal religions). Western theologians feel free to write on such "Asian issues," but Asian theologians who address other issues within their churches (e.g., healing, ethnic fragmentation, ecclesiastical politics, responding to persecution) or global issues (e.g., postmodernism, genetic technology, evolutionism, the Internet) tend to be marginalized in such anthologies. Moreover, only if one were to espouse the typical Western secular liberal agenda (e.g., same-sex

partnerships, prochoice, the equal validity of all religious worldviews) can one acquire the status of being a "progressive" theologian. Hence the huge gulf between those who profess to speak for the Third World church (in most ecumenical theological conferences) and the Third World church itself.

Postcolonial criticism has brought its deconstructive scrutiny to bear on the Bible.[86] Here the typical approach boils down to (1) reading the Bible as just another text on par with other literary and religious texts, carrying no special status or authority in the life of the academy, (2) showing up the contradictions in the biblical text and especially the places where the voices of the oppressed are silenced, (3) rewriting the text, or jettisoning whole texts altogether, in the service of a domination-free political agenda. Here the postcolonial critic simply mirrors the violence of colonial hermeneutics. He or she positions him- or herself above the text as its judge, extracts what is useful for his or her political purposes, and paradoxically wields the secularist liberal worldview of the academy (itself part of the colonial legacy) to outlaw all other theological voices. So, while difference is celebrated in theory, in practice differences tend be trivialized and subsumed under an old-style global humanism. There is nothing in the text, or any "other" beyond the text, that can anymore disturb and challenge the postcolonial reader's life world.

Moreover, there is surely a huge difference that the aims of biblical study make to the interpretation of the biblical text. Postcolonial criticism may be justified in approaching the Bible as a general text and not as the canonical, self-authorizing text of the church. Nevertheless, there is a world of difference in the power dynamics involved between, say, reading the Bible in order to hear God speaking to me and to discover what obedience to God means for me today, and reading it as a university lecturer in a religious studies department who is driven by the academic pressure to both defend the relevance of my subject and also be "original" and prolific in my publications so as to obtain tenure. It is strange that, for all its obsession with issues of power/knowledge, postcolonial biblical criticism has not applied its poststructural hermeneutics of suspicion to its own academic context.

8. Postcolonial criticism helps us to appreciate the hybridized and fluid nature of identity formation in many societies today under the impact of globalization and the flow of peoples. Some African and Asian attempts at

Christological reconstruction in the name of contextualization lack credibility. Their theological method begins with an African or Asian "reality" that is assumed to be given and unchanging, and then searches for a Christology that would be relevant or meaningful to that context. Cecie Kolie writes of fellow African theologians:

> Since their communities cannot name Christ personally without going to the Bible and the catechisms, they do just the opposite, and attribute to Christ the traditional titles of initiator, chief, great ancestor, and so on, that they would like to see him given in their communities. Once more we impose on our fellow Africans the way of seeing that we have learned from our Western masters.[87]

Kenneth Ross points out that this runs counter to the approach adopted by the Nicene theologians. The latter did not see their task as primarily one of creative construction but of articulating, faithfully and coherently, a reality that was already there, expressed in the life and worship of the believing community. Ross suggests that this offers a "liberating methodology" for African (and, I would add, other Third World) theologians:

> They are not required, on the one hand, to present a pre-packaged Christ who remains wrapped up in terminology and conceptuality that has been constructed elsewhere. Nor are they required, on the other hand, to work out their own Christology on the basis of their own assessment of what will be relevant to the African situation. Their task is, in fact, to bring to the clearest possible expression a reality which is already powerfully evident within African life, namely God's revelation in Jesus Christ.[88]

Ross's own field studies in northern Malawi showed how Christians there showed a marked preference for biblical titles such as Savior, Lord, Healer, even Messiah, over against those which most African theologians have advanced as truly African: ancestor, chief and so on. Such data could be interpreted as evidence of the intellectual passivity of the Christians, or it could be interpreted, as Ross himself does, "in terms of a community being drawn to biblical vocabulary and conceptuality as a means of accurately stating what it has to say about the reality of Jesus Christ."[89] Ross points out that a comparable development in patristic theology would be the way in which the initial cultural inclination to understand Jesus in terms of the Word *(logos)* gradually gave way to the Old Testament idiom of Son, as this could better articulate the relational understanding of God which was found in the gospel.

> So in African Christology it may well be that the categories which at first seem to make sense of Jesus in African terms gradually give way to the more biblical categories which are preferred. . . . As the Bible comes to occupy an increasingly formative place in the life of the community, its vocabulary and conceptuality may come to displace or revise the terms and categories which initially were predominant. It may be that we are entering a time when biblical vocabulary and concepts are no less indigenous than those derived from the African tradition![90]

Thus, as Jesus Christ enters as a participant into the vernacular world of a community, becomes known there and steadily comes to occupy a central place in the spiritual and moral universe of the people, his identity and significance comes to be recognized. In authentic contextualization, not only is there a conceiving of Jesus Christ in terms of traditional culture, there is also a reconception and reorientation of that culture in terms of the apostolic tradition.

9. Why are North American or British or German theologies never named as such, but Indian or Latin American or African theologies are? Western theologies are simply assumed to be universal, but non-Western theologies are "contextual." The insularity of most Western theological institutions is astonishing. The study of other cultures and societies is a marginal concern, despite the growth of Asian and African communities in the cities of Europe and North America. The only situation in which the typical theology student is likely to learn about other cultures, histories and religions is if he were to follow a course on missiology. In the more academic faculties, these courses do not exist. And in most missiology courses Asian religions are taught in an Orientalist style. Moreover, where chairs of mission or missiology have been established, these studies have become isolated from other parts of the theological task. They became what David Bosch calls "the theological insti-

tution's 'department of foreign affairs,' dealing with the exotic but at the same time the peripheral."[91]

There is a great need to develop local theologies and missionary practices that receive from all that is best in other cultures and contexts, while being relevant to one's own. In the church we now have a hermeneutical community that is global in scope and character, so we can test the local expressions of Christian faith against one another, thus manifesting the true catholicity of the body of Christ. The way we become truly global Christians is by seriously engaging with our local contexts as members of a global community that has redefined our identities and interests.

The implications for the way that we read church history are clear. The global diversity of world Christianity today requires a more diversified understanding of Christian tradition than that which is given in the dominant master narrative of Western Christianity. The historian Dale Irvin urges, rightly in my view, a "genealogical approach" to Christian history which "intentionally seeks to articulate its multiple origins, and uncover its significant ruptures, within a wider family of traditions."[92] An adequate historiography of the Christian church requires that "postcolonial, postmodern narratives of church history must be more global than the master narrative of modernism if we are not to remain captive to the political imperialism of Western Christendom."[93] Moreover, if the shared faith in Jesus Christ as Lord that is embodied in different Christian traditions is not to die of irrelevance, there will always be a significant measure of risk in every act of retraditioning that faith in new contexts.

This also implies, on the one hand, that no local theology (whether German, Brazilian or Korean) can ever become normative universally, even though it may have universal relevance. On the other hand, since all Christian theologies endeavor to speak truthfully (albeit, in broken speech) of the universal God whose triune nature is disclosed, salvific purpose effected, and divine authority mediated through a historically grounded narrative, the theologian—as a member of the Christian community—indwells that narrative him- or herself and seeks to articulate it in dialogue with other voices, past and present. Since Scripture invites us to see ourselves as living in the final (eschatological) act of the divine drama of redemption, we are at liberty, within that final act, to create new scenes as we experience new contexts. However, the test of the credibility of such new scenes is whether they (1) are faithful to the overall story line and (2) further our obedience to the original vision of how the play will end. What we are not at liberty to do is to act as if the play starts with us. If we change the story line, import scenes from other plays or rewrite the ending, we have another play and not the Christian one.

Musical improvisation too provides an apt analogy for Scripture reading and the theological task, as expressed so well by the New Testament scholar Bishop N. T. Wright:

> As all musicians know, improvisation does not at all mean a free-for-all where "anything goes," but precisely a disciplined and careful listening to all the other voices around us, and a constant attention to the themes, rhythms and harmonies of the complete performance so far, the performance which we are now called to continue. At the same time, of course, it invites us, while being fully obedient to the music so far, and fully attentive to the voices around us, to explore fresh expressions, provided they will eventually lead to that ultimate resolution which appears in the New Testament as the goal, the full and complete new creation which was gloriously anticipated in Jesus' resurrection. The music so far, the voices around us, and the ultimate multi-part harmony of God's new world: these, taken together, form the parameters for appropriate improvisation in the reading of scripture and the announcement and living out of the gospel it contains. All Christians, all churches, are free to improvise their own variations designed to take the music forwards. No Christian, no church, is free to play out of tune.[94]

In similar fashion, Kevin Vanhoozer reminds us, in an important essay on theological method in an era of world Christianity, that our Christian praxis "must correspond to the way of Jesus, that our stories must correspond to his story. . . . [T]he canonical text carries an authority that one's contemporary cultural context does not. Our deepest, truest identity is thus discovered in biblical narrative, not the so-called foundation narratives of this or that culture or this or that nation."[95]

Vanhoozer's final argument forms a fitting conclusion:

What ultimately gets translated, contextualized, or performed from culture to culture, then, is theodrama: the pattern of evangelical—gospel-centered—speech and action. How do we recognize theodramatic fidelity from one context to another? The operative term is direction. Doctrinal formulations must lead people in different contexts in the same basic direction, namely, in the way of truth and life as these are defined by the story of God's words and deeds that culminate in Jesus Christ. . . . The task of theology is to train speakers and doers of the Word, people who can render in contextually appropriate forms the poiesis and the praxis, the truth and the justice, of God or, in terms of the proposal set forth herein, people who can improvise the gospel of Jesus Christ.[96]

NOTES

Prologue

[1]Thornton Wilder, *The Bridge of San Luis Rey* (Harmondsworth, U.K.: Penguin, 1927).

[2]Vinoth Ramachandra, *Gods That Fail* (Carlisle, U.K.: Paternoster Press; Downers Grove, Ill: InterVarsity Press, 1996).

[3]John Milbank, "Sovereignty, Empire, Capital, and Terror," in *Strike Terror No More: Theology, Ethics and the New War*, ed. Jon L. Berquist (St. Louis: Chalice Press, 2002), p. 65.

[4]Jon Sobrino, *Where Is God? Earthquake, Terrorism, Barbarity, and Hope*, trans. Margaret Wilde (Maryknoll, N.Y.: Orbis, 2004), p. 69.

[5]Ibid., p. 3.

[6]Ibid., p. 31.

[7]Sam Harris, *The End of Faith: Religion, Terror, and the Future of Reason* (New York: W. W. Norton, 2005).

[8]Northrop Frye, *The Great Code* (London: Routledge, 1982), p. 32.

[9]Mary Midgley, *The Myths We Live By* (London and New York: Routledge, 2004), pp. 120-21.

[10]Vinoth Ramachandra, " 'Who Can Say What and To/For Whom?' Postcolonial Theory and Christian Theology," in *Mission and the Next Christendom*, ed. Timothy Yates (Sheffield, U.K.: Cliff College Publishing, 2005).

[11]Harry Wilce, "Young Minds in Hi-Tech Turmoil," *The Independent* (London), November 30, 2006.

Chapter 1: Myths of Terrorism

[1]In an interview in 1988, Zbigniew Brzezinski, President Carter's National Security Advisor, admitted that Washington had lied about the American role. "According to the official version of history," he said, "CIA aid to the mujahedin began during 1980, that is, after the Soviet army invaded Afghanistan. . . . But the reality, secretly guarded

until now, is completely otherwise" (*Le Nouvel Observateur*, January 15-21, 1998, cited in John Pilger, *The New Rulers of the World* [London and New York: Verso, 2002], p. 151).

[2]In 1893 Britain arbitrarily fixed the border between an invincible Afghanistan and British India, establishing the tribal trust territories as a turbulent buffer between them. After the partition of India in 1947, the new government in Pakistan, recognizing its inability to control its 1,500 kilometer western borders and the aggressive Pashtun clans that spilled over on both sides, left the tribal trust territories under Pashtun customary law.

[3]For the full story, meticulously researched, of the mujahedin divisions and the rise of the Taliban movement, see Michael Griffin, *Reaping the Whirlwind: The Taliban Movement in Afghanistan* (London: Pluto Press, 2001).

[4]Ibid., p. 147.

[5]Griffin, *Reaping the Whirlwind*, p. 26.

[6]*Wall Street Journal*, cited in Lance Selfa, "Behind the Fog of Deception: Washington's Real War Aims," *International Socialist Review* 20, November-December 2001.

[7]Dick Cheney, cited in George Monbiot, "America's Pipe Dream," *The Guardian*, October 23, 2001. See also <www.monbiot.com/archives/2001/10/23/americas-pipe-dream>.

[8]Bill Richardson, cited in Stephen Kinzer, "On Piping Out Caspian Oil, US Insists the Cheaper, Shorter Way Isn't Better," *New York Times*, November 8, 1998.

[9]Griffin, *Reaping the Whirlwind*, pp. 116-17. See also Michael T. Klare, *Resource Wars* (New York: Henry Holt, 2001), esp. pp. 1-50, 81-108, for a description of the great power machinations in the Caspian Sea region.

[10]Francis Robinson, "Present Shadows, Past Glory," *The Times Literary Supplement*, September 6, 2002, pp. 14-15. Robinson is a specialist in South Asian Islam.

[11]John L. Esposito and John O. Voll, *Makers of Contemporary Islam* (New York: Oxford University Press, 2001), p. 39.

[12]Between 1830 when the French occupied Algeria and 1920 when the League of Nations subjected the Arab provinces of the Ottoman Empire to European occupation under the mandate system, every part of the Middle East and North Africa, except Turkey, succumbed to European imperial domination.

[13]Esposito and Voll, *Makers of Contemporary Islam*, p. 16.

[14]Richard W. Bulliet, *The Case for Islamo-Christian Civilization* (New York: Columbia University Press, 2004), pp. 87-90.

[15]Ibid., p. 84.

[16]Ibid., p. 92.

[17]Maulana Mawdudi, quoted in T. N. Madan, *Modern Myths, Locked Minds: Secularism and Fundamentalism in India* (New Delhi, India: Oxford University Press, 1998), p. 141.

[18]In the aftermath of the devastating earthquake in northern Pakistan in October 2005, it was Islamist development organizations that stepped in to help the survivors, while the Pakistani government dragged its feet.

[19]Robert W. Hefner, "Secularization and Citizenship in Modern Indonesia," in *Religion, Modernity and Postmodernity,* ed. Paul Heelas (Oxford: Blackwell, 1998), p. 148. For a large-scale survey of widely divergent attitudes in four Muslim-majority countries, including Indonesia, see Riaz Hassan, *Faithlines: Muslim Conceptions of Islam and Society* (New York: Oxford University Press, 2002).

[20]Deobandism is a South Asian strand within the broader nineteenth-century movement known as Salafism. The latter refers to those who follow the salaf or al-salaf-al-saalih, the prophet Mohammad's contemporary followers, known as his Companions, and the next two generations of Muslims. A Salafi is an early Muslim who had access, it is believed, to a purer interpretation of the revelation of the Qur'an and therefore understood its message more clearly. Salafism does not necessarily advocate political violence. It does, however tend to view the world in Manichaean terms, with the West the source of all the impurities that have contaminated the world of Islam and obscured the message of God. Osama bin Laden considers himself a salafist.

[21]See Pilger, *New Rulers of the World,* p. 66.

[22]For the sources of these and other figures, see ibid., chap. 2.

[23]Jonathan Belke, "Years Later, US Attack on Factory Still Hurts Sudan," *Boston Globe,* August 22, 1999.

[24]Phil Rees, *Dining with Terrorists: Meetings with the World's Most Wanted Militants* (London: Pan Macmillan, 2005), p. 27.

[25]Abdel Aziz Rantisi, quoted in ibid., p. 272.

[26]George Orwell, "Politics and the English Language," in *The Collected Essays, Journalism and Letters of George Orwell,* ed. Sonia Orwell and Ian Angus (Harmondsworth, U.K.: Penguin, 1970), 4:170.

[27]Ibid., p. 166.

[28]Ibid., p. 157.

[29]Richard Boucher, cited in Rees, *Dining with Terrorists,* p. 66.

[30]George W. Bush, "Address to a Joint Session of Congress and the American People," *WhiteHouse.gov,* September 20, 2001 <www.whitehouse.gov/news/releases/2001/09/20010920-8.html>.

[31]George W. Bush, "President Discusses War Against Terrorism: Address to the Nation," *WhiteHouse.gov,* November 8, 2001 <www.whitehouse.gov/news/releases/2001

/11/20011108-13.html>.

[32]George W. Bush, "President Bush Announces Major Combat Operations in Iraq have Ended," *WhiteHouse.gov,* March 1, 2003 <www.whitehouse.gov/news/releases/2003 /05/20030501-15.html>.

[33]Irfan Awas, interviewed by Phil Rees in his *Dining with Terrorists,* p. 328.

[34]Robespierre, cited in John Dunn, *Setting the People Free: The Story of Democracy* (London: Atlantic Books, 2005), p. 118.

[35]The Tamil Tigers's full name is Liberation Tigers of Tamil Eelam, usually abbreviated to LTTE or just Tamil Tigers. For a history of the movement, see M. R. Narayan Swamy, *Tigers of Lanka: From Boys to Guerrillas* (Colombo, Sri Lanka: Vijitha Yapa, 1994). For more general historical background to the war, see K. M. De Silva, *Reaping the Whirlwind: Ethnic Conflict, Ethnic Politics in Sri Lanka* (New Delhi, India: Penguin, 1998); Stanley J. Tambiah, *Buddhism Betrayed? Religion, Politics, and Violence in Sri Lanka* (Chicago and London: University of Chicago Press, 1992); Stanley J. Tambiah, *Leveling Crowds: Ethnonationalist Conflicts and Collective Violence in South Asia* (Berkeley: University of California Press, 1996), chap. 4.

[36]See Jo Becker, "Funding the Final War: LTTE Intimidation and Extortion in the Tamil Diaspora," *Human Rights Watch* 18, no. 1(C) (2006).

[37]For a survey of peace initiatives over the past two decades, see *Negotiating Peace in Sri Lanka: Efforts, Failures and Lessons,* vols. 1 and 2, ed. Kumar Rupesinghe (Colombo, Sri Lanka: Foundation for Co-Existence, 2006).

[38]"National Strategy for Combating Terrorism," *WhiteHouse.gov,* September 2006 <www .whitehouse.gov/nsc/nsct/2006>.

[39]George Monbiot, "America's Terrorist Training Camp," *The Guardian,* October 30, 2001. See also <www.monbiot.com/archives/2001/10/30/americas-terrorist-training-camp>.

[40]Oliver O'Donovan, *The Just War Revisited* (Cambridge: Cambridge University Press, 2003), pp. 30, 64-65.

[41]Ibid., pp. 45-46.

[42]Ibid., pp. 41, 42.

[43]Cf. Noam Chomsky, *Imperial Ambitions: Conversations on the Post-9/11 World* (New York: Metropolitan Books, 2005).

[44]The October 2006 issue of the British medical journal *The Lancet* claimed that around 650,000 Iraqi civilians had been killed (by all sides) since the invasion began, though the U.S. government vigorously disputed the claim. However, neither the Iraqi nor U.S. governments came up with alternative figures.

[45]O'Donovan, *Just War Revisited,* p. 71.

[46]Ibid., p. 73.

[47]Ibid., p. 77.

[48]See Raymond Bonner, "The CIA's Secret Torture," *New York Review of Books*, January 11, 2007.

[49]O'Donovan, *Just War Revisited*, p. 51.

[50]Jürgen Moltmann, "Hope in a Time of Arrogance and Terror," in *Strike Terror No More: Theology, Ethics, and the New War*, ed. Jon L. Berquist (St. Louis: Chalice Press, 2002), p. 184.

[51]Paulo Freire, *Pedagogy of the Oppressed*, 30th anniversary edition (New York and London: Continuum, 2003), p. 55. Originally printed in 1970.

[52]"Arms Without Borders—Why a Globalized Trade Needs Global Controls," Oxfam International, October 2, 2006 <www.oxfam.org/en/policy/pa2006>.

[53]"A More Secure World: Our Shared Responsibility," *Report of the Secretary-General's High-Level Panel on Threats, Challenges and Change* (New York: United Nations Publications, 2004), p. 4.

[54]Ibid., pp. 57-58.

[55]Not only have its various agencies played an indispensable role in tackling global poverty, helping refugees, fighting the HIV/AIDS pandemic and restricting trade in small arms, but the UN weapons inspection process in Iraq actually succeeded in ridding that country of WMDs—a fact quickly forgotten and not acknowledged by those who went to war because they alleged that the UN process was ineffective!

[56]Moltmann, "Hope in a Time of Arrogance and Terror," p. 185.

[57]John Paul Lederach, *The Moral Imagination: The Art and Soul of Building Peace* (Oxford: Oxford University Press, 2005), p. 172.

[58]Ibid., pp. 34-39.

[59]From *The Oxford Book of Prayer* (Oxford: Oxford University Press, 1985), p. 80, quoted in Oliver O'Donovan, *Peace and Certainty: A Theological Essay on Deterrence* (Grand Rapids: Eerdmans, 1989), p. 114. See also his commentary on it, pp. 114-16.

Chapter 2: Myths of Religious Violence

[1]Nabil Matar, *Turks, Moors, and Englishmen in the Age of Discovery* (New York: Columbia University Press, 1999), p. 9.

[2]Linda Colley, *Captives: Britain, Empire and the World, 1600-1850* (London: Pimlico, 2002), p. 122.

[3]Cf. Nabil Matar, *Islam in Britain, 1558-1685* (Cambridge: Cambridge University Press, 2001).

[4]Richard W. Bulliet, *The Case for Islamo-Christian Civilization* (New York: Columbia University Press, 2004), p. 45 (emphasis is Bulliet's).

[5]Edward Said, *Orientalism* (Harmondsworth, U.K.: Penguin, 1978), pp. 1-2.

[6]For Islamic influences in technology, art and literature on medieval Europe, see Jack Goody, *Islam in Europe* (Cambridge: Polity Press, 2004), pp. 66-74.

[7]Cf. Bat Ye'or, *The Decline of Eastern Christianity Under Islam: From Jihad to Dhimmitude,* trans. Miriam Kochan and David Littman (Cranbury, N.J.: Associated University Presses, 1996), p. 233.

[8]Ibid., p. 217.

[9]Ibid., pp. 231-32.

[10]Ibid., p. 265.

[11]For instance, until around 1780 there was no such "religion" as Hinduism in India but rather a vast, extended family of systems of belief, philosophies, rituals and techniques for harnessing esoteric power. The identification of "nonviolence" and "tolerance" with "Hinduism" is a result of nineteenth-century Western scholarship. Similarly, the Marian dogmas were promulgated as official Roman Catholic teaching only in 1854 and 1950. Papal infallibility was first defined at the Vatican Council of 1870.

[12]William T. Cavanaugh, " 'A Fire Strong Enough to Consume the House': The Wars of Religion and the Rise of the State," *Modern Theology* 11, no. 4 (1995): 403.

[13]Mark Juergensmeyer, *Terror in the Mind of God: The Global Rise of Religious Violence,* 3rd ed. (Berkeley: University of California Press, 2003), pp. 191, 151.

[14]Ibid., p. 197.

[15]Vinoth Ramachandra, "Globalization, Nationalism, and Religious Resurgence," in *Globalizing Theology: Belief and Practice in an Era of World Christianity,* ed. Craig Ott and Harold Netland (Grand Rapids: Baker Academic, 2006), p. 215.

[16]Ian Buruma and Avishai Margalit, *Occidentalism: A Short History of Anti-Westernism* (London: Atlantic Books, 2004), p. 63.

[17]Fred Halliday, *Two Hours That Shook the World: September 11, 2001—Causes and Consequences* (London: Saqi Books, 2002), p. 126.

[18]Anantanand Rambachan, "Keynote Address, Hindu-Christian Consultation, Varanasi, India, October 23-27, 1997," *Current Dialogue* 31 (1998): 34.

[19]The legendary Pali chronicles, the Dipavamsa and the Mahavamsa, have assumed a canonical status among the island's Buddhists. They depict the triumphs in battle of Buddhist kings over Hindu invaders.

[20]See Stanley J. Tambiah, *Buddhism Betrayed? Religion, Politics, and Violence in Sri Lanka* (Chicago and London: University of Chicago Press, 1992); Stanley J. Tambiah, "Buddhism, Politics, and Violence in Sri Lanka," in *Fundamentalisms and the State: Remaking Politics, Economies, and Militance,* The Fundamentalism Project 3, ed. Martin E. Marty and R. Scott Appleby (Chicago and London: University of Chicago Press, 1991); Ga-

nanath Obeyesekere, "Buddhism, Nationhood, and Cultural Identity: A Question of Fundamentals," in *Fundamentalisms Comprehended,* The Fundamentalism Project 5, ed. Martin E. Marty and R. Scott Appleby (Chicago and London: University of Chicago Press, 1993).

[21]Rajmohan Ramanathapillai, *Sacred Symbols and the Adoption of Violence in Tamil Politics in Sri Lanka* (master's thesis, McMaster University, Hamilton, Ont., 1991).

[22]Ibid., p. 134.

[23]See K. M. deSilva, "The Islamic Factor," in *Reaping the Whirlwind: Ethnic Conflict, Ethnic Politics in Sri Lanka* (New Delhi, India: Penguin, 1998).

[24]In the 1667 Treaty of Breda, the formerly British-held island of Run in the Banda Islands was ceded to the Dutch in exchange for Manhattan Island in the British colony of America.

[25]Farsijana Risakotta-Adeney, "Politics, Ritual and Identity in Indonesia: A Moluccan History of Religion and Social Conflict," (Ph.D. diss., Radboud University, Nijmegen, Netherlands, May 2005), esp. chaps. 3 and 5; also available online at <http://webdoc .ubn.ru.nl/mono/r/risakotta_f/poliriani.pdf>.

[26]*The Sydney Morning Herald* of January 27, 2001, reported that on six islands affected by the conflict, 3,928 Christians were forced to convert to Islam.

[27]The international media spotlighted the beheading of four Christian schoolgirls on October 29, 2005. Killings of Muslims in reprisal for attacks on Christians have also been brutal. But the judicial execution of Christians responsible for murder has been swift, while very few Muslim ringleaders have been brought to justice.

[28]Christopher Hitchens, quoted in "Christopher Hitchens: You Ask the Questions," *The Independent,* March 2, 2002.

[29]Richard Dawkins, "Religion's Misguided Missiles," *The Guardian,* September 15, 2001.

[30]Jessica Stern, *Terror in the Name of God: Why Religious Militants Kill* (New York: HarperCollins, 2003), p. 26.

[31]Walter Wink, *The Powers That Be: Theology for a New Millennium* (New York: Doubleday, 1998), p. 42.

[32]The military historian John Keegan notes that "The First World war killed at least ten million people in battle, most of them young or very young men, and millions more died from war-related causes. The Second World War killed fifty million, of whom fewer than half were servicemen in uniform' (*War and Our World* [New York: Vintage, 1998, p. 2]).

[33]George W. Bush, "Address to the Joint Session of Congress and the American People," *WhiteHouse.gov,* September 20, 2001 <www.whitehouse.gov/news/releases/2001 /09/20010920-8.html>.

[34]J. Hoagland, "An Old Trooper's Smoking Gun," *Washington Post,* February 6, 2003.

[35]Buruma and Margalit, *Occidentalism,* p. 72.

[36]Ibid., p. 58.

[37]Christopher D. Marshall, "For God's Sake: Religious Violence, Terrorism, and the Peace of Christ" (paper presented at the Micah Network Conference, Chiang Mai, Thailand, September 11-16, 2006), p. 9.

[38]Greg Austin, Todd Kranock and Thomas Oommen, *God and War: An Audit and Exploration* (Bradford, U.K.: Department of Peace Studies, University of Bradford, 2004), cited in ibid., p. 8.

[39]Marshall, "For God's Sake," p. 8.

[40]Alister McGrath, *The Twilight of Atheism: The Rise and Fall of Disbelief in the Modern World* (London: Rider, 2004), pp. 183-84 (my emphasis).

[41]R. Scott Appleby, *The Ambivalence of the Sacred: Religion, Violence and Reconciliation* (New York: Rowman & Littlefield, 2000), p. 7. See chap. 4 of this book for some case studies of nonviolent religious militancy in action.

[42]Ibid., p. 8.

[43]David Barrett, George T. Kurian and Todd M. Johnson, *World Christian Encyclopaedia: A Comparative Survey of Churches and Religions in the Modern World,* 2nd ed. (Oxford: Oxford University Press, 2001), 1:11.

[44]Philip Jenkins, *The Next Christendom: The Coming of Global Christianity* (New York: Oxford University Press, 2002), p. 163.

[45]The eleventh and twelfth century "Crusades" to recapture Jerusalem from the Muslim invaders have received much press coverage since the rise of Islamic radicalism in recent times. But what is often not noted (in either the Western or Muslim media) is that it was the Greek-speaking Christian church in Byzantium that suffered the greatest barbarity and cruelty at the hands of the Western crusaders in the twelfth century. They seized the opportunity to plunder and destroy much of the city and its churches. There was much more going on than Christian-Muslim hostility.

[46]Ellen T. Charry, "The Uniqueness of Christ in Relation to Jewish People: The Eternal Crusade," in *Christ the One and Only,* ed. Sung Wook Chung (Milton Keynes, U.K.: Paternoster, and Grand Rapids: Baker, 2005), p. 145.

[47]M. Douglas Meeks, "What Can We Hope for Now?" in *Strike Terror No More: Theology, Ethics and the New War,* ed. John Berquist (St. Louis: Chalice Press, 2002), p. 261.

[48]Kate Zebiri, *Muslims and Christians Face to Face* (Oxford: Oneworld, 1997), p. 173.

[49]Ibid., p. 174.

[50]Anthony O'Mahony, "Christianity, Inter-Religious Dialogue and Muslim-Christian Relations," in Anthony O'Mahony and Michael Kirwan, *World Christianity: Politics, Theology, Dialogues* (London: Fox Communications, 2004), p. 81 (my emphasis).

[51]Appleby, *Ambivalence of the Sacred*, p. 16.

[52]Miroslav Volf, "Guns and Crosses," *Christian Century*, May 17, 2003.

[53]This account is taken from David W. Shenk, "The Gospel of Reconciliation Within the Wrath of Nations," *International Bulletin of Missionary Research* 32, no. 1 (2008): 3-9.

Chapter 3: Myths of Human Rights

[1]I am greatly indebted, for the following account, to Nicholas Wolterstorff, "Christianity and Social Justice," *Christian Scholar's Review* 16, no. 3 (1987).

[2]John Dunn, *Setting the People Free: The Story of Democracy* (London: Atlantic Books, 2005), p. 176.

[3]John Rawls, *Political Liberalism* (New York: Columbia University Press, 1993), pp. 19, 103-4.

[4]Wolterstorff, "Christianity and Social Justice," p. 221.

[5]Ibid., p. 222.

[6]Michael J. Perry, *The Idea of Human Rights: Four Inquiries* (Oxford: Oxford University Press, 1998), p. 35.

[7]Ibid., p. 39.

[8]Jean-Jacques Rousseau, *Émile, or On Education*, trans. Barbara Foxley (London and New York: Dent & Dutton, 1966), bk. 5, p. 359.

[9]Ibid., p. 332.

[10]Fundamental to the Christian gospel from its inception was the conviction that "there is no longer Jew or Greek, there is no longer slave or free, there is no longer male and female; for all of you are one in Christ Jesus" (Galatians 3:28). This radical equality had to be translated into the conditions of Greco-Roman society, and the early church often compromised shamefully with prevalent custom, so diluting the gospel. However, Paul and the other apostles followed their Master, Jesus, in encouraging women to be educated. Paul counted many women leaders as his "fellow workers" in the early mission churches of the Mediterranean world. His admonitions against women in teaching roles become more intelligible when the background of the churches, and particularly the educational status of women, is taken into consideration. The literature is vast. See, e.g., Craig S. Keener, *Paul, Women and Wives* (Peabody, Mass.: Hendrickson, 1992).

[11]Darrel W. Amundsen, "Medicine and the Birth of Defective Children: Approaches of the Ancient World," in *Euthanasia and the Newborn*, ed. Richard C. McMillan, H. Tristram Engelhardt Jr., and Stuart F. Spicker (Dordrecht, Holland: D. Reidel, 1987), p. 15.

[12]Ronald Dworkin, "In Defence of Equality," in *Liberalism*, ed. Richard J. Arneson (Hants, U.K.: Edward Elgar, 1992), 3:537.

[13]Friedrich Nietzsche, *The Anti-Christ* 43, in *The Portable Nietzsche,* trans. and ed. Walter Kauffmann (Harmondsworth, U.K.: Penguin, 1968), p. 619.

[14]Friedrich Nietzsche, *Will to Power* 734, trans. W. Kauffmann and R. J. Hollingdale (London and New York: Random House, 1967).

[15]Duncan B. Forrester, *On Human Worth: A Christian Vindication of Equality* (London: SCM Press, 2001), p. 109.

[16]J. Andrew Kirk, *What Is Mission? Theological Explorations* (London: Darton, Longman & Todd, 1999), p. 71.

[17]V. S. Azariah, "An Open Letter to Our Countrymen Who Are Classified as Belonging to the Depressed Classes," *Indian Witness,* September 17, 1936, p. 598.

[18]Forrester, *On Human Worth,* p. 31.

[19]Ibid., p. 109. Alasdair MacIntyre observes that "the distinctive values of equality and of the criteria of need which Christianity in large part begot could not possibly commend themselves as general values for human life until it began to appear possible for the basic material inequalities of human life to be abolished" (Alasdair MacIntyre, *A Short History of Ethics* [London: Routledge, 1967], p. 115). This is not the same as arguing that the concern for equality only arose after material progress had been made. Social reform presupposes that material inequalities are a problem, not a divinely ordered state of affairs.

[20]Richard Bauckham, "Egalitarianism and Hierarchy in the Bible," in *God and the Crisis of Freedom: Biblical and Contemporary Perspectives* (Louisville, Ky.: Westminster John Knox Press, 2002), p. 118.

[21]For instance, the famous dying words of Richard Rumbold, a Leveller (a seventeenth-century English political movement) leader, delivered (in face of considerable resistance from his captors) at the Market Cross in Edinburgh in June 1685, shortly before he was hung, drawn and quartered for his part in the conspiracy to kill King Charles II—"I am sure there was no Man born marked of God above another; for none comes into the World with a Saddle on his Back, neither any Booted and Spurred to ride him" (Dunn, *Setting the People Free,* p. 211).

[22]Friedrich Nietzsche, *Twilight of the Idols* 36, in *The Portable Nietzsche,* trans. and ed. Walter Kauffmann (Harmondsworth, U.K.: Penguin, 1968).

[23]John Chrysostom, *On Wealth and Poverty,* trans. Catherine Roth (Crestwood, N.Y.: St. Vladimir's Seminary Press, 1984), pp. 49-55.

[24]Basil of Caesarea, quoted in C. Avila, *Ownership: Early Christian Teaching* (Maryknoll, N.Y.: Orbis, 1983), p. 50.

[25]Thomas Aquinas, *Summa Theologiae* II-II, Q66, art. 7, trans. Fathers of the English Dominican Province (New York: Benziger, 1948).

[26]Even John Locke's individualist property rights were not absolute. He imposed two

constraints—against waste and demanding that the taker leave "enough and as good for others." He believed that when a childless father dies, his property should revert to the commons. Locke also spoke of a right to subsistence on the part of the propertyless, who can take from the surplus of the wealthy what they need to survive: "Men, being once born, have a right to their preservation, and consequently to Meat and Drink, and other such things, as nature affords for their subsistence" (John Locke, *Two Treatises of Government* [Cambridge: Cambridge University Press, 1968], 2nd treatise, p. 25).

[27]Wolterstorff, "Christianity and Social Justice," p. 228.

[28]Alexis de Tocqueville, *Democracy in America,* abridg. with intro. by Patrick Renshaw (1841; reprint, Herts, U.K.: Wordsworth Editions, 1998), p. 120.

[29]Ibid., p. 84.

[30]*2005 Global Refugee Trends* (Geneva: United Nations High Commissioner for Refugees, 2006); United Nations General Assembly, *International Migration and Development, Report of the Secretary-General,* May 18, 2006.

[31]Immanuel Kant, "Perpetual Peace," in *On History,* ed. and trans. Louis White Beck (New York: Macmillan, 1963), pp. 102-3.

[32]Hannah Arendt, *The Origins of Totalitarianism* (1951; reprint, New York: Harcourt, Brace and Jovanovich, 1968), pp. 296-97.

[33]It is a moot point, though, whether "Holocaust denial" (banned in Austria) is defensible in the same way. All definitions of what is "offensive" behavior are open to the charge of hypocrisy and double standards. Hence the need for wide-ranging public debate before such laws are passed.

[34]Oliver O'Donovan, *The Desire of the Nations: Rediscovering the Roots of Political Theology* (Cambridge: Cambridge University Press, 1996), p. 263.

[35]Mary Jo Leddy, *Radical Gratitude* (Maryknoll, N.Y.: Orbis, 2002), p. 117.

[36]For the Christian natural law tradition from Thomas Aquinas to John Locke and Hugo Grotius, it is divine law that is primary and rights secondary. The latter are derived from God's will, either revealed or discovered through our created natural needs. I have followed Wolterstorff in departing from this mainstream and situating rights not primarily in God's will but in God's love for his human creatures.

[37]"Human Rights and Human Development," *United Nations Human Development Report 2000* (Oxford: Oxford University Press, 2000), p. 25.

[38]Daniel A. Bell, *East Meets West: Human Rights and Democracy in East Asia* (Princeton, N.J.: Princeton University Press, 2000), p. 42.

[39]Neera Chandhoke, *Beyond Secularism: The Rights of Religious Minorities* (New Delhi, India: Oxford University Press, 1999), p. 190.

[40]Joan Lockwood O'Donovan, "Subsidiarity and Political Authority in Theological Per-

spective," in *Studies in Christian Ethics* 6, no. 1 (1998): 29-30.

[41]Rowan Williams, *Lost Icons: Reflections on Cultural Bereavement* (Edinburgh: T & T Clark, 2000), p. 93.

[42]Martin Luther King Jr., quoted in Charles Marsh, *The Beloved Community: How Faith Shapes Social Justice, from the Civil Rights Movement to Today* (New York: Basic Books, 2005), p. 6.

[43]Marsh, *Beloved Community*, p. 137.

[44]Desmond Tutu, "Religion and Human Rights," in *Yes to a Global Ethic*, ed. Hans Küng (London: SCM, 1996), p. 174.

[45]J. Waldron, "Religious Contributions in Public Deliberations," *San Diego Law Review* 30 (1993), cited in Duncan B. Forrester, *On Human Worth: A Christian Vindication of Equality* (London: SCM Press, 2001), p. 73.

[46]Ibid.

[47]Christoph Schwöbel, "Recovering Human Dignity," in *God and Human Dignity*, ed. R. Kendall Soulen and Linda Woodhead (Grand Rapids and Cambridge: Eerdmans, 2006), p. 58.

Chapter 4: Myths of Multiculturalism

[1]Pittu Laungani, *Asian Perspectives in Counselling and Psychotherapy* (Hove, U.K. and New York: Brunner-Routledge, 2004), pp. 32-33.

[2]Pittu Laungani, "East Meets West," *CPJ*, October 2004, p. 21.

[3]"Botswana Bushmen Win Land Ruling," *BBC News*, December 13, 2006 <http://news .bbc.co.uk/go/pr/fr/-/2/hi/africa/6174709.stm>.

[4]Ian Buruma, *Murder in Amsterdam* (New York: Penguin, 2006).

[5]Timothy Garton Ash, "Islam in Europe," *New York Review of Books*, October 5, 2006, p. 34.

[6]Figures on living languages and ethno-linguistic groups are from the Joshua Project website <www.joshuaproject.net>.

[7]In the American case, what were called "culture wars" on college campuses in the 1990s were bloodless wranglings over the curriculum in humanities departments (whether Seinfeld should replace Shakespeare and so on). For a more interesting "culture war" in the United States over rival moral visions and vocabularies, which cuts across boundaries of ethnicity, age, economic class, political and religious affiliation, see Gertrude Himmelfarb, *One Nation, Two Cultures* (New York: Vintage Books, 2001).

[8]Nigel Harris, *Thinking the Unthinkable: The Immigration Myth Exposed* (New York: IB Tauris, 2002), pp. 9-10.

[9]Raymond Williams, *The Long Revolution* (1961; reprint, Harmondsworth, U.K.: Pen-

guin, 1965), p. 42.

[10]Margaret Archer, *Culture and Agency* (Cambridge: Cambridge University Press, 1996), p. 1.

[11]Ethnicity often carries connotations of color and other physiognomic features which are absent in discussions of culture. However, it is a problematic concept in sociology.

[12]In Victorian Britain, culture as art ("highbrow culture") became an elitist, surrogate religion in the hands of persons like Matthew Arnold. It disdainfully stood aloof from politics and therefore lacked the political critique that the major faith traditions have carried.

[13]Bhikhu Parekh, *Rethinking Multiculturalism: Cultural Diversity and Political Theory* (Basingstoke, U.K., and New York: Palgrave, 2000), p. 175. I have found Parekh's work particularly illuminating on a number of issues dealt with in this chapter.

[14]Kathryn Tanner, *Theories of Culture: A New Agenda for Theology* (Minneapolis: Augsburg Fortress, 1997), p. 55.

[15]Charles Taylor, "The Politics of Recognition," in *Multiculturalism: Examining the Politics of Recognition,* ed. Amy Gutman (Princeton, N.J.: Princeton University Press, 1994), p. 66. Taylor warns both against an arrogant dismissal of cultures other than our own, and, at the other extreme, "peremptory and inauthentic judgments of equal value" (p. 73).

[16]Michael Ignatieff, *Blood and Belonging* (London: Viking, 1993), p. 188.

[17]Will Kymlicka, *Politics in the Vernacular: Nationalism, Multiculturalism, and Citizenship* (Oxford: Oxford University Press, 2001), p. 219 n. 13.

[18]Ibid., p. 244.

[19]C. A. Bayly, *The Birth of the Modern World, 1780-1914* (Oxford: Blackwell, 2004), p. 207.

[20]Linda Colley, *Britons: Forging the Nation 1707-1837* (New Haven, Conn., and London: Yale University Press, 1992), pp. 5-6.

[21]Bayly, *Birth of the Modern World,* p. 266.

[22]Ibid., p. 243.

[23]Daniel Patrick Moynihan, quoted in Gertrude Himmelfarb, *One Nation, Two Cultures* (New York: Vintage Books, 2001), p. 59.

[24]Himmelfarb, *One Nation, Two Cultures,* p. 62.

[25]Stephen L. Carter, *Civility: Manners, Morals, and the Etiquette of Democracy* (New York: Basic Books, 1998), p. 208.

[26]Will Kymlicka, *Liberalism, Community and Culture* (Oxford: Oxford University Press, 1991), p. 165.

[27]Oliver O'Donovan, *The Desire of the Nations: Rediscovering the Roots of Political Theology*

(Cambridge: Cambridge University Press, 1996), p. 267.

[28]Ibid., p. 268.

[29]Charles West, *Power, Truth and Community in Modern Culture* (Harrisburg, Penn.: Trinity Press International, 1999), p. 89.

[30]Lamin Sanneh, *Encountering the West* (London: Marshall Pickering, 1993), p. 119.

[31]Lamin Sanneh, *Whose Religion Is Christianity? The Gospel Beyond the West* (Grand Rapids: Eerdmans, 2003), pp. 105-6.

[32]Parekh, *Rethinking Multiculturalism*, p. 236.

[33]Ibid., pp. 262-63.

[34]Ellis Close, *The Rage of a Privileged Class* (New York: HarperCollins, 1993), p. 111.

[35]This example is from Kymlicka, *Politics in the Vernacular*, p. 197.

[36]Ibid., p. 118.

[37]The Indian Constituent Assembly in 1951 refused to accept that Muslim personal law was an inseparable part of the Islamic religion but, as a compromise, left the objective of a uniform civil code for India as a "Directive Principle" included in the constitution, which stated that "the state shall endeavour to secure for the citizens a uniform civil code throughout the territory of India" (art. 44). This Directive Principle, however, was long left in abeyance. However in 1986, in a celebrated case involving a Muslim woman's (Shah Bano's) appeal for alimony, the Supreme Court ruled in her favor against her husband. The Indian government, under the prime ministership of Rajiv Gandhi, overruled the Supreme Court decision. This angered the Hindu nationalists, led to waves of sectarian violence and eventually swept into political power the Hindutva party known as the BJP.

[38]Seyla Benhabib, *The Rights of Others: Aliens, Residents, and Citizens* (Cambridge: Cambridge University Press, 2004), p. 197.

[39]O'Donovan, *Desire of the Nations*, p. 270.

[40]Benhabib, *Rights of Others*, p. 179.

[41]Stephen Carter notes how, in recent years, "liberal theorists have spent much effort in crafting rules for public dialogue that leave well outside the universe of discourse points of view with which liberalism is uncomfortable— religious argument, for one" (*Civility*, p. 134).

[42]Timothy Garton Ash, "Islam in Europe," *New York Review of Books*, October 5 2006, p. 34.

[43]Cf. Alison Kesby, "The Shifting and Multiple Border and International Law," *Oxford Journal for Legal Studies* 27, no. 1 (spring 2007): 101-19.

[44]Interestingly, in my experience of Britain, once South Asian immigrants have settled into their new identities as British citizens, many of them become more resistant to

new immigrants, especially asylum seekers, than the older native population. Is this an expression of their own insecurity, fearing that their jobs will be threatened by new migrants? Or is it simply testimony to the fact that racist or ethnic prejudice bedevils all human communities?

[45]Harris, *Thinking the Unthinkable,* pp. 84, 79-80.

[46]Benhabib, *Rights of Others,* p. 43.

[47]Ibid., p. 177.

[48]Theodore W. Jennings Jr., *Reading Derrida/Thinking Paul: On Justice* (Stanford, Calif.: Stanford University Press, 2006), p. 120.

[49]Jacques Derrida, *On Cosmopolitanism and Forgiveness,* trans. Mark Dooley and Michael Hughes (New York: Routledge, 2001), p. 19, cited in ibid., p. 121.

[50]Jacques Derrida, *Negotiations,* trans. Elizabeth Rottenberg (Stanford, Calif.: Stanford University Press, 2001), pp. 374-75, cited in Theodore W. Jennings Jr., *Reading Derrida/Thinking Paul. On Justice* (Stanford, Calif.: Stanford University Press, 2006), p. 120

[51]*The Analects of Confucius,* bk. 12.7, trans. Arthur Waley (New York: Everyman's Library, 2000).

[52]John Dunn, *Setting the People Free: The Story of Democracy* (London: Atlantic Books, 2005), p. 180.

[53]Ibid., p. 181.

[54]Raymond Plant, *Politics, Theology and History* (Cambridge: Cambridge University Press, 2001), pp. 216-17.

[55]Francis Fukuyama, *Trust* (London: Hamish Hamilton, 1995), p. 11.

[56]Jonathan Sacks, *The Dignity of Difference* (London and New York: Continuum, 2002), p. 200.

[57]John Plamenatz, *Man and Society* (London: Longman, 1963), 1:50, cited in ibid., p. 199.

[58]Plant, *Politics, Theology and History,* chap. 8. Cf. Charles Taylor, "What's Wrong with Negative Liberty?" *Philosophy and the Human Sciences: Philosophical Papers*, vol. 2 (Cambridge: Cambridge University Press, 1985); Amartya Sen, *Development as Freedom* (New York: Anchor Books, 1999).

[59]Plant, *Politics, Theology and History,* p. 220.

[60]Dietrich Bonhoeffer, *Creation and Fall: A Theological Exposition of Genesis 1-3,* quoted in Clifford Green, "Human Sociality and Christian Community," *Cambridge Companion to Dietrich Bonhoeffer,* ed. John W. de Gruchy (Cambridge: Cambridge University Press, 1999), p. 117.

[61]I owe this insight to Richard Bauckham, *God and the Crisis of Freedom: Biblical and Contemporary Perspectives* (Louisville, Ky.: Westminster John Knox Press, 2002), chap.

2. What follows is influenced by Bauckham's discussion.

[62]Ibid., p. 39.

[63]Ibid., p. 192.

Chapter 5: Myths of Science

[1]Primo Levi, *The Periodic Table*, trans. Raymond Rosenthal (London: Sphere Books, 1986), p. 42.

[2]George Orwell, "What Is Science?" in *The Collected Essays, Journalism and Letters of George Orwell*, ed. Sonia Orwell and Ian Angus (London: Penguin, 1970), 4:27-28.

[3]Rudolf Carnap, *The Logical Structure of the World*, trans. R. George (Berkeley: University of California Press, 1967), p. 290.

[4]Tapan Raychaudhuri, "The Pursuit of Reason in Nineteenth-century Bengal, in *Mind Body and Society: Life and Mentality in Colonial Bengal*, ed. Rajat Kanta Ray (Calcutta, India: Oxford University Press, 1995), p. 60.

[5]For further details see C. A. Russell, *Cross-Currents: Interactions Between Science and Faith* (Leicester, U.K.: Inter-Varsity Press, 1985), chap. 9; O. Chadwick, *The Secularization of the European Mind in the Nineteenth Century* (Cambridge: Cambridge University Press, 1975).

[6]Jawaharlal Nehru, *Proceedings of the National Institute of Science of India*, vol. 27 (1960): 564, cited in Mary Midgley, *The Myths We Live By* (London and New York: Routledge, 2004), p. 14 (emphasis is Midgley's).

[7]See George Perkovich, *India's Nuclear Bomb: The Impact on Global Proliferation* (Berkeley: University of California Press, 1999).

[8]Midgley, *Myths We Live By*, p. 16.

[9]Ibid., p. 16.

[10]E. O. Wilson, *On Human Nature* (Cambridge, Mass.: Harvard University Press, 1978), pp. 201-7.

[11]Anti-evolution hysteria is an American religious phenomenon, but is increasingly promoted globally by televangelists and well-endowed conservative organizations. For evangelical critiques of "creationism" (or what is misleadingly called "creation science") see Denis Alexander, *Rebuilding the Matrix: Science and Faith in the 21st Century* (Oxford: Lion, 2001), chap. 9; Ernest Lucas, *Can We Believe Genesis Today? The Bible and Questions of Science* (Leicester, U.K.: Inter-Varsity Press, 2001).

[12]Charles Darwin, *The Autobiography of Charles Darwin, 1809-1882, With Original Omissions Restored*, ed. Nora Barlow (New York: Harcourt, Brace, & World, 1958), p. 395. Darwin, however, was often inconsistent. In the fifth chapter of his later book *The Descent of Man* (1871), he did offer an account of the development of human morality based

on group selection. However, he agreed that the moral sense was a distinctive feature of humans as compared with other animals, and that moral progress was achieved through education and imitation—in other words, cultural inheritance.

[13]For a representative variety of other approaches to biological evolution, see Stuart Kauffman, *At Home in the Universe* (London: Penguin, 1996); Lynn Margulis, *The Symbiotic Planet* (London: Phoenix, 1998); James Lovelock, *Gaia: The Practical Science of Planetary Medicine* (London: Gaia Books, 1991); William Dembski and Michael Ruse, eds., *Debating Design: From Darwin to DNA* (Cambridge: Cambridge University Press, 2004).

[14]Simon Conway Morris, *Life's Solution: Inevitable Humans in a Lonely Universe* (Cambridge: Cambridge University Press, 2003).

[15]Ibid., p. 11.

[16]Notwithstanding the exaggerated claims of the origin-of-life industry (going back to the classical experiments of Miller and Urey in the 1950s) to have replicated the prebiotic chemical conditions of the early earth and produced the molecular precursors to life, we are as far as ever from creating a single living cell. (In any case, even if we do, it will be as a result of intelligent human agency.) For origin-of-life theories and the lack of experimental progress, see chap. 4 of Morris, *Life's Solution;* also Robert Shapiro, *Origins: A Skeptic's Guide to the Creation of Life on Earth* (New York: Bantam, 1987); Irene Fry, *The Emergence of Life on Earth: A Historical and Scientific Overview* (London: Free Association Books, 1999).

[17]The general problem is referred to as the C-value paradox, C being the amount of DNA in a cell. Cf. Morris, *Life's Solution,* pp. 237ff.

[18]Richard Dawkins, *The Selfish Gene* (Oxford: Oxford University Press, 1976), pp. x, 2, 215 (my emphasis).

[19]Steven Rose, *Lifelines: Biology, Freedom, Determinism* (London: Penguin, 1997), pp. 125-27, 169.

[20]Probably the best critical discussion of evolutionary psychology is the collection of essays *Alas, Poor Darwin!* ed. Steven Rose and Hilary Rose (London: Jonathan Cape, 2000).

[21]Colin Blakemore, *The Mind Machine* (London: BBC, 1988), pp. 269-71.

[22]Jerry Fodor, *In Critical Condition: Polemical Essays on Cognitive Science and the Philosophy of Mind* (Cambridge, Mass.: MIT Press, 1998), p. 145. See also pp. 86-89.

[23]Chandra Wickramasinghe, "An Astronomer's View of the Universe and Buddhist Thought," *Ceylon Daily News,* May 15, 1992.

[24]G. K. Chesterton, *Orthodoxy* (1908; reprint, San Francisco: Ignatius Press, 1995), p. 39.

[25]Charles Darwin, letter to W. Graham, July 3, 1881, in *The Life and Letters of Charles*

Darwin, ed. Francis Darwin (New York: Basic Books, 1959), p. 285.

[26]Blaise Pascal, *Pensées,* trans. A. J. Krailsheimer (London: Penguin, 1966), no. 113.

[27]Paul Davies, *The Cosmic Blueprint* (London: Unwin Hyman, 1989), p. 203.

[28]Denis Alexander, *Rebuilding the Matrix: Science and Faith in the 21st Century* (Oxford: Lion, 2001), p. 416.

[29]Morris, *Life's Solution,* p. xii.

[30]Ibid., p. 307.

[31]This should not be taken in an anthropocentric way. Numerous biblical passages such as Psalm 104 and Job 38—41 make plain that God relates with the nonhuman world quite independently of human beings. God would have sported with dinosaurs and flown with the pterodactyls long before the human was formed.

[32]Timothy Ferris, *Coming of Age in the Milky Way* (New York: William Morrow, 1988), p. 385.

[33]John F. Haught, *Is Nature Enough? Meaning and Truth in the Age of Science* (Cambridge: Cambridge University Press, 2006), p. 95.

[34]Ibid., pp. 104-5.

[35]Thomas F. Torrance, *Christian Theology of Scientific Culture* (New York: Oxford University Press, 1981), p. 63.

[36]Michael Ruse and Edward O. Wilson, "The Evolution of Ethics," *New Scientist* 108 (1985): 51.

[37]Francis Crick, *The Astonishing Hypothesis: The Scientific Search for the Soul* (New York: Simon & Schuster, 1994), p. 3.

[38]Richard Dawkins, "The Ultraviolet Garden," Royal Institution Christmas Lecture, no. 4, London, 1991.

[39]Steve Jones, introduction to *The Language of the Genes* (London: HarperCollins, 1993).

[40]The philosopher Colin McGinn honestly admits that no one today has any idea how consciousness and physical brains come together, and is humble enough to recognize that this may be an insoluble problem: "We are suffering from what I called 'cognitive closure' with respect to the mind-body problem. Just as a dog cannot be expected to solve the problems of space and time and the speed of light that it took a brain like Einstein's to solve, so maybe the human species cannot be expected to understand how the universe contains mind and matter in combination. . . . As Socrates always maintained, it is always the wise man who knows his own ignorance" (*The Making of a Philosopher: My Journey Through Twentieth-Century Philosophy* [London: Simon & Schuster, 2002], p. 182).

[41]Etienne Gilson, *From Aristotle to Darwin and Back Again: A Journey in Final Causality, Species, and Evolution,* trans. John Lyon (Notre Dame, Ind.: University of Notre Dame

Press, 1984), p. 105.

[42]Haught, *Is Nature Enough?* pp. 103-4.

[43]John Polkinghorne, *Quarks, Chaos and Christianity,* 2nd ed. (London: SPCK, 2005), pp. 10-11.

[44]John Polkinghorne, *Science and Christian Belief* (London: SPCK, 1994), p. 41.

[45]Robert Oppenheimer, quoted in Freeman Dyson, *Disturbing the Universe* (London: Pan, 1979), p. 78.

[46]Dyson, *Disturbing the Universe,* p. 91.

[47]Ibid., p. 30.

[48]United Nations Development Program, *Human Development Report 2001* (Oxford and New York: Oxford University Press, 2001), p. 98.

[49]Derek Bok, *Universities in the Marketplace* (Princeton, N.J.: Princeton University Press, 2003).

[50]Richard Horton, "The Dawn of McScience," *New York Review of Books,* March 11, 2004, pp. 8-12.

[51]See David J. Rothman, "The Shame of Medical Research," in *The New York Review of Books,* November 30, 2000, pp. 60-64.

[52]Maureen L. Condic, "What We Know About Embryonic Stem Cells," *First Things,* January 2007, p. 26.

[53]There is a burgeoning body of Christian ethical and theological reflection in this area. See C. Deane-Drummond, *Theology and Biotechnology: Implications for a New Science* (London: Geoffrey Chapman, 1997); A. Holland and A. Johnson, eds., *Animal Biotechnology and Ethics* (London: Chapman & Hall, 1998); M. J. Reiss and R. Straughan, *Improving Nature? The Science and Ethics of Genetic Engineering* (Cambridge: Cambridge University Press, 1996); John Bryant and John Searle, *Life in Our Hands: A Christian Perspective on Genetics and Cloning* (Leicester, U.K.: Inter-Varsity Press, 2004).

[54]Midgley, *Myths We Live By,* p. 105.

[55]Ibid., p. 107.

[56]See, for instance, the definitive study by Jean Dreze and Amartya Sen, *Hunger and Public Action* (Oxford: Clarendon Press, 1989).

[57]Between them, Europe and the United States subsidise their farmers by $350 billion a year, which allows their surpluses to flood cheaply into poor countries, depress prices and undermine local farming. About 20 percent of Africa's food now comes from rich countries, though it could easily grow its own.

[58]Claude Alvarez, *Science, Development and Violence* (New Delhi, India: Oxford University Press, 1994), p. 43.

[59]Michael S. Northcott, " 'Behold I Have Set the Land Before You' (Deut 1.8): Chris-

tian Ethics, GM Foods, and the Culture of Modern Farming," in *Re-Ordering Nature: Theology, Society and the New Genetics,* ed. Celia Deane-Drummond and Bronislaw Szerszynski with Robin Grove-White (London and New York: T & T Clark, 2003), p. 99.

[60]Wendell Berry, *Sex, Economy, Freedom, and Community* (New York: Pantheon Books, 1992), p. 98, quoted in Northcott, ibid., p. 102.

[61]T. S. Eliot, *Murder in the Cathedral* (New York: Harcourt Brace Jovanovich, 1935), p. 86.

[62]Cf. Richard L. Fern, *Nature, God and Humanity: Envisioning an Ethics of Nature* (Cambridge: Cambridge University Press, 2002), pp. 201ff.; Jürgen Moltmann, *God in Creation,* trans. Margaret Kohl (Minneapolis: Fortress Press, 1993), pp. 276ff.

[63]Francis Galton, quoted in R. Kendall Soulen, "Cruising Toward Bethlehem: Human Dignity and the New Eugenics" in *God and Human Dignity,* ed. R. Kendall Soulen and Linda Woodhead (Grand Rapids and Cambridge: Eerdmans, 2006), pp. 107-8.

[64]For what follows, see Philip J. Sampson, *6 Modern Myths About Christianity and Western Civilization* (Downers Grove, Ill.: InterVarsity Press, 2001), pp. 67-70.

[65]Gilbert Meilaender, "Designing Our Descendants," *First Things* 109 (January 2001): 25.

[66]Soulen, "Cruising Toward Bethlehem," p. 113.

[67]Ibid., pp. 116-17.

[68]Condic, "What We Know About Embryonic Stem Cells," p. 29.

[69]Ron McKay, quoted in ibid.

[70]Lee Silver, *Remaking Eden* (New York: Avon Books, 1997), p. 237f.

[71]Susan Greenfield, *Tomorrow's People: How 21st-Century Technology Is Changing the Way We Think and Feel* (London: Penguin, 2004), p. 143.

[72]Gregory Stock, *Redesigning Humans: Changing Our Children's Genes* (London: Profile Books, 2002), pp. 1, 13.

[73]Elaine L. Graham, "The 'End' of the Human or the End of the 'Human'?" in *God and Human Dignity,* ed. R. Kendall Soulen and Linda Woodhead (Grand Rapids and Cambridge: Eerdmans, 2006), p. 267.

[74]Nick Bostrom, "Transhumanist Values," *World Transhumanist Association* <www .transhumanism.org/index.php/ WTA/more/transhumanist-values>.

[75]Stock, *Redesigning Humans,* p. 173.

[76]Eric Davis, *Techgnosis: Myth, Magic and Mysticism in the Age of Information* (London: Serpent's Tail, 1998), cited in Elaine L. Graham, "The 'End' of the Human or the End of the 'Human'?" in Soulen and Woodhead, *God and Human Dignity,* p. 274.

[77]Thomas F. Torrance, *Reality and Scientific Theology* (Edinburgh: Scottish Academic Press, 1982), p. 68.

Chapter 6: Myths of Postcolonialism

[1]Ulrich Beck, *What Is Globalization?* trans. Patrick Camiller (Cambridge: Polity Press, 2000), p. 11.

[2]I have found the following particularly useful, C. A. Bayly, *The Birth of the Modern World, 1780-1914* (Oxford: Blackwell, 2004); John M. Hobson, *The Eastern Origins of Western Civilization* (Cambridge: Cambridge University Press, 2004); A. G. Hopkins, ed., *Globalisation in World History* (London: Pimlico, 2002); Felipe Fernández-Armesto, *Millennium* (London: Black Swan, 1996); Peter van der Veer, *Imperial Encounters: Religion and Modernity in India and Britain* (Princeton, N.J.: Princeton University Press, 2001); Jack Goody, *Islam in Europe* (Cambridge: Polity Press, 2004).

[3]Bayly, *Birth of the Modern World*, p. 86.

[4]Ibid., p. 88.

[5]Ibid., p. 1.

[6]Ibid., p. 21.

[7]Robert J. Holton, *Globalization and the Nation-State* (London: Macmillan, 1998), p. 28.

[8]Linda Colley, *Captives: Britain, Empire and the World 1600-1850* (London: Jonathan Cape, 2002); Peter van der Veer, *Imperial Encounters: Religion and Modernity in India and Britain* (Princeton, N.J.: Princeton University Press, 2001).

[9]Hobson, *Eastern Origins of Western Civilization*, p. 36.

[10]Ibid., p. 2.

[11]Gavin Menzies, *1421: The Year China Discovered the World* (London: Bantam Press, 2002). chap. 4.

[12]Ibid., p. 10.

[13]Michael Edwardes, *East-West Passage* (New York: Taplinger, 1971), p. 85, quoted in Hobson, *Eastern Origins of Western Civilization,* p. 132.

[14]For the story of the impact of the Jesuit mission on Europe, see Donald F. Lach and Edwin J. Van Kley, *Asia in the Making of Europe,* vol. 3 (Chicago: University of Chicago Press, 1993).

[15]For an account of specific agricultural and industrial machines and processes that Europe learned from China, see Hobson, *Eastern Origins of Western Civilization,* pp. 201-15.

[16]Walter Rostow and Perry Anderson, quoted in ibid., p. 191.

[17]See, apart from Bayly and Hobson, Eric L. Jones, *Growth Recurring* (Oxford: Clarendon Press, 1988).

[18]Paul Bairoch, quoted in Hobson, *Eastern Origins of Western Civilization,* pp. 75, 76.

[19]Hobson, *Eastern Origins of Western Civilization,* p. 192. Francesca Bray writes that "Western writers and innovators plagiarised each other's ideas shamelessly . . . [and] we

may be sure that they had no scruples in passing off as their own, ideas that had come from the other side of the world" (Francesca Bray, *Science and Civilization in China,* [Cambridge: Cambridge University Press, 1984] 6:571, cited in ibid., p. 201).

[20]Bayly, *Birth of the Modern World,* p. 63.

[21]Van der Veer, *Imperial Encounters,* p. 160.

[22]Johan Huizinga, *Erasmus and the Age of Reformation* (1924; reprint, London: Phoenix Press, 2002), p. 194.

[23]See Giles Milton, *Nathaniel's Nutmeg* (London: Hodder & Stoughton, 1999), pp. 309ff.

[24]Hobson, *Eastern Origins of Western Civilization,* p. 211. It was wood rather than steel that was the basis for much of Britain's early industrialization. Hobson points out that, on the eve of the 1851 Great Exhibition held in London's Crystal Palace and designed to show British industrial superiority to the rest of the world, 90 percent of Britain's warships were still made of wood (p. 216).

[25]Felipe Fernández-Armesto, *Millennium* (London: Black Swan, 1996), pp. 361, 386-87.

[26]Frantz Fanon, *The Wretched of the Earth,* trans. Constance Farrington (London: Penguin, 1967), pp. 76-81.

[27]Mohammed Iqbal, *Persian Psalms,* quoted in Francis Robinson, "Present Shadows, Past Glory," *The Times Literary Supplement,* September 6, 2002, p. 15.

[28]Antonio Gramsci, *Selections from the Prison Notebooks,* ed. and trans. Quintin Hoare and Geoffrey Nowell Smith (London: Lawrence & Wishart, 1971).

[29]George Nathaniel Curzon, quoted in A. P. Thornton, *The Imperial Idea and Its Enemies* (New York: St. Martin's Press, 1966), p. 72.

[30]George Lamming, quoted in P. Hulme, "The Profit of Language," in *Recasting the World: Writing After Colonialism,* ed. J. White (Baltimore and London: John Hopkins University Press, 1993), p. 120.

[31]Jorge Klor de Alva, "The Postcolonization of the Latin American Experience," in *After Colonialism: Imperial Histories and Postcolonial Displacements,* ed. G. Prakash (Princeton, N.J.: Princeton University Press, 1995), p. 245.

[32]Gauri Viswanathan, *Masks of Conquest: Literary Study and British Rule in India* (London: Faber, 1987), p. 2.

[33]Ania Loomba, *Colonialism/Postcolonialism* (London and New York: Routledge, 1998), pp. 96-97.

[34]Ibid., p. 97.

[35]Edward Said, *Orientalism: Western Conceptions of the Orient* (London: Penguin, 1978).

[36]Ibid., pp. 81-85.

[37]Ibid., pp. 43-46.

[38]Charles Allen, *The Buddha and the Sahibs* (London: John Murray, 2002), p. 4.

[39]For representative critiques, see Michael Sprinker, ed., *Edward Said: A Critical Reader* (Oxford: Blackwell, 1992); Carol A. Breckenridge and Peter van der Veer, eds., *Orientalism and the Postcolonial Predicament* (Philadelphia: University of Pennsylvania Press, 1993).

[40]Linda Colley, *Captives: Britain, Empire and the World 1600-1850* (London: Jonathan Cape, 2002; Pimlico edition, 2003), p. 310.

[41]Ibid., p. 316.

[42]Bayly, *Birth of the Modern World*, p. 111.

[43]Thomas Babington Macauley, "Minute on Indian Education" (1835), in *The Post-Colonial Studies Reader*, ed. Bill Ashcroft, Gareth Griffiths and Helen Tiffin (London and New York: Routledge, 1995), p. 430.

[44]Sheldon Pollock, quoted in David Smith, *Hinduism and Modernity* (Oxford: Blackwell, 2003), p. 92.

[45]Richard King, *Orientalism and Religion: Postcolonial Theory, India and "the Mystic East"* (London and New York: Routledge, 1999), p. 158.

[46]Allen, *Buddha and the Sahibs*, pp. 4-5.

[47]Ibid., p. 292.

[48]Wilhelm Halbfass, *India and Europe* (Albany, N.Y.: SUNY Press, 1988), pp. 403-18.

[49]Swami Radhakrishnan, quoted in ibid., p. 409.

[50]King, *Orientalism and Religion*, p. 156.

[51]Van der Veer, *Imperial Encounters*, p. 132.

[52]Frits Staal, *Rules Without Meaning: Rituals, Mantras and the Human Sciences*, Toronto Studies in Religion 4 (New York: Peter Lang, 1989), p. 393.

[53]Michel Foucault, *History of Sexuality* (Harmondsworth U.K.: Penguin, 1978), 1:94.

[54]Homi Bhabha, "Signs Taken for Wonders: Questions of Ambivalence and Authority Under a Tree in Delhi, May 1817," *Critical Inquiry* 12, no. 1 (1985): 144-65; abridged version in *The Post-Colonial Studies Reader*, ed. Ashcroft et al (London: Routledge, 1995). Homi Bhabha, "The Other Question: Difference, Discrimination and the Discourse of Colonialism," in *Literature, Politics and Theory*, ed. Francis Barker (London: Methuen, 1986). Reprinted in *Contemporary Postcolonial Theory: A Reader*, ed. Padmini Mongia (London: Hodder Headline Press, 1996).

[55]Bhabha, "Signs Taken for Wonders," p. 36.

[56]Benita Perry, "Problems in Current Theories of Colonial Discourse," *Oxford Literary Review* 9 (1987): 43, abridged version in *The Post-Colonial Studies Reader*, ed. Ashcroft et al (London: Routledge, 1995), p. 43.

[57]Loomba, *Colonialism/Postcolonialism*, p. 179.

[58]Arif Dirlik, "The Postcolonial Aura: Third World Criticism in the Age of Global Cap-

italism," *Critical Inquiry* 20, no. 2 (winter 1994), pp. 328-356.

[59]Loomba, *Colonialism/Postcolonialism*, p. 180.

[60]Dirlik, "The Postcolonial Aura," p. 342.

[61]Kwame Anthony Appiah, "Is the Post in Postmodernism the Post in Postcolonialism?' in *Contemporary Postcolonial Theory: A Reader*, ed. Padmini Mongia (London: Arnold, 1996), pp. 62-63.

[62]Arun Shourie, *Missionaries in India: Continuities, Changes, Dilemmas* (New Delhi, India: ASA Publications, 1994), p. 3.

[63]Antonio Gramsci used the term *subaltern* in referring to rural peasant groups in southern Italy. Departing from the classic Marxist view of the unified consciousness of the urban working class, Gramsci stressed the unsystematic, unorganized nature of rural peasant resistance to the state. Ranajit Guha, one of the founders of the Subaltern Studies Collective, inaugurated the widespread use of the term in postcolonial studies. He defined *subaltern* as "the general attribute of subordination in South Asian society, whether this is expressed in terms of class, caste, age, gender and office or in any other way." It became so expansive as to refer to "the demographic difference between the total Indian population and all those we have defined as elite" (see Ranajit Guha, "On Some Aspects of the Historiography of Colonial India," in *Subaltern Studies*, ed. Ranajit Guha, vol. 1 [New Delhi, India: Oxford University Press, 1982], reprinted in *Selected Subaltern Studies*, ed. Ranajit Guha and Gayatri Chakravorty Spivak [Oxford: Oxford University Press, 1988] pp. 37-44).

[64]Gayatri Chakravorty Spivak, "Can the Subaltern Speak?" in *Marxism and the Interpretation of Culture*, ed. Cary Nelson and Larry Grossberg (Urbana: University of Illinois Press, 1988), p. 287.

[65]R. O'Hanlon and D. Washbrook, "After Orientalism: Culture, Criticism and Politics in The Third World," quoted in Ania Loomba, *Colonialism/Postcolonialism* (London and New York: Routledge, 1998), pp. 241-42.

[66]Nancy Hartsock, "Foucault on Power: A Theory for Women?' in *Feminism/Postmodernism*, ed. Linda J. Nicholson (London: Routledge, 1990), p. 163.

[67]Edward Said, interview in *Criticism in Society* by Imre Salusinzsky (London: Methuen, 1987) p. 137, cited in Richard King, *Orientalism and Religion: Postcolonial Theory, India and "the Mystic East"* (London and New York: Routledge, 1999), p. 84.

[68]Herbert Butterfield, *The Whig Interpretation of History*, quoted in David Brown, *Tradition and Imagination: Revelation and Change* (Oxford: Oxford University Press, 1999), p. 22.

[69]I. M. Lewis, *Islam in Tropical Africa* (London: n.p., 1966), cited in John Mbiti, *African Religions and Philosophy* (Nairobi: n.p., 1989), p. 256.

[70]Andrew F. Walls, "Structural Problems in Mission Studies," in *The Missionary Move-*

ment in Christian History: Studies in the Transmission of Faith (Edinburgh: T & T Clark and New York: Orbis, 1996), p. 150.

[71]For these accounts see, for example, the essays by Jane Samson and Brian Stanley in *Christian Missions and the Enlightenment,* ed. Brian Stanley (Grand Rapids and Cambridge: Eerdmans, 2001). Also see Andrew Porter, *Religion Versus Empire? British Protestant Missionaries and Overseas Expansion, 1700-1914* (Manchester, U.K.: Manchester University Press, 2004).

[72]Hugh Tinker, *The Ordeal of Love: C. F. Andrews and India* (Oxford: Oxford University Press, 1979; Oxford India Printing, 1998), pp. 168-69, 189, 228.

[73]Ibid., p. 314.

[74]Lamin Sanneh, *Encountering the West* (London: Marshall Pickering, 1993), p. 19.

[75]David W. Smith, *Against the Stream: Christianity and Mission in an Age of Globalization* (Leicester, U.K.: Inter-Varsity Press, 2003), p. 95.

[76]Fred Halliday, *Islam and the Myth of Confrontation: Religion and Politics in the Middle East* (London: I. B. Tauris, 1996), p. 5.

[77]Hartsock, "Foucault on Power," p. 167.

[78]Bayly, *Birth of the Modern World,* pp. 280-81.

[79]Gustavo Gutiérrez, *A Theology of Liberation,* rev. ed. (London: SCM, 1988), p. xxxviii.

[80]Smith, *Against the Stream,* pp. 105-6.

[81]Cf. Gayatri Chakravorty Spivak, "Subaltern Studies: Deconstructing Historiography," in *Selected Subaltern Studies,* ed. Ranajit Guha and Gayatri Chakravorty Spivak (Oxford: Oxford University Press, 1988), pp. 3-33.

[82]Russell Jacoby, *The End of Utopia: Politics and Culture in an Age of Apathy* (New York: Basic Books, 1999), pp. 149, 151.

[83]Hans Urs von Balthasar, *The Theology of Karl Barth* (San Francisco: Ignatius Press, 1992), p. 126, quoted in Richard L. Fern, *Nature, God and Humanity* (Cambridge: Cambridge University Press, 2002), p. 160.

[84]Jacoby, *End of Utopia,* pp. 121-22.

[85]Cf. Spivak, "Can the Subaltern Speak?"

[86]Cf. Fernando F. Segovia, ed., *Interpreting Beyond Borders,* The Bible and Postcolonialism 3 (Sheffield, U.K.: Sheffield Academic Press, 2000); R. S. Sugirtharajah, *Postcolonial Criticism and Biblical Interpretation* (Oxford: Oxford University Press, 2002).

[87]Cecie Kolie, "Jesus the Healer," in *Faces of Jesus in Africa,* ed. Robert J. Schreiter (London: SCM, 1992), pp. 141-42.

[88]Kenneth Ross, *Here Comes Your King! Christ, Church and Nation in Malawi* (Blantyre, Malawi: Christian Literature Association, 1998), p. 31.

[89]Ibid., p. 24.

[90]Ibid., p. 25.

[91]David J. Bosch, *Transforming Mission: Paradigm Shifts in Theology of Mission* (Maryknoll, N.Y.: Orbis, 1991), p. 492.

[92]Dale T. Irvine, *Christian Histories, Christian Traditioning: Rendering Accounts* (Maryknoll, N.Y.: Orbis, 1998), p. xii.

[93]Ibid., p. 104.

[94]N. T. Wright, *Scripture and the Authority of God* (London: SPCK, 2005), p. 93.

[95]Kevin J. Vanhoozer, " 'One Rule to Rule Them All?' Theological Method in an Era of World Christianity," in *Globalizing Theology: Belief and Practice in an Era of World Christianity,* ed. Craig Ott and Harold Netland (Grand Rapids: Baker Academic, 2006), pp. 112-13.

[96]Ibid., p. 124.

Name Index

Adelman, Kenneth, 76
Alexander II, 38
Alexander, Dennis, 183
Al-Banna, Hasan, 25
Al-Mansur, Ahmad, 57
Ali, Muhammad, 12
Alighieri, Dante, 136
Allen, Charles, 233, 235
Alvares, Claude, 201
Ambedkar, Bhimrao
 Ramji, 243
Ambrose, 43, 84
Anderson, Perry, 222
Andrews, C. F., 248
Angier, Natalie, 11
Appiah, Anthony Kwame,
 241
Appleby, Scott, 80, 89
Arafat, Yasser, 36
Archer, Margaret, 132
Arendt, Hannah, 114
Aristotle, 94, 219
Ash, Timothy Garton,
 129, 156
Augustine, 43, 84
Azariah, V. S., 103
Baker, James, 23
Bairoch, Paul, 223
Bandaranaike, S. W. R.
 D., 70
Basil of Caesarea, 107
Bauckham, Richard, 104,
 166-67
Bayly, Christopher,
 140-41, 218, 234
Beck, Ulrich, 217
Bediako, Kwame, 248
Beethoven, Ludwig van,

189
Begin, Menachem, 38, 50
Bell, Daniel, 121
Benhabib, Seyla, 153,
 159-60
Bentinck, William, 247
Berlin, Isaiah, 165
Berry, Wendell, 202-3
Beschi, Constanzo, 247
Bhabha, Homi, 173,
 239-40
Bhindranwale, Jarnail
 Singh, 66
Bibi, Mukhtaran, 91
Bin Laden, Osama, 20,
 22-23, 25, 30-31, 33,
 36-37, 50
Blair, Tony, 85, 155
Blakemore, Colin, 179,
 181, 187
Bok, Derek, 194
Bonaparte, Napoleon, 218,
 228, 231-32
Bonhoeffer, Dietrich, 166
Bostrom, Nick, 211
Boucher, Richard, 35
Bouyeri, Mohammed, 129
Buber, Martin, 105
Bulliet, Richard, 24-25, 58
Burke, Edmund, 228
Buruma, Ian, 67
Bush, George H. W., 23,
 29
Bush, George W., 22-23,
 33, 36, 41, 50, 76
Butterfield, Herbert, 246
Buxton, Thomas Foxwell,
 238

Caldwell, Robert, 247
Carey, William, 247
Carlson, Ron, 11
Carnap, Rudolf, 171
Carter, Stephen, 142
Cavanaugh, William, 65
Chandhoke, Neera, 121
Charles I, 57
Charry, Ellen, 83
Cheney, Dick, 22, 23
Chesterton, G. K., 104,
 182
Cicero, 43
Clinton, Bill, 23, 30, 210
Close, Ellis, 150
Colley, Linda, 219, 233
Comte, August, 171
Condic, Maureen, 196,
 208
Copernicus, Nicolaus, 172
Crick, Francis, 177-78, 187
Curzon, George, 228
Da Gama, Vasco, 61
Dante. See Alighieri, Dante
Darwin, Charles, 170,
 172, 175, 182, 204-5
Darwin, Leonard, 204
Davies, Paul, 183
Dawkins, Richard, 11, 75,
 170, 177, 187
Derrida, Jacques, 160, 253
Dharmapala, Anagarika,
 238
Dirlik, Arif, 241
Dunn, John, 96, 162
Dworkin, Ronald, 100
Dyson, Freeman, 193
Elizabeth I, 57-58

Erasmus, Desiderius, 224

Esposito, John, 24

Fanon, Frantz, 226

Feith, Douglas, 76

Fernandez-Armesto,
Felipe, 226

Ferris, Timothy, 185

Feuerbach, Ludwig, 79

Fodor, Jerry, 180

Ford, Henry, 197

Forrester, Duncan, 101,
104

Fortuyn, Pim, 129

Foucault, Michel, 232,
238-39, 251

Freire, Paulo, 51

Frye, Northrop, 12-13

Fukuyama, Francis, 164

Gaddafi, Muammar, 52

Galilei, Galileo, 172

Galton, Francis, 172, 204,
206

Gandhi, Mohandas, 236,
248

Gates, Bill, 197

Gilson, Etienne, 190

Gould, Stephen Jay, 184

Graham, Billy, 29

Graham, Elaine, 211

Gramsci, Antonio, 227,
230

Greenfield, Susan, 16, 209

Griffin, Michael, 21, 23

Grotius, Hugo, 43

Gutiérrez, Gustavo, 250

Habibie, B. J., 73

Halbfass, Wilhelm, 236

Halliday, Fred, 68, 249

Harris, Nigel, 159

Harris, Sam, 11-12, 75

Hartsock, Nancy, 245, 250

Hawking, Stephen, 185

Haught, John, 186, 191

Hayek, Friedrich, 165

He, Zheng, 221

Hefner, Robert, 28

Hekmatyar, Gulbuddin,
19

Hian, Fa, 235

Hirsi Ali, Ayaan, 129

Hitchens, Christopher, 75

Hitler, Adolf, 38, 171

Hobson, John, 220

Hopkins, A. G., 217

Hopkins, Gerard Manley,
7

Holton, Robert, 219

Horton, Richard, 195

Hugo, Victor, 232

Huizinga, Johan, 224

Huntington, Samuel, 26

Hussein, Saddam, 29, 36,
46

Huxley, T. H., 172

Hwang, Woo-Suk, 196-97

Ignatieff, Michael, 139

Iqbal, Mohammed, 226

Irvin, Dale, 259

Jacoby, Russell, 251, 254

Jefferson, Thomas, 25

Jenkins, Philip, 81

John Chrysostom, 107

Jones, Steve, 188

Juergensmeyer, Mark, 66

Kant, Immanuel, 114,
159-60

Kennedy, John F., 45

Keynes, John Maynard,
204

Khomeini, Ayatollah, 24

King, Martin Luther, Jr.,
101, 123

Klor de Alva, Jorge, 229

Kolie, Cecie, 257

Kruhonja, Katarina, 89

Kymlicka, Will, 139, 143

Lamming, George, 229

Laungani, Pittu, 127

Lay, Ken, 23

Lederach, Jean Paul, 55-56

Leibniz, Gottfried, 222

LeMay, Curtis, 45

Levi, Primo, 170

Levinas, Emmanuel, 160

Lewinsky, Monica, 30

Lewis, I. M., 246

Lewontin, Richard, 11

Livingstone, David, 238

Locke, John, 63, 96, 165

Loomba, Ania, 231, 240

Louis XIV, 222

Mandela, Nelson, 50

Mann, Josiah, 15

Margalit, Avishai, 67

Marsh, Charles, 123-24

Marshall, Chris, 79

Marx, Karl, 25, 170, 213,
254

Matar, Nabil, 58

Mawdudi, Maulana, 26

McGrath, Alister, 79

McKay, Ron, 208-9

McNamara, Robert, 45

Mccks, Donald, 85

Meilaender, Gilbert, 206

Midgley, Mary, 13,
173-74, 199

Milbank, John, 10

Milton, John, 165

Moltmann, Jürgen, 50, 55

Morris, Simon Conway, 176, 184
Mossadeq, Mohammed, 17
Mountbatten, Louis, 248
Moynihan, Daniel Patrick, 142
Mugabe, Robert, 36
Muhammad, 25
Müller, Max, 237
Mussolini, Benito, 38
Nasser, Gamal Abdel, 26
Nehru, Jawaharlal, 172-73
Nietzsche, Friedrich, 100, 105, 170
Nolde, Frederick, 107
Northcott, Michael, 202
O'Donovan, Joan Lockwood, 122
O'Donovan, Oliver, 43-49, 118, 144-45
O'Hanlon, Rosalind, 244
O'Mahony, Anthony, 87
Olcott, Henry, 238
Oppenheimer, Robert, 192
Orwell, George, 33-34, 37, 170-71
Parekh, Bhikhu, 135, 144, 148
Pascal, Blaise, 183
Paul, 99, 109, 160-61
Perle, Richard, 76
Perry, Benita, 240
Perry, Michael, 97, 101
Plant, Raymond, 163-65
Plato, 94
Plütschau, Henry, 247
Polkinghorne, John, 192
Pol Pot, 54
Pope, George, 247

Popper, Karl, 165
Powell, Colin, 77
Qutb, Sayyid, 25-26
Ramanathapillai, Rajmohan, 71
Rambachan, Anantanand, 69
Rantisi, Abdel Aziz, 33
Rawls, John, 96
Reagan, Ronald, 18, 29, 50
Rees, Phil, 31
Ricci, Matteo, 222
Richardson, Bill, 23
Risakotta-Adeney, Farsijana, 73
Robespierre, Maximilien, 37
Rose, Steven, 178
Ross, Kenneth, 257
Rostow, Walter, 222
Rousseau, Jean-Jaques, 98
Roy, Ram Mohan, 247
Rumsfeld, Donald, 76
Rushdie, Salman, 15
Russell, Bertrand, 170, 204
Sacks, Jonathan, 165
Said, Edward, 58, 231, 233-35, 245, 250
Sanneh, Lamin, 146-47, 248
Schwartz, Christian Friedrich, 247
Schwöbel, Christoph, 124
Scowcroft, Brent, 23
Sen, Amartya, 165
Shakespeare, William, 136
Shaw, George Bernard, 204
Shariati, Ali, 25

Sharon, Ariel, 36, 65
Shourie, Arun, 242
Silver, Lee, 209-10
Smith, David, 248, 250
Sobrino, Jon, 10-11
Soulen, Kendall, 206-7
Spencer, Herbert, 172
Spivak, Gayatri, 229, 244, 251
Staal, Frits, 237
Stalin, Joseph, 38
Stern, Jessica, 75, 77
Stock, Gregory, 210, 212
Straw, Jack, 155
Suárez, Francisco, 43
Suharto, 27, 73
Suzuki, D. T., 236
Tanner, Kathryn, 136
Tantawi, Sayyid, 31
Taylor, Charles, 136, 165
Thalib, Jafar Umar, 74
Thatcher, Margaret, 19, 29
Thomas Aquinas, 43, 108
Torrance, Thomas F., 187
Toynbee, Polly, 75
Tsang, Huan, 235
Tutu, Desmond, 124
Ul-Haq, Zia, 19
Van Gogh, Theo, 129
Vanhoozer, Kevin, 260-61
Veer, Peter van der, 219, 224
Viswanathan, Gauri, 230
Vitoria, Francisco de, 43
Vivekananda, Swami, 236-237
Volf, Miroslav, 89
Voll, John, 24
Waldron, Jeremy, 124
Webb, Sidney, 204

Wells, H. G., 204

West, Charles, 146

Wickramasinghe, Chandra, 182

Wigner, Eugene, 185

Williams, Raymond, 131

Williams, Rowan, 122-23

Wilder, Thornton, 9

Wilson, Edward, 174, 177, 209

Wink, Walter, 75

Wolfowitz, Paul, 76

Wolterstorff, Nicholas, 95-97

Wright, N. T., 260

Yassin, Ahmed, 33

Ye'or, Bat, 60

Zawahri, Ayman, 20, 31

Zebiri, Kate, 87

Zigenbalg, Bartholomew, 247

Subject Index

Afghanistan, 17-18, 20-23, 32, 35-36, 42, 45, 66-67, 129

African Americans, 10, 100, 123, 142, 149, 205, 229

al-Qa'ida, 20-22, 25, 28, 31-33, 35, 42, 45, 48, 74, 76, 129

Amish, 144

Amnesty International, 55

Amoco, 23

asylum, 66, 113, 157-58, 160

atheism, 15, 76, 82, 97, 181, 186

atheist polemics, 74-80

Auschwitz, 79-80

Australian Aboriginals, 144

Basque separatists, 35, 41

blowback, 17

Bosnia, 28, 81, 129

Bridge of San Luis Rey, The, 9

British East India Company, 141, 225, 247

British Petroleum, 23

Buddhism, Buddhists, 27, 63, 67, 69-70, 76, 80, 132, 140, 154, 182, 235-38, 246, 255

Bushmen. *See* Sana people

capitalism, 13, 62, 141, 164, 213, 217, 229, 241, 244, 254

caste system, 63, 71, 91, 94, 101, 120, 150, 225, 242-43

Cargill, 201

Chevron, 23

China, 15, 36, 48, 53, 55, 61, 67, 76, 114, 173, 218, 220-26, 228

Christian hope, 10, 52, 56, 103, 147, 191, 213

Christian missions, 99, 104, 146-47, 205, 235, 238, 247

Christian theology, 13, 42-43, 64, 68, 84, 101, 107, 125, 145, 203, 214, 233, 245-61

Christianity, American, 55, 78, 85, 110, 278

Christianity and the state, 62-65, 82, 104-05

Christians in the Third World, 59-61, 63-65, 67-68, 70, 72-74, 76, 81, 90, 103, 155-56, 236, 242, 246-47, 255

civil rights movement, 101, 123

Civil War, American, 10, 218

CNN, 29

Cold War, 22, 28, 53, 73

colonialism, colonialists, 12, 15, 22, 29, 61-62, 70, 103, 116, 136, 141, 205, 218, 224-36, 238-45, 247, 251, 253-54, 256

colonialism, contemporary, 229-30

creation, biblical doctrine of, 12, 63, 83, 102-3, 174, 184, 190, 203, 207, 212, 215

creationism, creationists, 11, 174, 278

criminals, criminalization, 45-47, 51, 112-13

cultural determinism, 174

culture, cultures, 14, 24-25, 27, 59-60, 62-64, 66-67, 73, 79, 81, 84, 87-88, 90, 100, 104-5, 115-17, 119, 128-56, 161-64, 167, 169, 186, 195, 210, 217, 229-34, 247-50, 258-61

culture, definition of, 130-37

culture, public (public culture), 152-54

dalits ("untouchables"), 63, 101, 103, 243, 247

Darwinianism, 182, 186

Darwinists, Social, 170, 205

Declaration of Independence, 100-101

Democratic Party, Democrats (U.S.), 77, 82-83

democracy and capitalism, 164

democracy, liberal democracy, 22, 28, 33, 36-37, 49, 51, 53, 55, 62, 76, 83, 85, 96, 110, 115, 120, 122, 125, 136, 138, 148, 153-54, 160-64, 198, 207, 228

dissent, political, 27, 53,
    110-11, 144, 243
diversity, cultural, 117,
    133-34, 143, 145, 149,
    153, 233, 240
Dutch East India
    Company, 72, 225
El Salvador, 10-11
End of Faith, The, 11
Enlightenment, the, 86,
    98, 101, 139, 156, 172,
    211, 224, 245, 252
eugenics, 204-9
evil (theology), 84-86,
    102-3, 151, 249-51
evolution, evolutionism,
    11, 13, 15, 23, 75,
    174-78, 182, 210-12,
    214, 255
Exxon, 23
Fog of War, The, 45
freedom, ethics of, 161-68
freedom of expression, 110
fundamentalism
    religious, 14, 18, 22,
        77, 174
    secularist, 15, 154-56
genetic determinism,
    177-78
genetic engineering, 13,
    197-204
Geneva Protocols, 46-47
global media, 11, 16, 69,
    81, 142
globalism, globalization,
    15, 50, 113, 125, 160,
    217-24, 256
Gnosticism, Gnostics, 155,
    212
Gods That Fail, 9

Good Friday Agreement,
    40
Greece, 221
Green Revolution, 200-1
Guatemala, 11
Gulf War, the, 29
Hague Conventions,
    46-47
human cloning, 196-97
human rights. *See* rights,
    human
Human Rights Watch, 55
humanism, humanists,
    156, 176, 204, 211, 235,
    244-45, 251-54, 256
Hurricane Katrina, 11
Hurricane Stan, 11
idolatry, idols, 9-10, 12,
    58, 82, 84, 87, 89, 145,
    172, 214
imago Dei, image of God,
    99-105, 191, 203
immigrants, 111-15, 119,
    129-30, 147, 151, 157-60,
    229, 241
India, 15, 18, 29, 34-35,
    39, 53-54, 61, 63, 66,
    69-70, 103, 127, 130-31,
    140-42, 149, 151-52,
    162, 166, 172-73, 200,
    217-18, 220-21, 223-26,
    228-32, 234-37, 239,
    241-44, 247-48, 254
individualism, 27, 121-22,
    138, 167, 170, 222
Indonesia, 27, 32, 37, 62,
    67-68, 72-74, 78, 81, 90,
    139, 142
insurgencies,
    counterinsurgencies, 46,

48, 70, 243-44
international law, 43, 47,
    53, 111, 158
International Monetary
    Fund, 200
international relations, 14
Iran, 17-18, 20-21, 23-25,
    28-29, 32, 113
Iranian Revolution, 28
Irish Republican Army
    (IRA), 41, 46
Islam, Islamicists,
    Islamization, 12, 19,
    21-22, 24-33, 37, 57-59,
    64, 66-68, 72-75, 78,
    87-88, 90-91, 129, 133,
    137, 156-57, 162, 232,
    237, 246-47, 255
Islamist militancy, 24-33
ius ad bellum, 43, 49, 54
Japan, 34, 45, 55, 67, 114,
    223, 236-38
Jews, Judaism, 28, 58-60,
    75-77, 83-84, 88, 99,
    101, 129, 170, 205, 212,
    217
just-war theory, 42-49,
    84-85
Kuwait, 29, 31-32
liberal democracies, 53,
    62, 85, 138, 148, 163-64,
    207
liberal political philosophy,
    116, 138
liberal theory, 93-99
liberty, 27, 38, 52-53, 83,
    95-96, 109-10, 139, 154,
    157, 165, 260
marginalization, 24, 63,
    89, 101, 135, 139, 254-55

market system, 13
Marx, Karl; Marxism, 13,
    25, 35, 62, 131, 138, 162,
    170, 178, 213, 222, 227,
    241, 243-44, 251, 254
meaning-seeking, 49, 186
media, 11-12, 15, 25, 30,
    32, 34, 36, 40-41, 47,
    49-50, 52, 73-74, 76-78,
    87, 89, 104, 110, 133,
    148, 153-55, 196-97,
    208, 247
Middle East, 18, 22,
    24-28, 58, 64, 72, 162,
    231
migrants, 88, 96, 112-13,
    118, 155, 158, 249
Mind Machine, The, 179
Mobil, 23
Monsanto, 201
moral responsibility, 50,
    54, 160, 192-97, 202, 253
multicultural
    nationhood, 138-43
    society, defense of, 14,
    117, 143-47
    state, 14, 147-54
multiculturalism, 14, 117,
    127-68
Muslim Brotherhood,
    25-26, 28, 33
Muslims, 18-19, 23-29,
    31-33, 36, 48, 57-62,
    65-68, 72-76, 87-90,
    129-30, 132, 137,
    140-41, 149, 151-52,
    154-56, 221, 232,
    236-37, 242, 248
nationalism, 62, 70, 82,
    140-42, 154, 236-37,

243, 248, 250
Nazi, Nazism, 33, 76, 78,
    114, 170, 205
Nineteen Eighty-Four, 33
niqab, 155
Northern Ireland, 35, 40,
    49
oil (petrolium), 17, 22-23,
    28-29, 44, 79, 113, 171,
    189, 238
Oklahoma City, 10
Operation Desert Storm,
    29, 31
Origin of Species, The, 175,
    205
Ottoman Empire, 29, 220
Pakistan, 18, 19, 21-23,
    29, 33, 39, 50, 54, 68, 91,
    113, 226, 241
pluralism, 28, 125, 149,
    154, 253
political language, 33-34
political violence, 35, 38,
    43
postcolonialism, 15, 70,
    139, 142, 217-61, 286
post-Enlightenment, 62,
    87, 124
posthumanism, 15, 211,
    213
proportionality, 43-44
public square, 154
Qur'an, 19, 24, 33, 64,
    129, 137, 152, 265
racism, 12, 152, 206, 240,
    248
reductionism, 188-89, 191
refugees, 19, 22, 39, 56,
    60, 67, 96, 112-13, 119,
    156-61, 205, 255

Republicans (U.S.), 77, 83
right
    to life, 105-6, 108-9,
    119
    to private property, 94,
    108
rights,
    civil, 39, 150
    collective, 117-20, 139,
    150
    cultural, 14
    human, 12, 14, 27,
    39-40, 48, 55, 91-125,
    136, 148, 157-60,
    162, 207
    individual, 105-17, 122,
    150
    language of, 91-93, 99,
    121-22
    legislating, 119-23
    property, 95-96, 98,
    106-8, 157, 188, 201,
    203, 209, 228, 234
rights of the poor, 106
Rwanda, 54
Salafi, 28, 72, 265
Sana people, 128
Saudi Arabia, 20-23,
    27-29, 31, 66, 72
science, 15, 59, 67, 93, 148,
    169-215, 222
    and atheism, 15, 181-87
    and eugenics, 204-9
    and moral
    responsibility, 192-97
    and reductionism,
    187-92
    as ideology, 171-81
scientific materialism,
    174-75

self-determination, 122, 125, 166, 205, 211

Selfish Gene, The, 177

September 11, 2001, 10, 20, 32-36, 40, 42, 45-46, 50-51, 53, 61, 64, 66, 74-76, 85, 114, 129

shock and awe, 32

Sikhs, 35, 66, 149

Sinhalese, 39-40, 69-70, 72, 237-38

social contract theory, 13

sociobiology, 15, 174, 178, 214

Soviet Union, 18, 20, 33, 76

Sri Lanka, 14, 35, 38-40, 47, 66, 69-72, 142, 151, 162, 238

stem cell research, 196

Sudan, 24, 30, 48, 66, 81

Sunni Islam, 23

Taliban, 21-23, 35-36, 67, 98

Tamil nationalism, 70

Tamil Tigers, 35, 39-40, 47, 52, 71

telos, 175, 203

terrorism, 10, 14, 17-56, 75, 77-78, 130, 157

Third Reich, 148

Third World, 12, 15, 45, 51, 64, 195, 197, 226, 241, 255-57

transhumanism, 15, 209-13

UNICEF, 21

United Kingdom, 17, 29, 32, 39-40, 47, 53, 57, 63, 67, 75, 85, 130, 140-41, 149, 152, 156, 170, 172, 220, 222-23, 225, 228-29

United Nations, 29-32, 42, 49, 54, 77, 85, 93, 95, 107, 112-13, 116, 119-20, 158, 163

United States, 10, 15, 17-21, 23, 26, 29, 31-32,

35-36, 39-42, 47-50, 53, 55, 60-61, 69, 73, 75, 77-78, 89, 114, 130, 140, 149-50, 157, 159, 174-75, 200, 205, 212, 221, 228, 236, 238, 247

Universal Declaration of Human Rights (UN) 93, 107, 113, 116, 158, 163

untouchables. *See* dalits

violence, religious, 14, 57-90, 131

Wahhabis, 22, 28

war on terror, 12, 14, 33-42, 50, 53, 67

World Bank, 150, 200

worldviews, 13, 27, 65, 71, 74-76, 88, 162, 169, 174, 177, 181, 186-87, 191, 214, 256

Zeneca, 201

Zionism, Christian, 83